Chinese Characters

Chinese Characters

*Profiles of Fast-Changing Lives
in a Fast-Changing Land*

EDITED BY

Angilee Shah and Jeffrey Wasserstrom

Foreword by Pankaj Mishra

UNIVERSITY OF CALIFORNIA PRESS

Berkeley · Los Angeles · London

University of California Press, one of the most
distinguished university presses in the United States,
enriches lives around the world by advancing
scholarship in the humanities, social sciences, and
natural sciences. Its activities are supported by the UC
Press Foundation and by philanthropic contributions
from individuals and institutions. For more information,
visit www.ucpress.edu.

University of California Press
Berkeley and Los Angeles, California

University of California Press, Ltd.
London, England

For acknowledgments of previous publication for
chapters 2, 7, 9, 11, and 14, please see credits on
p. 231.

Library of Congress Cataloging-in-Publication Data

Chinese characters : profiles of fast-changing lives
in a fast-changing land / edited by Angilee Shah and
Jeffrey Wasserstrom ; foreword by Pankaj Mishra.
    p. cm.
  Includes bibliographical references.
  ISBN 978-0-520-27026-8 (cloth : alk. paper)
  ISBN 978-0-520-27027-5 (pbk. : alk. paper)
  1. National characteristics, Chinese. 2. China—
Social life and customs. I. Shah, Angilee.
II. Wasserstrom, Jeffrey N.
  DS799.4.C425 2012
  951—dc23
                              2012004374

Manufactured in the United States of America

21 20 19 18 17 16 15 14 13 12
10 9 8 7 6 5 4 3 2 1

In keeping with a commitment to support
environmentally responsible and sustainable printing
practices, UC Press has printed this book on Rolland
Enviro100, a 100% post-consumer fiber paper that is
FSC certified, deinked, processed chlorine-free, and
manufactured with renewable biogas energy. It is
acid-free and EcoLogo certified.

Contents

Foreword

Looking back four decades later at his years as a journalist in China in the 1940s, the historian John K. Fairbank blamed himself and his journalistic colleagues for "one of the great failures in history": "We had no knowledge, in other words, and no way to gain any knowledge, of the life of ordinary Chinese people. . . . Our reporting was very superficial. We could not educate or illuminate or inform the American people or the American leadership in such a way that we could modify the outcome."

What was this outcome he so regretted? Fairbank not only had in mind the American support for the Nationalist Party (Guomindang) and unstinting hostility to the Communists. He was also thinking of the way America reacted to the establishment of the People's Republic of China in 1949: that it had "lost" China to Communism.

Fairbank was targeted for his allegedly Communist sympathies, so he knew all too well that this anti-Communist obsession had serious consequences. The vengeful rage of budding cold warriors found ready scapegoats among diplomats and journalists—the many "China Hands"—who had correctly perceived the strengths of Mao Zedong's army and the weaknesses of America's ally Chiang Kai-shek. Promptly branded fellow travelers of Communism, they were purged from positions of influence in the government, universities, and the media—a self-mutilation that led to the intellectual and military fiascos of Korea and Vietnam, when the United States, drawn into ground wars in Asia by Cold War paranoia, could barely see its enemy.

Fairbank implicated himself and other American journalists in these wars, which he described as "a first-class disaster for the American people." Reading him now, you may wonder if he was exaggerating his own role in history. The general public may have been underinformed but to what extent could journalists be blamed for failures in American foreign policy making?

The West's understanding of China, a country always deemed more "inscrutable" than its Asian counterparts, had long been filtered through the varying interpretations of foreign writers in the country—right from the carefully detailed accounts of the first Jesuits in China to the jubilant news spread by American businessmen and publicists about the world's last unexplored market in the early twentieth century. In the 1920s and 1930s, Anna Louise Strong, Agnes Smedley, and Edgar Snow attempted to educate American progressives about left-wing currents in China. At the same time, children of American missionaries in China such as Pearl S. Buck and Henry Luce—the first a Nobel Prize–winning writer, the latter the publisher of *Time, Life,* and *Fortune* magazines—helped establish China in the popular imagination as a test case for America's engagement with the world.

It is largely forgotten today that China, apparently hapless before civil wars and foreign invasions in the early twentieth century, was adopted by many American do-gooders, who hoped that American democracy and culture might be transformative forces beyond the country's borders. Hence, the great fury when this needy orphan was, as it were, "lost" in 1949.

The new caretakers of China, of course, had no time for its aspiring foster parents in the West. They favored those foreign journalists—and there were quite a few of them—who sang the praises of the revolution. Narrative journalism about post–World War II China has been logistically possible only since the early 1980s, when the country began to emerge out of a long period of political and cultural isolation. But have contemporary writers on China done a better job than those Fairbank deplored?

The Cold War, during which China moved from "Yellow Peril" to "Red Menace," is over, even if some attitudes from it linger in the semi-hysterical predictions about the Chinese taking over the universe. There is no question that we have entered a multipolar world in which China is too big and strong to be patronized or pushed around. But it's too easy to say that the decline of old ideological certainties in West, and improved access to China, automatically makes for perceptive writing about the country. For post-Mao China is, in many ways, even more dauntingly—to use a much-abused word—inscrutable; and writing about it requires many skills not taught at journalism schools.

Most coverage of China in the mainstream press aims to alert the West to the promise and perils of rapid economic growth in the country. You might think that writing about a civilization with a long history in terms of whether its "rise" would help Westerners make or lose money is self-limiting. However, most journalists, especially correspondents of business periodicals, don't aim very high. At their most thoughtful, they might speculate about the timetable for the introduction of Western-style "democracy" in China.

Not surprisingly, their writings reveal very little about how most Chinese live or see themselves and the world, but very much about how certain ideological assumptions and prejudices of the "West," so strengthened by its supposed victory in the Cold War, have overwhelmed many journalists in Britain and America.

The Chinese, we are repeatedly told, have embraced capitalism and globalization. But the word "capitalism" scarcely describes an economic system in which a one-party state controls the major banks and companies and regulates the movement of capital. And while embracing globalization, China has surely also adopted commonplace Western practices such as the privatization and truncating of public services, deunionization, and the fragmenting and lumpenization of urban working classes.

Many in China's new middle classes have done very well out of two decades of capitalism, and the country's ruling elite struts across the world stage, browbeating its neighbors and standing up to America, as never before. But what does China's "rise" mean for the large majority of its population? What is one to make of the lingering reverence for Mao in the age of post-Mao prosperity? How does the embattled trade-union organizer in Guangzhou perceive Ai Weiwei and Liu Xiaobo, two "dissidents" celebrated in the West?

Plainly, any worthwhile discussion of the New China must continually dismantle ideological frameworks in both China and the West and focus on the diversity and many internal schisms of Chinese society. Even a commonplace triumphalism like "globalization has lifted hundreds of millions of Chinese above the poverty line" is freighted with particular assumptions. For it does not tell us what poverty, always a relative concept, means in the context of the world's biggest-ever transition from rural to urban areas. Or, how the awful boredom of collective stagnation, what Marx called the "idiocy of rural life," compares to the distress of extreme inequality and exploitation in urban areas. Does the rural migrant worker from Shanxi find his desolation in Wenzhou preferable to a hand-to-mouth existence with his family at home?

There are no simple answers to these questions, largely because the Chinese themselves, gaining some things, losing others, cannot but be internally split about the great changes in their society. As Jeffrey Wasserstrom shows in his introduction to this collection, the one constant about China today is rapid and bewildering changes in personal lifestyles and ideologies. Honoring this complexity is the fundamental task of any contemporary writer about China. As Fairbank pointed out: "Every journalist is walking on a fault line—of unresolved and ambivalent historic situations—trying to represent it some way in words. It is probably the essence of the journalistic profession . . . that reporters deal with ambivalent situations where the outcome is uncertain, the values are mixed, and the sides are in conflict."

This has never been as true as it is in the case of today's mercurial China. And, it's not an exaggeration to say that only journalism that aspires to the condition of literature can do justice to contemporary China: a mode of writing that creates in its readers not certainty of any kind but a profound sense of the ambiguity and irony inherent in human desires and aspirations. *Chinese Characters* rises to this challenge admirably. It has too many of my favorite writers for me to name them individually. Read together in this wonderfully rich anthology, they seem to me to herald a new golden age of journalism about a ceaselessly fascinating country.

Pankaj Mishra

Acknowledgments

The editors are grateful to the staff of the University of California Press for their support, and encouragement, especially to Reed Malcolm, who has worked with us closely throughout the project, and Sheila Levine, who was instrumental in the original conceptualization. We owe a large debt to all of the contributors, who made room in their busy schedules not only to write their chapters but also to respond to queries, brainstorm on various aspect of the book, and in, Pankaj Mishra's case, read the manuscript and carve out time, while finishing a book of his own, to write the Foreword. Tom Mullaney deserves a shout out for his contributions to a lively lunchtime brainstorming session on the book that ended with it being rechristened with its final title. We would also individually like to offer the following thanks:

Angilee Shah: My first experiences in China were possible because of a fellowship from Princeton in Asia, a program that gave me a practical, ground-level perspective on life in Asia and introduced me to the realities of one-party systems. I would especially like to thank PiA's executive director, Anastasia Vrachnos, for her support and insight. I am in debt as well to Anka Lee, who helped me access parts of China I could have never seen on my own and has been a sounding board and source of ideas for as long as I have worked on the country. Conversations with Anka, since we were editors together as students at the University of California, Berkeley, have helped shaped the kinds of narratives I seek and the questions I ask as an editor. Clayton Dube not only gave me my first job as an editor at *AsiaMedia* but has also been a mentor and a friend ever since. Brian Hu and Chi Tung gave me valuable feedback on chapters in this book and helped me work through ideas both conceptually and practically. Finally, I want to thank Sonia and Anil, Vicky and Joe, who always gave me a home and space to work while I transitioned from Asia back to the United States.

Jeffrey Wasserstrom: I am grateful to my China Studies and History colleagues at the University of California, Irvine, both graduate students and faculty, for providing an ideal setting in which to do the kind of work that makes books like this possible. In particular, I want to thank Ken Pomeranz, Kate Merkel-Hess, and Maura Cunningham, my main co-conspirators in the "China Beat" enterprise, since there is an integral connection between that blog and this volume; Catherine Liu, who has been an ardent supporter of campus events that bring scholars and journalists into dialogue; and Pierre Fuller who, despite the pressures of first-year teaching, gave me valuable advice on an early draft of the Introduction (as did Maura Cunningham). I am grateful as well to Jennifer Munger of the Journal of Asian Studies for serving as a thoughtful sounding board for ideas about the book, ranging from its contents to what its cover should look like, and to James Carter, who went over a draft of the Introduction with a fine-toothed comb. For inspiration from the other side of the Pacific and helping me find new ways to move between the world of the academy and the world of journalism and literature, I want to thank CET Academic Programs (http://cetacademicprograms.com) and also Michelle Garnaut and Tina Kanagaratnam of M on the Bund, the very special restaurant where the Shanghai International Literary Festival is held each year. Finally, as always, I am grateful to Anne Bock for, among many other things, introducing me to "Ms. Liu" in the 1980s and always being the first one to hear my stories—and letting me know which ones are worth telling a second time.

Introduction

"Who Are You This Time?"

JEFFREY WASSERSTROM

Each time I go back to China, I prepare myself to hear stories of surprising ways that the country has changed since I was last there. I also expect to hear equally surprising reports of personal transformations. It seems inevitable that at least a couple of friends whose lives seemed set to move in one direction will have had something completely unexpected happen to them since I last saw them. During the months since my previous trip to China, a professor who had no interest in business will have become an entrepreneur. A loyal bureaucrat within the Communist Party Youth League will have turned consultant to an international corporation (and now be a bit embarrassed by his earlier commitment to Marxist economics). Someone who considered all forms of religion mere superstition will have become first a fervent Buddhist and then a devout Christian. An earnest graduate student who once said that a visit to Hong Kong was probably the closest that she would ever get to going "abroad" will now regularly be taking trips to Europe.

China has become what the United States famously was a century ago, a land of reinvention. Rags-to-riches stories are as popular there now as they were in America in the days of Horatio Alger—and for similar reasons. I often feel that many of the people I know in China have lived out several lives while I have been making my way through just this one.

Consider the case of a longtime friend whom I shall call Ms. Liu for her privacy's sake. Before I met her in 1986, her life had already gone through dramatic twists and turns. She grew up in Shanghai, the child of intellectuals, but was sent to the countryside to learn from peasants late in the Cultural Revolution, an experience she still remembers with some fondness. She thought it instilled a respect for hard work and the ability to enjoy simple things that some people born later seem to lack. After returning to Shanghai, she was trained as a Russian-language teacher, only to have that career trajectory derailed by the dominance of English-language study in China. Ms. Liu was reassigned to the *waiban* (foreign affairs unit) of her university, where her main job was to take care of arrangements for and keep an eye on the activities of foreign teachers and students.

That would be enough reversals of fortune to constitute a life of ups and downs, but in the years since, she has continued on a protean course. By turns, Ms. Liu spent a year in central Europe as a visiting scholar, worked as a nanny in California for about the same amount of time, and lived for a time primarily on what she made as a day-trader on Shanghai's new stock exchange. She'd once assumed she'd always live in an apartment owned by her work unit, but the last time I saw her, she was the proud owner of a flat on the outskirts of Shanghai. The shifts in her beliefs, ideological and spiritual, also mark changes of the sort that we in the West might expect to see over the course of generations rather than of one life. And her child's life—like many of her generation, she has just one—has matched hers in its unpredictability. Her daughter studied in New Zealand and then worked in jobs that did not exist in China before the 1990s, often employed in the marketing divisions of international companies that until recently never expected to be making money selling their products in China.

Not all of the life stories that go to make up this book have much in common with Ms. Liu's or her daughter's when it comes to the details, but they all involve surprising transformations of individuals and communities. The chapters that follow remind us that China is now a place where identities can be taken on and shed with surprising ease, in ways that can be exciting or exhausting, traumatic or confusing, or, in many cases, all of those things at once.

The China revealed by the characters in this volume is a place where lives can suddenly be turned inside out as opportunities are seized or squandered, and change is by turns liberating and unsettling. The writing on contemporary China that appeals to me most is the kind that conveys the complexity of these transformations from the perspectives of those who live them. The essays of the journalists and scholars represented here are the kinds of pieces I love to read—and now can claim to love to help edit as well—for all beg a common question of their characters: "Who will they be next?"

These individuals are nothing if not varied. After spending time in their company, even readers who have never experienced China's human diversity firsthand should find themselves pausing whenever they come across statements that generalize about how "the Chinese" feel about a given issue..

THE FIRST "NEW" CHINA

In chapter 4, Harriet Evans introduces us to Old Lady Gao, the most senior of our *Chinese Characters*. In many regards, the country in which she drew her first breath in the early 1920s was a very different place from today's China. There was no People's Republic of China then—until the Chinese Communist Party (CCP) took control of the mainland in 1949, neither that name nor the acronym PRC existed. Gao was born in the Republic of China (ROC).

The revolutionary uprisings of 1911 had put an end to the long reign of the Qing Dynasty, the Manchu ruling family that had controlled China since the 1640s, and laid the groundwork for Sun Yat-sen to become the first president of the new republic. In the 1920s, and for many decades afterward, China was still an overwhelmingly rural place—whereas today roughly half of the country's people live in or around cities. The vast majority of Chinese were farmers and very poor before 1949. Today, while China still has a much lower per capita GDP than developed Western countries or Japan (it ranks roughly 100th among nations by this criterion), it is home to more millionaires than any other country, has a rapidly expanding middle class, and has become the world's biggest market for luxury goods.

Life was rough in China when Gao was born: very few men and many fewer women went to school; children routinely died in infancy; adults felt lucky if they made it past fifty; and women had no formal legal rights in marriage. However, a child born in Shanghai around the year 2000 had a better chance of living to attend elementary school than one born at the same point in time in New York City. It is common today for Chinese people to live into their seventh, eighth, or even ninth decades. When it comes to gender, there are a great many ways that women are still at a disadvantage in China, and the preference for sons over daughters remains strong, but there have been some improvements. When Old Lady Gao was in her twenties, for example, the Communist Party introduced a New Marriage Law that gave wives formal equality with their husbands to seek a divorce. It is no longer a novelty to see university classrooms with as many female as male students in Chinese cities.

The saying "5,000 years of continuous civilization"—a favorite trope of the Chinese official media, and of some nationalist writers and foreigners as well—encourages one to assume that the current map of the subcontinent-sized PRC delineates a set of timeless boundaries. The real story of China's borders is very different. Prior to the end of the imperial era, different dynasties, and even different emperors within dynastic periods, governed territories of widely diverging sizes. Sometimes the empire included Tibet, sometimes it didn't. The same goes for territories to the south near today's Burma, as well as northern areas such as Manchuria and, to its west, Inner Mongolia. The great expanse of land west of Mongolia and north of Tibet is now known as Xinjiang. But the name Xinjiang (the first character means "new," the second "border" or "frontier") only came into use during Qing times. During the final decades of the imperial period and the opening decades of the Republican era (1912–49), though officials sometimes issued maps that look like the ones we see today, many key territories were formally or effectively under foreign control. This included, from 1843 on, sections of several major port cities, including Shanghai, and all of Hong Kong.

When Old Lady Gao was born, there were many counties and provinces that were solidly under Chinese control, yet were not governed by the men who cycled in and out of the office of the presidency. This was a time of great disunity and weak central governments, sometimes called the Warlord Era in reference to military figures who seized power regionally. These "warlords" were a varied lot, including among them both men who promoted themselves as benevolent Confucian rulers steeped in Chinese traditions and the "Christian General" Feng Yuxiang, who baptized his troops with a fire hose. This political situation began to shift in the mid-1920s, when Sun Yat-sen, the hero of 1911 and leader of the Nationalist Party, or Guomindang (GMD), called for a military drive known as the Northern Expedition to reunify the country and get the derailed revolution back on track.

Sun dreamed up this campaign while operating from a regional base in the southern city of Guangzhou (Canton). Though a firm opponent of some aspects of Marxism—for example, he had no time for the concept of class struggle—Sun admired the Soviet Union and liked two key Leninist notions. One was that imperialism was responsible for much that was wrong with the world. The other was that the best hope for a developing country was to have its destiny guided by a tightly disciplined revolutionary organization. At the urging of Soviet advisers, who were willing to support Sun's cause if he made concessions to them, he welcomed members of the recently created Chinese Communist Party into the Northern Expedition campaign. Many important Communist leaders, including Mao Zedong, spent their early careers holding posts in both the Communist Party and the Nationalist Party.

The Northern Expedition's goals, which included toppling regional strongmen and bringing an end to foreign bullying and corruption within the national government, struck a powerful chord with many Chinese. Soon, the joint GMD–CCP military force was surging to a series of major victories against the warlords. A crucial one came in 1927, when a series of general strikes and worker uprisings orchestrated by Communist Party activists helped deliver Shanghai (except for two enclaves where foreigners held power) into the hands of the alliance. By then, however, Sun had died and his brother-in-law and protégé Chiang Kai-shek was head of the Nationalist Party. The brothers-in-law had agreed on many issues, but not on the value of working with the Communist Party. As soon as the Chinese-run districts of Shanghai came under his control, Chiang worked with local gangsters to carry out a vicious purge against his erstwhile comrades-in-arms. This put a bloody end to what came to be known as the "First United Front" (a second would start a decade later), and marked the opening salvo in a stop-and-start war between the Nationalists and the Communists, which would have truces but no full resolution until 1949.

CHIANG KAI-SHEK'S CHINA

Soon after his 1927 White Terror, which nearly exterminated the fledgling Communist Party, Chiang set up a central administration in Nanjing (whose name means "Southern Capital") to rival the one in Beijing ("Northern Capital"). Chiang insisted that his Nationalist government was China's only legitimate one, for it alone was carrying forward the revolutionary spirit of 1911 and honoring the legacy of Sun. The Nanjing Decade, when Chiang governed from that city, would later be derided in PRC textbooks as a time of oppression and mismanagement. In fact, it witnessed a series of state-building efforts and development drives that have a great deal in common with those that have been carried out recently in China.

The Nationalist Party's efforts to create a strong and prosperous "New China," a term revived yet again in 1927, were stymied by two things. One was the series of costly and ultimately unsuccessful "extermination campaigns" aimed at ridding the country of all remaining Communists, while downplaying concerns about foreign threats. Chiang took the line that foreigners, including the increasingly aggressive Japanese, were merely a "disease of the skin," while the "Reds" represented a sickness that struck right at the China's heart. So it was ironic that the second thing that undermined Chiang's grand plans of the Nanjing Decade was the full-scale Japanese invasion of North China. The invasions began in 1931 with encroachments into Manchuria and intensified greatly by 1937, as the battle lines moved into the heartland, eventually reaching Nanjing, where the most brutal Japanese military atrocities of the war were committed.

When Japanese troops committed the infamous Nanjing Massacre, or Rape of Nanking (December 1937–February 1938), the Communists were based far to the north, in the mountain stronghold of Yan'an in Shaanxi Province. This was the end point of their epic Long March, the 1934 trek over thousands of miles taken to escape Chiang's most determined Communist extermination campaign. Faced with the Japanese invasion and under intense pressure from non-allied regional military commanders and even some within his own party, Chiang finally grudgingly agreed to form a Second United Front with the Communists. This alliance between Chiang and Mao's forces was always plagued by mutual distrust. It was in many ways more of a halting of hostilities than a common fight against the foreign enemy.

In the 1940s, much of China was under the direct control of the Japanese military or their Chinese collaborators. Now routinely demonized as "traitors," these collaborators were people who decided, sometimes with great reluctance, to collude with rather than militantly oppose the invaders, convinced in many cases that their country would never again be completely free of Japanese control. China was nominally still run by Chiang's national government, but that government was no longer based in any traditional capital city. Japanese forces drove the Nationalists far inland from Nanjing, and Chiang finally had to set up a temporary wartime base of operations in the city of Chongqing in Sichuan.

In the first part of the decade, the Nationalists were allied not just with the Communists but also with the Americans, who came into the fight against Japan after Pearl Harbor. When Japan surrendered, the Second United Front, not surprisingly, immediately frayed. The rivalry between the Nationalists and Communists was fierce, despite—or perhaps in large part because of—how much they had in common. The Nationalists were just as Leninist in orientation as the Communists, but Chiang broke with Mao on other things. One was the issue of class struggle, which only the Communists thought of as something that drove history forward. Another point of disagreement related to Confucius. Chiang sought to combine Christian values (he converted only in adulthood, but his wife had been born a Christian) with Confucian ones. Mao, by contrast, had come of age during the iconoclastic New Culture Movement, which lasted from 1915 through 1923, and devoted some of his first essays to promoting the idea that reverence for Confucius was reactionary. Confucian ritual and hierarchy had kept China from becoming modern, Mao claimed as a youth and continued to assert later in life. Confucius was to blame for an unjust social system that gave scholars and officials too much power and transformed women into the virtual slaves of all their male relatives.

The Oxford historian Rana Mitter had this conflict in mind when he wrote in his lively and informative book *Modern China: A Very Short Introduction* (2007) that if the two leaders' ghosts floated above today's China, Chiang might be more pleased about what he saw on the ground than Mao. It is true that China is still run by a Communist Party, which would surely vex Chiang's ghost. It is a Communist Party, however, that has stopped celebrating class struggle—Mao's ghost would discover, much to his chagrin, that the pursuit of a "harmonious society" is what China's leaders today talk about most—and that is often willing to treat Confucius with veneration rather than scorn. This was certainly the case at the start of the 2008 Beijing Olympics; the Opening Ceremonies included a quotation from the sage's work (about the pleasure of friends coming from afar) and a set piece involving over two thousand members of the People's Liberation Army, which Mao once commanded, acting the part of the ancient philosopher's disciples.

The Nationalist and Communist armies fought a final battle for control of the Chinese mainland, and Chiang ultimately fled to Taiwan, where he died in 1975. In October 1949, Mao stood atop Tiananmen (The Gate of Heavenly Peace) in Beijing and announced the formation of the newest New China, but Chiang never gave up on the idea that the Nationalists had only staged a strategic retreat. The Nationalists under Chiang treated Taiwan as a temporary staging ground, and its capital city of Taipei as a kind of counterpart to Chongqing during World War II. The Communist Party's leaders on the mainland, meanwhile, spent that same period insisting that Taiwan should be seen as a renegade province, a part of the PRC that was temporarily out of Beijing's reach.

FROM MAO TO NOW

There are many ways to tell the story of the newest New China, a country that took shape under Mao's watch and has continued to evolve under his successors. There is, for example, the officially endorsed version of China's recent past, a "Glorious Quest" story that stresses continuities over time in the actions of the Communist Party, allowing for some mistakes. Most notably, the Cultural Revolution—a complex series of events that began as an orchestrated mass movement spearheaded by Mao to reassert his control of the country—is treated as a chaotic decade that was very bad for the country. But its focus is on progress toward an unchanging goal of national renewal after a "century of humiliation" (lasting from the Opium Wars of the mid-1800s through the Japanese invasions of the World War II era) and devastating periods of misrule by the Qing, then the warlords, and then a corrupt and despotic Nationalist Party.

In stripped-down form, the main theme in this story is simple: the Communist Party's leaders, who have demonstrated great wisdom and are motivated by love of the nation, have made strides to better the lot of ordinary people, modernize the country, and return China to its former status as the leading regional power and one of the world's most important states. In this tale, the late 1940s through the late 1950s was a time of great accomplishments. Land-reform brought about a more equal distribution of rural holdings, and the corrupt and impoverished cities of Chiang Kai-shek's time were replaced by cities that were better governed and free of beggars and exploited workers. Women were given new rights, while literacy rates and life expectancy rose dramatically. China even helped North Korea prevent the United States from turning the Korean peninsula into a virtual American colony during the Korean War.

In this official version of history, many of these accomplishments were due to Mao's vision and leadership. Mao is conceded to have made mistakes, especially during the Great Leap Forward, which began in the late 1950s and triggered a famine that continued into the early 1960s, and during the Cultural Revolution (1966–76). He is seen, though, as having done much more good for the nation than harm. Even in the later stages of his life, he developed a theoretical framework that made his country seem like the logical leader of struggles for liberation throughout the developing world. In the 1960s, he made it possible for China to join the circle of nations with atomic weapons, and in the early 1970s, he worked to reestablish ties with the United States and succeeded in having the PRC replace the Republic of China (Taiwan) as holder of the "Chinese" seat on the UN Security Council. In the end, the official line holds, his impact on the country was 70 percent positive and only 30 percent negative. Much of the blame for the mistakes he made in his dotage is laid at the feet of the "Gang of Four," a group made up of his wife Jiang Qing and three of her allies, who are portrayed as having taken unfair advantage of an old man.

The period following Mao's death, especially the so-called Reform Era after December 1978, when Deng Xiaopeng became China's paramount leader, is treated as a second age of great accomplishments. The pursuit of modernization and harmony rather than the promotion of equality became the main focus. In Chinese official rhetoric, the reforms introduced by Deng and his successors are all intended simply to bring to completion Mao's revolutionary goal of strengthening China. When the Gang of Four were punished for their crimes, they were not charged with being too revolutionary, but rather with being counterrevolutionary; that is, doing things that endangered the country's movement forward.

Among the many ways of telling the tale of the Mao years and the period after his death, two have gained prominence in the West. One might be called the "Troubling Path Corrected." It paints Mao and Deng as being as different as night and day. Deng was a pragmatist, whereas Mao was an ideologue. It was Deng's readiness to experiment with market reforms that allowed China finally to start shedding its longtime status as an impoverished nation. He is credited with steering China onto the right track by implementing reforms that encouraged entrepreneurship both in the countryside, where the decollectivization of agriculture allowed farmers to keep some of the profits from crops grown on private plots, and in joint ventures between Chinese companies and foreign investors in "special economic zones." The narrative treats Deng as a proponent of moderation, eager to move China into step with global norms, making it more open and less authoritarian. He might have talked about "socialism with Chinese characteristics," but what he was really doing was moving China toward capitalism—and liberalizing it slowly but steadily in the process.

This scenario lost favor in the West, however, in the aftermath of the Tiananmen struggle of 1989. Student-led protests in Beijing called for an end to corruption and increased personal freedoms. Soon urbanites from many walks of life were gathering en masse in Tiananmen Square in Beijing and the main plazas of scores of other cities. The government responded by imposing martial law, denouncing the demonstrators as "rioters" and "counterrevolutionaries," and the struggle became in large part a fight for the right to protest. Deng was instrumental in calling in troops to stop this inspiring struggle for change, and he is rightly seen as one of the main architects of the June 4th Massacre, when unarmed citizens were mowed down with automatic weapons on the streets near Tiananmen Square.

A contrasting Western narrative, which gained influence after the 1989 crackdown, stresses continuities between Mao's China and the PRC of today—but not positive ones of the sort found in China's official tale. This "Unchanging Dictatorship" scenario depicts the enormous death toll of the Great Leap Forward famine and the persecutions of the Cultural Revolution years as the defining phenomena of the early PRC. Promoters of this version of the past admit that Deng and his successors have done many things differently but argue that it is a mistake to forget some basic things that have never changed. The Party, for example, has never allowed any competing political organization to exist, has never stopped imprisoning those who speak out most forcefully against its rule, and has always been led by men (and they have nearly all been men) who enjoy special privileges.

This is not the place to parse all of the strengths and weaknesses of these story lines, but it is worth noting some things that are most misleading about each. The biggest problem with the official line is surely the way it minimizes and sometimes even denies the occurrence of truly horrific acts. The Great Leap Forward began with Mao's misguided call for China's people to focus all of their energy on the unrealistic goal of catching up with the West quickly in fields such as steel production. It was much more than just a misstep or miscalculation. The policy caused widespread starvation and malnutrition; local officials, obsessed with meeting impossible agricultural quotas, promoted foolish farming methods, and villagers, focused on smelting ore in backyard furnaces, stopped tending crops. Exact figures may vary, but there is a consensus now that the number of victims of these policies must have been in the tens of millions. The Cultural Revolution began when young Red Guards fiercely loyal to Mao denounced all officials they deemed insufficiently true to his vision. In the end, warring factions, each of whom claimed to be the only ones to truly understand the Great Leader's ideal, fought pitched battles for control of cities. The official narrative recognizes the Cultural Revolution as a troubling event, but avoids dealing with it in any detailed fashion. It denies that the June 4th Massacre even occurred. Many of the Communist Party's oppressive actions in Tibet and Xinjiang are badly distorted or ignored.

The Western tales I have described, though, have their own problems. For example, to give Deng and later leaders all the credit for China's economic boom glosses over the fact that the Mao years ended with a country whose population was primed for economic success. The economic takeoff that began under Deng reached new heights under his successor Jiang Zemin, who rose to the top spot in the Party hierarchy in the wake of the June 4th Massacre, and Hu Jintao, who became the country's paramount leader in 2002. There are many reasons why China prospered, but one thing that made this possible was that Mao left China with a large pool of relatively well-educated workers. Literacy rates far outstripped those of many other developing countries. It also helped greatly that these workers, thanks to improvements in public health, were often in relatively good physical shape.

What then of the Unchanging Dictatorship story? This, too, is flawed. There is no question that there are many limits on political freedom in today's China. Repression is especially severe in areas where there are significant numbers of disaffected residents, such as the Tibetan plateau, and the Party is in many ways the same kind of organization that it has always been. Still, the state has become a much less intrusive force in people's day-to-day lives, and there are many in China who feel much freer to express themselves in private settings—and certain public ones as well—than they did under Mao.

• • •

The pioneering historian and sociologist Charles Tilly, who did so much to illuminate the birth pangs of industrial modernity in Europe, wrote that the primary goal of social historians is to show how ordinary people "lived the big changes." China's politics will, of course, be further examined in the chapters of this book, but the stories focus primarily on social history.

The contributors sensibly steer clear of making predictions about a land that continually makes fools of prognosticators who speculate about what lies ahead. Instead, they simply tell the stories of individual *Chinese Characters* living through their country's remarkable rise after centuries of war and want. Taken together, these forays into charting the social history of the present illuminate today's China and may serve to contextualize the twists and turns the country will surely take in the future.

Doubters and Believers

One of the most important things separating the People's Republic of China of Maoist times from the China of the past few decades is the decline of faith in the official ideology of the Communist Party and the rise of faith in other creeds. Since Mao's death, there has been a dramatic uptick in the number of followers of various religions and philosophical schools of thoughts. Some of these systems of belief, such as Taoism and Confucianism, have deep historical roots in China but largely disappeared or went underground during the Cultural Revolution. Others, such as varieties of Protestantism, are experiencing their first great heyday in China. And still others, most famously the banned Falun Gong sect, are new religions altogether, albeit often made up of elements of several preexisting traditions. In some cases, skepticism about the old verities, including Mao's celebration of class struggle, has led to a simple embrace of materialism. But other kinds of beliefs, including an ardent form of nationalism that both supports and sometimes challenges the official rhetoric of the Communist Party, are also found in China today.

Part One uses the stories of a mountaintop quest, an encounter with a fervent young patriot, and the tale of a Tibetan who must choose between his ethnic heritage and his material future to introduce readers to some of the ways in which individual residents of the PRC are grappling with doubt about and belief in a country defined by both its traditions and its transitions.

CHAPTER 1

The North Peak

IAN JOHNSON

The "voluntary" insurance at the entrance had cost just two yuan, about thirty-five cents, but I had been fleeced all the way from Beijing and somehow this was the final straw. Why did everything have to be so crass and commercialized? I whined to myself. I knew the answers—all the nuanced reasons why so many religious sites in China had been reduced to a carnival—but was in too foul a mood to be rational. The view didn't help either. Once one of Taoism's holiest mountains, Mount Heng in Shanxi Province was a denuded wreck, seeming to consist of nothing but broken slate. I grumbled epitaphs as I climbed the steep trail wondering why I had bothered to come.

Then he appeared on the ridge above me, like something out of a Chinese kung fu thriller: a Taoist priest clad in a blue robe, white breeches, his hair up on his head in a bun. I hesitated for a second. He was moving so quickly that he was almost gone before I could blurt out: "Master, have you seen the priest known as Mysterious Forest?" He stopped, looked at me, and said the priest had moved on.

I didn't really care about Mysterious Forest. I had come to Mount Heng to meet Taoists and here was one. I told him I was researching Taoism and asked if he knew anything about the mountain. He didn't answer but immediately strode down the slate slope to my path, oblivious of the mini-landslide he was causing. "I can help you," he said, turning on his heel. "Follow me."

I rushed to catch up, trying not to let on that I was in un-Taoist-like bad shape, barely able to keep up with this man who must have been twenty years my senior. As we walked—it felt like cantering—he kept looking back and talking, as if his steady stream of chatter could lasso and draw me toward him.

"Have you noticed that Taoism has a lot of temples to Laozi?"

"Yes, sure," I said. "He's the religion's founder and wrote the *Daodejing,* which is a great work."

"Correct. Then tell me what is the second-greatest work of Taoism?"

"*Zhuangzi.* It has many colorful stories and is maybe even more profound than the *Daodejing.*"

"Exactly! Well put. It's even better than the *Daodejing.* It *is* better. It is much better. But have you ever noticed that there are no temples to Zhuangzi? There are hundreds of temples to Laozi but not one to Zhuangzi. Why is that?"

I shook my head. Both Laozi and Zhuangzi were mythical figures. Who knew why Laozi got all the incense burned in his name and Zhuangzi only got a book named after him.

"So here's my idea," he said, stopping at a bend and locking his eyes on mine. "We build a temple to Zhuangzi. You and I. We have met here on this road. It is fate. Foreigners can fund it. It will be China's first temple to Zhuangzi."

My heart began to sink. Not another con.

"It will be cheap," he said, continuing. "Zhuangzi is from my hometown in Henan Province. I know people there and we can get the land for free. The gate receipts can pay back the investors. The officials there are very interested."

Another cockamamie scheme. No wonder Taoists have a reputation for being slippery. I argued to myself that I was being unfair. Then I got a grip; no, I wasn't being unfair, and I started to walk ahead quickly. I needed to find some real Taoists and ditch this guy. But he followed me, talking incessantly as I tried to block out his voice. "It's the twenty-first century. It's the century of Zhuangzi. Last century was Laozi's century but this is Zhuangzi's." Shut up, shut up, I countered in a loud internal voice. Where can I find a real Taoist?

. . .

Chinese religion is so different from Western belief systems that some experts have argued that for most of their history, the Chinese have been a people little concerned with the spiritual. Nothing could be more wrong. Up until the twentieth century, China was a land imbued with religion and the spiritual. The problem is that it wasn't rooted in and controlled by powerful institutions like a church with a clergy but instead consisted of a system of daily practices, including ancestor worship, veneration of mountains and streams, worship of famous people or local gods, belief in fate and fortune-telling, and techniques of physical cultivation like tai chi and qigong. For millennia, this amalgam of practices—often called "folk religion" or "popular religion"—dominated China's spiritual landscape. Organized religions existed but were imports: it was under the pressure of Buddhism, for example, that some of China's indigenous religious practices coalesced around the second century C.E. into an organized religion that loosely became known as Taoism.

For much of the next two thousand years, Taoism (sometimes written as "Daoism") ran a distant second to Buddhism, which was better organized and had a devout cadre of monks who zealously spread their creed around the empire. Buddhism was also a more intellectualized religion and more acceptable for high-ranking officials than Taoism, which seemed a hodgepodge of esoteric and earthy beliefs.

Many religions also combine high philosophy with simple rituals. Catholicism boasts the works of St. Augustine and St. Thomas Aquinas but also rosary beads and saying the "Hail Mary" to atone for sins. But Taoism might take it further than most. Laozi's *Daodejing—The Classic of the Way and Its Power*—is a work on governing written in such a spare, metaphorical style that it can be read as a way to conduct one's own life. The *Zhuangzi* is full of allegories and parables, including some of the most memorable in the Chinese language. But if one takes the entire body of Taoist writing—for example, the 1,400 texts gathered in a compendium known as the *Taoist Canon*—most are works of liturgy and ritual. These include how to summon gods, fast, cure diseases, extend the lifespan, purify vessels, pray, or channel energy around the body. In the West, Taoism has become synonymous with going with the flow *(The Tao of Pooh)* and maximizing pleasure *(The Tao of Sex)*, but throughout most of its history it's been a religion that seeks union with the "way" through carefully scripted rituals and principled living.

I got interested in Taoism because I saw in it a way to understand many different parts of Chinese culture. Taoist principles underlie Chinese calligraphy, painting, poetry, and many great works of literature, such as Wu Cheng'en's *Journey to the West,* which is ostensibly about a Buddhist's monk's journey to India but on a deeper level is a book on Taoist longevity practices. I thought of Taoism as the DNA of Chinese culture, and while I later learned that this was a bit of a stretch, I found I learned a lot about China by looking at its only indigenous religion.

I quickly realized, however, that Taoism had suffered the most of China's religions. The nineteenth and twentieth centuries were brutal for China, with the country unable to ward off the West's and then Japan's unstoppable combination of science and advanced capitalism. The country was being carved up piece by piece, and the problem seemed to lie deeper than just in outdated military technology. Reformers began to cast doubt on everything Chinese, especially the country's religions. Influenced by Western definitions of religion and superstition, some Chinese thinkers decided that most Chinese belief was mere "superstition" and only a few narrow practices—basically more intellectualized and organized forms of Buddhism and Taoism—were real religions worthy of the name. The rest had to be destroyed.

What followed was one of the most sustained assaults on religion in modern history. Starting with the reform movement of 1898 and picking up speed when the last emperor was overthrown in 1911, a wave of violence was visited upon Buddhist, Taoist, and Confucian places of worship. Islam and Christianity also suffered, but Islam is closely tied to specific minority groups, and Christianity was at times protected and at other times persecuted because of its close ties to Western colonialists. At the turn of the twentieth century, the best estimate is that China had one million places of worship. When the Communists took over in 1949, half of those had been destroyed, turned into schools, or commandeered for other purposes. As the most radical of the groups that advocated destroying the past, the Communists continued the attack with even more zeal. By the time radical communists were overthrown at the end of the 1970s, almost no place of worship was open. Priests, monks, imams, and nuns had been driven out of their churches and mosques and forced to work in factories or the fields. Many of those practicing celibacy were forced to marry.

Yet what followed was a dramatic revival of religious life. China was still run by a Communist Party that is officially atheist, but starting in the 1980s, religion was tolerated. Communist leaders saw this as a concession to mainly elderly worshippers who, they thought, would die out anyway. What happened shocked authorities: young people began to believe, and religion, far from dying out, flourished. The best guesstimate is that China today has one hundred thousand places of worship, although many of these are simply informal meeting places. That's still just 10 percent of the figure at the end of the nineteenth century, but a significant change from the late 1970s. Opinion polls also reflect a return of belief. Over two-thirds of Chinese say they believe in a higher being, while a quarter say that over the past year, they have experienced the presence of a deity. Those are figures similar to those for Western countries like the United States or Britain.

Why does the government tolerate this revival? One reason is the recognition that belief alone does not threaten the Communist Party's rule. Many government officials also realize that the country suffers from a lack of public morality—for too many people, all that matters is the prosperity of immediate family and the acquisition of riches. Religion, even Party officials grudgingly admit, can instill values. And then there's money: for local governments, holy mountains and temples can help fill coffers, aiding an area's tourist industry. Entrance tickets—and even insurance—are sold, and the local government siphons off a good chunk of the profits.

This was the case at Mount Heng, also known as the North Peak, one of the five holy mountains that marked the extent of civilization in very early Chinese history. The mountains were seen as pillars holding up the Chinese world; even the emperor worshipped them at the Temple of the Earth in Beijing. But when I made this trip to visit it in 2000, the North Peak had only been officially open for a year and was mostly in the hands of greedy government officials, who sold tickets and tourism "insurance" policies and harassed the few Taoists who tried to live there. Soon into my trip, I was pretty sure that the rich Taoist traditions I'd come searching for had been extinguished.

• • •

We soon arrived at the main halls, one of the most down-at-heel temple complexes I'd seen at a major Taoist site. I hadn't expected much. My friend Brock, an American businessman who runs a charity devoted to helping renovate Taoist sites, had visited a few years earlier, and he told me it was a wreck. Still, this was one of Taoism's holy mountains, and I thought something might have survived the past century's tumult.

"This is the North Peak," the Taoist announced as we looked at the temples, which were so weather-beaten that they seemed to sag under some enormous historical weight. I generally like old buildings, but these were sad, more like corpses than relics of a glorious past. The

Taoist began to talk again but my inner voice blocked him out. Taoists, I thought; there must be some real ones here like Mysterious Forest. Brock had met him, and they meditated together. That seemed like a real experience. This seemed like a waste of time. But my Taoist's voice was loud and persistent. I glanced at his name card: Xianfo Shengren.

"Shengren means saint," I said. "Is this a title?"

"It's a goal," he said, waving off my question. "Some people call me that."

I stifled a laugh as we stepped inside the main hall, an unimposing building about thirty feet long and twenty feet deep, with a ten-foot-high ceiling. The cramped feeling was reinforced by red ropes that kept us in a small area directly in front of the altar. Most temples allow visitors to walk around, but this limited access to the front of the main altar. It seemed annoying, but as I stood there I began to see why. The altar had only three statues, but the central one was a Ming dynasty sculpture of the god of the North Peak. The statues of the acolytes flanking him were new, but the main deity was a genuine piece of art, covered in dark gold leaf, at least 400 years old. That made it a rarity for a Chinese temple—over the past century, anti-religious zealots had singled out statues for destruction, acting as if they were missionaries eager to wipe out pagan idols. But, somehow, here was the real thing, a dark, brooding god that could stand up to any piece of religious art I had seen. It was protected by glass, and the ropes made sure we kept our distance. A single stick of incense smoldered. The trip was beginning to feel more worthwhile.

Xianfo pointed to the statue. "During the Cultural Revolution, a Red Guard tried to smash the god, but he broke his arm when he struck the statue. Another Red Guard fell to his death ascending the mountain. After that, everyone fled, and the god was saved."

I wondered what really happened and imagined something very dramatic: angry villagers pushing a Red Guard off the sheer precipices or beating one of Mao's fanatics before his club could strike the statue. Maybe locals simply told the Red Guards the most dangerous way up the mountain, which in places can be treacherously steep. Some had died and the rest had given up. Stories about temples in the Cultural Revolution often involved miracles. For the Maoists, their leader himself was nearly a god, and they began circulating miraculous stories. Following Mao's thoughts could increase production, cause fruit to stop rotting, and even raise the dead. His "Little Red Book" of quotations was treated like a religious text, and young believers undertook what can only be described as pilgrimages to see him, even just for a split second.

But the victims had their miracles too. I had visited a temple outside Beijing once and the groundskeeper had told me that when Red Guards were assaulting a statue, a ceiling panel fell and crushed the young attackers. Behind the panel was a carving of a dragon, and the story was born of the dragon god defending the temple. These tales are told privately and rarely recorded—part of the untold history of the rural, uneducated oppressed. The Party is willing to admit that its first thirty years in power were a series of disasters, but it doesn't want its face rubbed in it. Instead, one is supposed to forget its crimes and move forward. Most people do this. It is sensible, but it has caused a collective amnesia to settle over the country.

I felt Xianfo's gaze on me and realized my mind had wandered. "There are miracles," he said. "You have to open your eyes. Look in front of us. The god of the North Peak existed. He was a real person. He died, and his body didn't decompose. So people thought he was a spirit. His body is inside the statue," Xianfo said, lifting up his left arm with a flourish. He shook his sleeves so that his index finger, pointing at the statue, dramatically appeared out of the garments. I had to smile, but I knew he wasn't trying to be funny. He was being dramatic, because for him this was a truth that he was trying to make me understand.

"I can show you a lot of dead bodies in the mountains. Hermits go into the hills to meditate, die, and their bodies don't decompose," Xianfo said, turning away from the statue to look out of the door at the endless mountains stretching across the yellow plateau. "It's common."

"Yes," I said absently. "It's very dry here in North China." Then I caught myself. This was the wrong attitude. I was ruining it—the same game authorities played when they tried to distinguish between religion and superstition. He was trying to tell me something. He cast a glance at me and went on. "You have to know where to look. There are people in the mountains of the Central Plains who have gone to the hills for centuries. They die, but no one finds their body, just their staff. They have gone to heaven, immortal. This is my goal."

He fixed his eyes on me and said steadily, "You don't believe me, but I lived with them in the mountains. They were my teachers." Xianfo walked outside toward the mountains, and I followed. My eyes teared in the cold, bright light, and I furrowed my brow in concentration, for the first time trying to listen.

"Here's another strange thing," Xianfo said. A huge elm tree grew on the terrace in front of the temple, its roots sticking out of the ground. It had grown at such an angle that it was almost parallel to the earth and jutted out into the air above the slope below us. "It is named after Zhang Guolao, one of the Eight Immortals. We call it the Guolao Elm. During the Cultural Revolution, some people hacked at its branches and tried to uproot it," he said, pointing at the dead roots sticking out of the ground. "It seemed dead but then after the Cultural Revolution ended in 1976, it sprouted new shoots and leaves."

We contemplated the tree for a while and walked back inside the temple to the altar and the beautiful god. "Have a seat," he said, kicking the kneeler out toward me. I hesitated, thinking it sacrilegious to sit on something people knelt on to pray, but he waved his arms dismissively and pulled a tin tray off the altar. It held a few apples and dry cookies, the locals' meager offerings to the god.

"Have an apple." I looked aghast, but then laughed at his casual attitude to the formal practice of his religion. He had lived in the mountains with immortals, I thought; he must know Taoist etiquette better than I. "We can't waste them," he said. "Eat one. They're local products. Very good."

He sat on the kneeler too and we faced each other, straddling the wood. He drew closer until our feet intertwined. "It's fate that has drawn us here," he started, and I wondered if he was about to make another sales pitch for a temple. But then I relaxed and told myself to shut up.

"You know, I don't care about the temple to Zhuangzi too much. It was just an idea I had back then, although I do think that Zhuangzi deserves a temple. But let's forget it; I can see you are not an entrepreneurial person. The problem is how to save Taoism. The Cultural Revolution brainwashed people. They don't understand anything about their own religion. We have Taoist philosophy, which is widely admired, and the religion, which is looked down on by everyone except the peasants. That was why I brought up the Zhuangzi temple. We could link the philosophy to the religion and bring more prestige to Taoism.

"Local officials don't understand this. They just want money. They wanted to reopen this for tourism and didn't want Taoists in the temples. They reopened the temple last year, but I was here already. I was here before they permitted it to be reopened. I had been here for years, sitting in my room playing the *erhu* [a two-stringed fiddle] and practicing internal alchemy [a kind of meditation] for two hours a day. I said we Taoists would stay here, and that without us there would be no [religious] atmosphere. They eventually relented."

I remembered what he said about living in the mountains and began to understand. "When did you come here?" I asked, guessing at the answer.

"I spent the Cultural Revolution practicing martial arts and medicine in the Kunlun Mountains"—the Kunlun Mountains, I thought, the axis mundi of traditional China, the abode of gods and mythical creatures. They are at the other end of the Central Plains, about six hundred miles south, a refuge overlooking the turmoil below.

"Many people went to the mountains at that time. I had a master, much older than I. He had lived on the North Peak. He had found the Tao here and had a strong attachment to this mountain. He knew when the turmoil was over but said he was too old to leave the Kunlun Mountains and return here. So he said, go to the North Peak and rebuild it. I arrived in 1980. I was fifty years old."

I could not believe he was seventy already; he seemed so vigorous. I asked how he had managed to start such an ambitious project at that age.

"I know medicine and treated people. I opened a clinic and a consulting company telling fortunes. I got rich; I invested one million yuan [almost US$160,000], basically all my money into preventing these halls from collapsing. This was before the government got interested. The money wasn't really mine; it was to follow my master's orders. The peak had to be rebuilt. Can you understand this?"

It was late afternoon, and the light was less harsh. The mountain wasn't that high, about 6,000 feet, but it had a quiet grandeur. Even though denuded, and featuring nothing but dilapidated buildings, this had once been a beautiful part of the country and a majestic place of worship. I could see why it had been one of China's five holy mountains and why someone would devote the last part of his life to saving it. Xianfo was born in 1930 and wasn't even twenty when the Communists took over. His faith must have been strong for him to have survived the next thirty years of persecution. He got up and nodded to me. "Let me introduce you to more Taoists."

I followed him toward a set of doors in the back of the temple. He raised one hand and like a Taoist master in a movie seemed to push them open with a burst of energy. They flew apart, and in front of us was a scene that made me believe. It was his team: an even older man, who looked like a caretaker, a young girl with a deformed arm, and a boy with skin hardened like a carapace. They were sitting around a table drinking thin soup and eating buns. The room had a concrete floor and two bunk beds up against the wall, with four thin quilts neatly folded. Clearly, they all slept here, even Xianfo. The old man and the girl continued to eat. The boy looked up, solemnly grave as if about to perform a ceremony.

My eyes locked on the boy, and I suddenly realized the beauty of the mountain, the temple, and Xianfo's life.

"His name is Qing Feng," Xianfo said. The name means Clear Wind and it seemed a perfect name for a Taoist.

"His parents?" I asked.

"His parents abandoned him in our care three years ago, and he was hopeless. He had a terrible disease. We tried to cure him. We took him to a hospital, but it was no use. But after a year on the mountain, he recovered. He's six now and in good health."

The boy looked vigorous but withered. His face was terribly dark, his hands gnarled and hardened into claws. I gestured at the robes. How could a child be a Taoist priest?

"He has experienced enough. He is a Taoist," Xianfo said with finality.

I nodded quickly in agreement. Then a voice spoke, a husky unearthly sound that seemed to come out of the ground beneath us. I looked up, startled, and realized it had come from the boy.

"Master, lunch is ready."

CHAPTER 2

The New Generation's Neocon Nationalists

EVAN OSNOS

On the morning of April 15, 2008, a short video entitled "2008 China Stand Up!" appeared on Sina, a Chinese web site. The video's origin was a mystery: unlike the usual YouTube–style clips, it had no host, no narrator, and no signature except the initials "CTGZ."

It was a homespun documentary, and it opened with a Technicolor portrait of Chairman Mao, sunbeams radiating from his head. Out of silence came an orchestral piece, thundering with drums, as a black screen flashed, in both Chinese and English, one of Mao's mantras: "Imperialism will never abandon its intention to destroy us." Then a cut to present-day photographs and news footage, and a fevered sprint through conspiracies and betrayals, the "farces, schemes, and disasters" confronting China today. The sinking Chinese stock market (the work of foreign speculators who "wildly manipulated" Chinese stock prices and lured rookie investors to lose their fortunes). Shoppers beset by inflation, a butcher counter where "even pork has become a luxury." And a warning: this is the dawn of a global "currency war," and the West intends to "make Chinese people foot the bill" for America's financial woes.

A cut, then, to another front: rioters looting stores and brawling in Lhasa, the Tibetan capital. The music crescendos as words flash across the scenes: "So-called peaceful protest!" A montage of foreign press clippings critical of China—nothing but "rumors, all speaking with one distorted voice." The screen fills with the logos of CNN, the BBC, and other news organizations, which give way to a portrait of Joseph Goebbels. The orchestra and the rhetoric climb toward a final sequence: "Obviously, there is a scheme behind the scenes to encircle China. A new Cold War!" The music turns triumphant with images of China's Olympic hurdler Liu Xiang standing in Tiananmen Square, raising the Olympic torch, "a symbol of Peace and Friendship!" But, first, one final act of treachery: in Paris, protesters attempt to wrest the Olympic torch from its official carrier, forcing guards to fend them off—a "long march" for a new era. The film ends with the image of a Chinese flag, aglow in the sunlight, and a solemn promise: "We will stand up and hold together always as one family in harmony!"

The video, which is just over six minutes long and was later posted on YouTube, captured the mood of nationalism that surged through China after a Tibetan uprising sparked foreign criticism of China's hosting of the 2008 Summer Olympics. Citizens were greeting the criticism with rare fury. Thousands demonstrated in front of Chinese outlets of Carrefour, a French supermarket chain, in retaliation for what they considered France's sympathy for pro-Tibetan activists. Charles Zhang, who holds a Ph.D. from the Massachusetts Institute of Technology (MIT) and is the founder and CEO of Sohu, a leading Chinese search engine, called for a boycott of French products "to make the thoroughly biased French media and public feel losses and pain." When U.S. Speaker of the House Nancy Pelosi denounced China's handling of Tibet, Xinhua, China's official news service, called her "disgusting." State-run media revived language from another age: the magazine *Outlook Weekly* warned that "domestic and foreign hostile forces have made the Beijing Olympics a focus for infiltration and sabotage." In the anonymity of the web, decorum deteriorated. "People who fart through the mouth will get shit stuffed down their throats by me!" one commentator wrote in a forum hosted by a semi-official newspaper. "Someone give me a gun! Don't show mercy to the enemy!" wrote another. The comments were an embarrassment to many Chinese, and they were difficult for foreign journalists, who had begun receiving threats, to ignore. (An anonymous letter to my fax machine in Beijing warned, "Clarify the facts on China . . . or you and your loved ones will wish you were dead.")

In its first week and a half, the video by CTGZ drew more than a million hits and tens of thousands of favorable comments. It rose to the site's fourth-most-popular rating. (A television blooper clip of a yawning news anchor was no. 1.) On average, the film attracted nearly two clicks per second. It became a manifesto for a self-styled vanguard in defense of China's honor, a patriotic swath of society that the Chinese call the *fen qing,* the angry youth.

Nineteen years after the crackdown on student-led protests in Tiananmen Square, China's young elite rose again this spring—not in pursuit of liberal democracy but in defense of sovereignty and prosperity. Nicholas Negroponte, the founder of MIT's Media Laboratory and one of the early ideologists of the Internet, once predicted that the global reach of the web would transform the way we think about ourselves as countries. The state, he predicted, will evaporate "like a mothball, which goes from solid to gas directly" and "there will be no more room for nationalism than there is for smallpox." In China, things have gone differently.

A young Chinese friend of mine, who spends most of his time online, traced the screen name CTGZ to an e-mail address. It belonged to a 28-year-old graduate student in Shanghai named Tang Jie, and it was his first video. A couple of weeks later, I met Tang Jie at the gate of Fudan University, a top Chinese school situated on a modern campus that radiates from a pair of thirty-story steel-and-glass towers that could pass for a corporate headquarters. He wore a crisp powder-blue oxford shirt, khakis, and black dress shoes. He had bright hazel eyes and rounded features—a baby face, everyone tells him—and a dusting of goatee and mustache on his chin and upper lip. He bounded over to welcome me as I stepped out of a cab, and he tried to pay my fare.

Tang spends most of his time working on his dissertation, which is on Western philosophy. He specializes in phenomenology; specifically, in the concept of "intersubjectivity" as theorized by Edmund Husserl, the German philosopher who influenced Sartre, among others. In addition to Chinese, Tang reads English and German easily, but he speaks them infrequently, so at times he swerves, apologetically, among languages. He is working on his Latin and ancient Greek. He is so self-effacing and soft-spoken that his voice can drop to a whisper. He laughs sparingly, as if he were conserving energy. For fun, he listens to classical Chinese music, though he also enjoys screwball comedies by the Hong Kong star Stephen Chow. He is proudly unhip. The screen name CTGZ is an adaptation of two obscure terms from classical poetry: *changting* and *gongzi,* which together translate as "the noble son of the pavilion." Unlike some elite Chinese students, Tang has never joined the Communist Party, for fear that it would impugn his objectivity as a scholar.

Tang lives alone in a sixth-floor walkup, a studio of less than seventy-five square feet, which could be mistaken for a library storage room occupied by a fastidious squatter. Books cover every surface and great mounds list from the shelves above his desk. His collections encompass, more or less, the span of human thought: Plato leans against Lao-tzu, Wittgenstein, Bacon, Fustel de Coulanges, Heidegger, the Quran. When Tang wanted to widen his bed by a few inches, he laid plywood across the frame and propped up the edges with piles of books. Eventually, volumes overflowed the room, and they now stand outside his front door in a wall of cardboard boxes.

Tang slumped into his desk chair. We talked for a while, and I asked if he had any idea that his video would be so popular. He smiled. "It appears I have expressed a common feeling, a shared view," he said.

Next to him sat Liu Chengguang, a cheerful, broad-faced Ph.D. student in political science who recently translated into Chinese a lecture on the subject of "Manliness" by the conservative Harvard professor Harvey Mansfield. Sprawled on the bed, wearing a gray sweatshirt, was Xiong Wenchi, who earned a Ph.D. in political science before taking a teaching job last year. And to Tang's left sat Zeng Kewei, a lean and stylish banker, who picked up a master's degree in Western philosophy before going into finance. Like Tang, each of his friends was in his twenties, was the first in his family to go to college, and had been drawn to the study of Western thought.

"China was backward throughout its modern history, so we were always seeking the reasons for why the West grew strong," Liu said. "We learned from the West. All of us who are educated have this dream: Grow strong by learning from the West."

Tang and his friends were so gracious, so thankful that I'd come to listen to them, that I began to wonder if China's anger of last spring should be viewed as an aberration. They implored me not to make that mistake.

"We've been studying Western history for so long, we understand it well," Zeng said. "We think our love for China, our support for the government and the benefits of this country, is not a spontaneous reaction. It has developed after giving the matter much thought."

In fact, their view of China's direction, if not their vitriol, is consistent with the Chinese mainstream. Almost nine out of ten Chinese approve of the way things are going in the country—the highest share of any of the twenty-four countries surveyed by the Pew Research Center in 2008. (In the United States, by comparison, just two out of ten voiced approval.) As for the more assertive strain of patriotism, scholars point to a Chinese petition against Japan's membership in the UN Security Council. At last count, it had attracted more than forty million signatures, roughly the population of Spain. I asked Tang to show me how he made his film. He turned to face the screen of his Lenovo desktop PC. "We must thank Bill Gates," he said.

When people began rioting in Lhasa in March 2008, Tang followed the news closely. As usual, he was receiving his information from American and European news sites, in addition to China's official media. Like others his age, he has no hesitation about tunneling under the government firewall, a vast infrastructure of digital filters and human censors that blocks politically objectionable content from reaching computers in China. Younger Chinese friends of mine regard the firewall as they would an officious lifeguard at a swimming pool; an occasional, largely irrelevant, intrusion.

To get around it, Tang detours through a proxy server—a digital way station overseas that connects a user with a blocked web site. He watches television exclusively online. Tang also receives foreign news clips from Chinese students abroad. (According to the Institute of International Education, the number of Chinese students in the United States—some 67,000—has grown by nearly two-thirds in the past decade.) He's baffled that foreigners might imagine that people of his generation are somehow unwise to the distortions of censorship.

"Because we are in such a system, we are always asking ourselves whether we are brainwashed," he said. "We are always eager to get other information from different channels." Then he added, "But when you are in a so-called free system you never think about whether you are brainwashed."

At the time, news and opinion about Tibet was swirling on Fudan's electronic bulletin board, or BBS. The board was alive with criticism of foreign coverage of Tibet. Tang had seen a range of foreign press clippings deemed by Chinese web users to be misleading or unfair. A photograph on CNN.com, for instance, had been cropped around military trucks bearing down on unarmed protesters. But an uncropped version showed a crowd of demonstrators lurking nearby, including someone with an arm cocked, hurling something at the trucks. To Tang, the cropping looked like a deliberate distortion. (CNN disputed this and said that the caption fairly describes the scene.)

"It was a joke," Tang said bitterly. That photograph and others crisscrossed China by e-mail, scrawled with criticism, while people added more examples from the *Times of London,* Fox News, German television, and French radio. It was a range of news organizations and, to those inclined to see it as such, it smacked of a conspiracy. It shocked people like Tang, who put faith in the Western press, but, more important, it offended them: Tang thought that he was living in the moment of greatest prosperity and openness in his country's modern history, and yet the world still seemed to view China with suspicion. As if he needed confirmation, Jack Cafferty, a CNN commentator, called China's government "the same bunch of goons and thugs they've been for the last 50 years," a quote that rippled across the front pages in China, and CNN later apologized. Like many of his peers, Tang couldn't figure out why foreigners were so agitated about Tibet, an impoverished backwater, as he saw it, that China had tried for decades to civilize. Boycotting the Beijing Games in the name of Tibet seemed as logical to him as shunning the Salt Lake City Olympics to protest America's treatment of the Cherokee.

Tang scoured YouTube in search of a rebuttal, a clarification of the Chinese perspective, but he found nothing in English except pro-Tibet videos. He was already busy—under contract from a publisher for a Chinese translation of Leibniz's *Discourse on Metaphysics* and other writings—but he couldn't shake the idea of speaking up on China's behalf.

"I thought, OK, I'll make something," he said.

Before Tang could start, however, he was obligated to go home for a few days. His mother had told him to be back for the harvest season. She needed his help in the fields, digging up bamboo shoots.

. . .

Tang is the youngest of four siblings from a farming family near the eastern city of Hangzhou. For breaking China's one-child policy, his parents paid fines measured in grain: Tang's birth cost them 200 kilos of unmilled rice. ("I'm not very expensive," he says.)

Neither his mother nor his father could read or write. Until the fourth grade, Tang had no name. He went by Little Four, after his place in the family order. When that became impractical, his father began calling him Tang Jie, an abbreviated homage to his favorite comedian, Tang Jiezhong, half of a popular act in the style of Abbott and Costello.

Tang was bookish, and in a large, boisterous household, he said little. He took to science fiction. "I can tell you everything about all those movies, like *Star Wars,*" he told me. He was a good, though not spectacular student, but he showed a precocious interest in ideas. "He wasn't like other kids, who spent their pocket money on food. He saved all his money to buy books," said his sister Tang Xiaoling, who is seven years older. None of his siblings had studied past the eighth grade, and they regarded him as an admirable oddity. "If he had questions that he couldn't figure out, then he couldn't sleep," his sister said. "For us, if we didn't get it, we just gave up."

In high school, Tang improved his grades and had some success at science fairs as an inventor. But he was frustrated. "I discovered that science can't help your life," he said. He happened upon a Chinese translation of a fanciful Norwegian novel, *Sophie's World,* by the philosophy teacher Jostein Gaarder, in which a teenage girl encounters the history of great thinkers. "It was then that I discovered philosophy," Tang said.

Patriotism was not a particularly strong presence in his house, but landmarks of national progress became the backdrop of his adolescence. When Tang was in junior high, the Chinese were still celebrating the country's first major freeway, completed a few years before. "It was famous. We were proud of this. At last we had a highway!" he recalled one day, with a laugh, as we whizzed down an expressway in Shanghai. "Now we have highways everywhere, even in Tibet."

Supermarkets opened in his home town, and, eventually, so did an Internet café. (Tang, who was eighteen at the time, was particularly fond of the web sites for the White House and NASA, because they had kids' sections that used simpler English sentences.) Tang enrolled at Hangzhou Normal University. He came to credit his country and his family for opportunities that his siblings had never had. By the time he reached Fudan, in 2003, he lived in a world of ideas. "He had a pure passion for philosophy," said Ma Jun, a fellow philosophy student who met him early on. "A kind of religious passion."

. . .

The Internet had barely taken root in China before it became a vessel for nationalism. At the Atlanta Olympics in 1996, as the Chinese delegation marched into the stadium, the NBC announcer Bob Costas riffed on China's "problems with human rights, property right disputes, the threat posed to Taiwan." Then he mentioned "suspicions" that Chinese athletes used performance-enhancing drugs. Even though the web in China was in its infancy (there were just five telephone lines for every hundred people), comments spread instantly among Chinese living abroad. The timing couldn't have been more opportune: after more than fifteen years of reform and Westernization, Chinese writers were pushing back against Hollywood, McDonald's, and American values. An impassioned book by a group of young intellectuals titled *Zhongguo keyi shuo bu* (China Can Say No) came out that spring and sold more than a hundred thousand copies in its first month. It decried China's "infatuation with America," which had suppressed the national imagination with a diet of visas, foreign aid, and advertising. If China didn't resist this "cultural strangulation," it would become "a slave," extending a history of humiliating foreign incursions that stretched back to China's defeat in the first Opium War and the British acquisition of Hong Kong in 1842. The Chinese government, which is wary of fast-spreading new ideas, eventually pulled the book off the shelves, but not before a raft of knockoffs (Why China Can Say No; China Still Can Say No; China Always Says No) sought to exploit the same mood.

Groups claiming to represent more than seventy thousand overseas Chinese wrote to NBC asking for an apology for the Costas remarks, according to *Chinese Cyber Nationalism* by Xu Wu, a former journalist in China who now teaches at Arizona State University. They collected donations online and bought an ad in the *Washington Post,* accusing Costas and the network of "ignominious prejudice and inhospitality." NBC apologized and Chinese online activism was born.

The government treated online patriots warily. The activists placed their pride in the Chinese nation, not necessarily in the Party, and leaders rightly sensed that the passion could swerve against them. After a nationalist web site was shut down by censors in 2004, one commentator wrote, "Our government is as weak as sheep!" The government permitted nationalism to grow at some moments but strained to control it at others. The following spring, when Japan approved a new textbook that critics claimed glossed over wartime atrocities, patriots in Beijing drafted protest plans and broadcast them via chat rooms, bulletin boards, and text messages. As many as ten thousand demonstrators took to the streets, hurling paint and bottles at the Japanese Embassy. Despite government warnings to cease these activities, thousands more marched in Shanghai the following week—one of China's largest demonstrations in years—and vandalized the Japanese consulate. At one point, Shanghai police cut off cell-phone service in downtown Shanghai.

"Up to now, the Chinese government has been able to keep a grip on it," Xu Wu told me. "But I call it the 'virtual Tiananmen Square.' They don't need to go there. They can do the same thing online and sometimes be even more damaging."

. . .

Tang was at dinner with friends one night in 2004 when he met Wan Manlu, an elegantly reserved Ph.D. student in Chinese literature and linguistics. Her delicate features suited her name, which includes the character for the finest jade. They sat side by side, but barely spoke. Later, Tang hunted down her screen name—gracelittle—and sent her a private message on Fudan's bulletin board. They worked up to a first date: an experimental opera based on "Regret for the Past," a Chinese story.

They discovered that they shared a frustration with China's unbridled Westernization. "Chinese tradition has many good things, but we've ditched them," Wan told me. "I feel there have to be people to carry them on." She came from a middle-class home, and Tang's humble roots and old-fashioned values impressed her. "For him, from that kind of background, with nobody educated in his family, nobody helping him with schoolwork, with great family pressure, it's not easy to get where he is today," she said.

They were engaged in the spring of 2008. In their years together, Wan watched Tang fall in with a group of students devoted to a charismatic 39-year-old Fudan philosophy professor named Ding Yun, a translator of Leo Strauss (1899–1973), the political philosopher whose admirers include the Harvard political thinker Harvey Mansfield and other neoconservatives. A Strauss student, Abram Shulsky, who co-authored a 1999 essay titled "Leo Strauss and the World of Intelligence (By Which We Do Not Mean Nous)," ran the Pentagon's Office of Special Plans before the invasion of Iraq. Since then, other Strauss disciples have vigorously ridiculed suggestions of a connection between Strauss's thought and Bush-era foreign policy.

Professor Ding teaches a Straussian regard for the universality of the classics and encourages his students to revive ancient Chinese thought. "During the 1980s and 90s, most intellectuals had a negative opinion of China's traditional culture," he told me recently. He has close-cropped hair and stylish rectangular glasses, and favors the conspicuously retro loose-fitting shirts of a Tang-dynasty scholar. When Ding grew up, in the early years of reform, "conservative" was a derogatory term, just like "reactionary," he said.

But Ding and others have thrived in recent years amid a new vein of conservatism that runs counter to China's drive for integration with the world. Just as America's conservative movement in the 1960s capitalized on the yearning for a post-liberal retreat to morality and nobility, China's classical revival draws on a nostalgic image of what it means to be Chinese. Ding met Tang in 2003, at the entrance interview for graduate students. "I was the person in charge of the exam," Ding recalled. "I sensed that this kid is very smart and diligent." He admitted Tang to the program, and watched with satisfaction as Tang and other students pushed back against the onslaught of Westernization. Tang developed an appetite for the classics. "The fact is we are very Westernized," he said. "Now we started reading ancient Chinese books, and we rediscovered the ancient China."

This renewed pride has also affected the way Tang and his peers view the economy. They took to a theory that the world profits from China but blocks its attempts to invest abroad. Tang's friend Zeng smiled disdainfully as he ticked off examples of Chinese companies that have tried to invest in America.

"Huawei's bid to buy 3Com was rejected," he said. "CNOOC's bid to buy into Unocal and Lenovo's purchase of part of IBM caused political repercussions. If it's not a market argument, it's a political argument. We think the world is a free market—"

Before he could finish, Tang jumped in. "This is what you—America—taught us," he said. "We opened our market, but when we try to buy your companies, we hit political obstacles. It's not fair."

Their view, which is popular in China across ideological lines, has validity: American politicians have invoked national security concerns, with varying degrees of credibility, to oppose Chinese direct investment. But Tang's view, infused with a sense of victimhood, also obscures some evidence to the contrary: China has succeeded in other deals abroad (its sovereign wealth fund has stakes in the Blackstone Group and in Morgan Stanley), and though China has taken steps to open its markets to foreigners, it remains equally inclined to reject an American attempt to buy an asset as sensitive as a Chinese oil company.

Tang's belief that the United States will seek to obstruct China's rise—"a new Cold War"—extends beyond economics to broader American policy. Disparate issues of relatively minor importance to

Americans, such as support for Taiwan and Washington's calls to raise the value of the yuan, have metastasized in China into a feeling of strategic containment.

. . .

In the spring of 2008, Tang stayed at his family's farm for five days before he could return to Shanghai and finish his movie. He scoured the web for photographs on the subjects that bother him and his friends, everything from inflation to Taiwan's threats of independence. He selected some of the pictures because they were evocative—a man raising his arm in a sea of Chinese flags reminded him of Delacroix's *Liberty Leading the People*—and chose others because they embodied the political moment—a wheelchair-bound Chinese amputee carrying the Olympic flame in Paris, for instance, fending off a protester who was trying to snatch it away.

For a soundtrack, he typed "solemn music" into Chinese search engine Baidu and scanned the results. He landed on a piece by Vangelis, a Yanni-style pop composer from Greece who is best known for his score for the movie *Chariots of Fire*. Tang's favorite Vangelis track was from Ridley Scott's *1492: Conquest of Paradise,* a film about Christopher Columbus. He watched a few seconds of Gérard Depardieu (as Columbus) standing manfully on the deck of a tall ship coursing across the Atlantic. Perfect, Tang thought: "It was a time of globalization."

Tang added scenes of Chairman Mao and the Olympic track star Liu Xiang, both icons of their eras. The film was six minutes and sixteen seconds long. Some title screens in English were full of mistakes, because he was hurrying, but he was anxious to release it. He posted the film to Sina and sent a note to the Fudan bulletin board. As the film climbed in popularity, Ding rejoiced. "We used to think they were just a postmodern, Occidentalized generation," Ding said. "Of course, I thought the students I knew were very good, but the wider generation? I was not very pleased. To see the content of Tang Jie's video, and the scale of its popularity among the youth, made me very happy. Very happy."

Not everyone was pleased. Young patriots are so polarizing in China that some people, by changing the intonation in Chinese, pronounce "angry youth" as "shit youth."

"How can our national self-respect be so fragile and shallow?" Han Han, one of China's most popular young writers, wrote on his blog, in an essay about nationalism. "Somebody says you're a mob, so you curse him, even want to beat him, and then you say, 'We're not a mob.' This is as if someone said you were a fool, so you held up a big sign in front of his girlfriend's brother's dog, saying 'I Am Not a Fool.' The message will get to him, but he'll still think you're a fool."

If the activists thought that they were defending China's image abroad, there was little sign of success. After weeks of patriotic rhetoric emanating from China, a 2008 poll sponsored by the *Financial Times* showed that Europeans ranked China as the greatest threat to global stability, surpassing America.

But the eruption of the angry youth has been even more disconcerting to those interested in furthering democracy. By age and education, Tang and his peers inherit a long legacy of activism that stretches from 1919, when nationalist demonstrators demanded "Mr. Democracy" and "Mr. Science," to 1989, when students flooded Tiananmen Square, challenging the government and erecting a sculpture inspired by the Statue of Liberty. The year 2009 marked the twentieth anniversary of that movement, but the events of the spring of 2008 suggest that prosperity, computers, and Westernization have not driven China's young elite toward tolerance but, rather, persuaded more than a few of them to postpone idealism as long as life keeps improving. The students in 1989 were rebelling against corruption and abuses of power. "Nowadays, these issues haven't disappeared but have worsened," Li Datong, an outspoken newspaper editor and reform advocate, told me. "However, the current young generation turns a blind eye to it. I've never seen them respond to those major domestic issues. Rather, they take a utilitarian, opportunistic approach."

One caricature of young Chinese holds that they know virtually nothing about the crackdown at Tiananmen Square—known in Chinese as "the June 4th incident"—because the authorities have purged it from the nation's official history. It's not that simple, however. Anyone who can click on a proxy server can discover as much about Tiananmen as he chooses to learn. And yet many Chinese have concluded that the movement was misguided and naïve.

"We accept all the values of human rights, of democracy," Tang told me. "We accept that. The issue is how to realize it."

I met dozens of urbane students and young professionals the spring that Tang posted his video. We often got to talking about Tiananmen Square. In a typical conversation, one college senior asked whether she should interpret the killing of protesters at Kent State in 1970 as a fair measure of American freedom. Liu Yang, a graduate student in environmental engineering, said, "June 4th could not and should not succeed at that time. If June 4th had succeeded, China would be worse and worse, not better."

Liu, who is twenty-six, once considered himself a liberal. As a teenager, he and his friends happily criticized the Communist Party. "In the 1990s, I thought that the Chinese government is not good enough. Maybe we need to set up a better government," he told me. "The problem is that we didn't know what a good government would be. So we let the Chinese Communist Party stay in place. The other problem is we didn't have the power to get them out. They have the army!"

When Liu got out of college, he found a good job as an engineer at an oil services company. He was earning more money in a month than his parents, retired laborers living on a pension, earned in a year. Eventually, he saved enough money that, with scholarships, he was able to enroll in a Ph.D. program at Stanford University. He had little interest in the patriotic pageantry of the Olympics until he saw the fracas around the torch in Paris. "We were furious," he said, and when the torch came to San Francisco, he and other Chinese students surged toward the relay route to support it. When I was in San Francisco, we arranged to meet at a Starbucks near his dorm in Palo Alto. He arrived on his mountain bike and wore a Nautica fleece pullover and jeans.

The date, we both knew, was June 4th, nineteen years since soldiers had put down the Tiananmen uprising. The overseas Chinese students' bulletin board had been alive all afternoon with discussions of the anniversary. Liu mentioned the famous photograph of an unknown man standing in front of a tank—perhaps the most provocative image in modern Chinese history.

"We really acknowledge him. We really think he was brave," Liu told me. But, of that generation, he said, "They fought for China, to make the country better. And there were some faults of the government. But, finally, we must admit that the Chinese government had to use any way it could to put down that event."

"Chinese people have begun to think, one part is the good life, another part is democracy," Liu went on. "If democracy can really give you the good life, that's good. But, without democracy, if we can still have the good life, why should we choose democracy?"

. . .

When the Olympic torch returned to China in May for its final journey to Beijing, the Chinese seemed determined to make up for its woes abroad. Crowds overflowed along the torch's route. One afternoon, Tang and I set off to watch the torch traverse a suburb of Shanghai.

At the time, the country was still in a state of shock following the May 12 earthquake in the mountains of Sichuan Province, which killed more than sixty-nine thousand people and left millions homeless. It was the worst disaster in three decades, but it also produced a rare moment of national unity. Donations poured in, revealing the positive side of the patriotism that had erupted weeks earlier.

The initial rhetoric of that nationalist outcry contained a spirit of violence that anyone old enough to remember the Red Guards—or the rise of skinheads in Europe—could not casually dismiss. And that spirit had materialized in ugly episodes: when the Olympic torch reached South Korea, Chinese and rival protesters fought in the streets. The Korean government said it would deport Chinese agitators, though a Chinese Foreign Ministry spokeswoman stood by the demonstrators' original intent to "safeguard the dignity of the torch." Chinese students overseas emerged as some of the most vocal patriots. According to *The New York Times*, at the University of Southern California they marshaled statistics and photographs to challenge a visiting Tibetan monk during a lecture. Then someone threw a plastic water bottle in the monk's direction and campus security removed the man who tossed it. At Cornell, an anthropology professor who arranged for the screening of a film on Tibet informed the crowd that, on a web forum for Chinese students, she was "told to 'go die.'" At Duke University, Grace Wang, a Chinese freshman, tried to mediate between pro-Tibet and pro-China protesters on campus. But online she was branded a "race traitor." People ferreted out her mother's address, in the seaside city of Qingdao, and vandalized their home. Her mother, an accountant, remains in hiding. Of her mother, Grace Wang said, "I really don't know where she is, and I think it's better for me not to know."

In the end, nothing came of the threats to foreign journalists. No blood was shed. After the chaos around the torch in Paris, the Chinese efforts to boycott Carrefour fizzled. China's leaders, awakening to their deteriorating image abroad, ultimately reined in the students with a call for only "rational patriotism."

"We do not want any violence," Tang told me. He and his peers had merely been desperate for someone to hear them. They felt no connection to Tiananmen Square, but, in sending their voices out onto the web, they, too, had spoken for their moment in time. Their fury, newspaper editor Li Datong told me, arose from "the accumulated desire for expression—just like when a flood suddenly races into a breach." Because a flood moves in whatever direction it chooses, the young conservatives are, to China's ruling class, an unnerving new force. Harvey Mansfield described the conservatives after a visit to young admirers in China. They "are acutely aware that their country, whose resurgence they feel and admire, has no principle to guide it," he told me. "Some of them see . . . that liberalism in the West has lost its belief in itself, and they turn to Leo Strauss for conservatism that is based on principle, on 'natural right.' This conservatism is distinct from a status-quo conservatism, because they are not satisfied with a country that has only a status quo and not a principle."

In the weeks after Tang's video went viral, he made a series of others, about youth, the earthquake, China's leaders. None of his follow-ups generated more than a flicker of the attention of the original. The web had moved on to newer nationalist films and other distractions. As Tang and I approached the torch relay route in Shanghai, he said, "Look at the people. Everyone thinks this is their own Olympics."

Venders were selling T-shirts, headbands, and big and mini Chinese flags. Tang told me to wait until the torch had passed, because hawkers would then cut prices by up to 50 percent. He fished around in a plastic bag he was carrying for a bright-red scarf of the kind that Chinese children wear to signal membership in the Young Pioneers, a kind of Socialist Boy Scouts. He tied it around his neck, grinned, and offered one to a passing teenager, who politely declined.

The air was stagnant and thick beneath a canopy of haze, but the mood was exuberant. Time was ticking down to the torch's arrival and the town was coming out for a look: a man in a dark suit, sweating and smoothing his hair; a construction worker in an orange helmet and farmer's galoshes; a bellboy in a vaguely nautical getup.

Some younger spectators were wearing T-shirts inspired by China's recent troubles: "Love China, Oppose Divisions, Oppose Tibetan Independence," read a popular one. All around us, people strained for a better perch. A woman hung off a lamppost. A young man in a red headband climbed a tree. The crowd's enthusiasm seemed to brighten Tang's view of things, reminding him that China's future belongs to him and to those around him. "When I stand here, I can feel, deeply, the common emotion of Chinese youth," he said. "We are self-confident."

Police blocked the road. A frisson swept through the crowd. People surged toward the curb, straining to see over one another's heads. But Tang hung back. He is a patient man.

CHAPTER 3

Out of Tibet

ALEC ASH

When Tashi calls, I am in a temple overlooking Xining, the capital of Qinghai Province in western China. Loud, slurred, distraught, he asks me to come quickly.

Tongren, or Rebkong in Tibetan, is eight bumpy hours south, high on the eastern edge of the Tibetan plateau, and the next bus is at noon. When I arrive, it is dusty evening. Tibetans in cowboy hats or Adidas beanies walk the markets, where Hui Muslims in characteristic white hats sell fried chicken and chilled Coke to Han Chinese immigrants. Monks from the Tongren monastery stretch their legs, trainers poking out from underneath their dark crimson robes. Although this region is not politically defined as Tibet ("China's Tibet," the autonomous region established by Beijing in 1965, is many miles to the southwest), ethnically and historically, it is firmly Tibetan. It is Tibet out of Tibet.

I find Tashi in a bar on the outskirts, in the middle of a self-hating drunk. He is in his mid twenties, with dark Tibetan skin, brown puppy dog eyes, and a greasy waterfall of black hair. On the table in front of him is a small Everest of cigarette butts and a display of beer and liquor that would make the poet Li Bai, famous for his verses on wine, blush.

"I'm an animal," Tashi says, looking up. "She left me."

. . .

I first met Tashi—not his real name—eighteen months before that night, in his home village of Shuangpengxi, half an hour's drive north-east of Tongren. To go there by taxi costs fifty yuan (about US$8), but passengers often pool together so that no one pays more than the cost of noodles and a beer. Taxis making the return journey are scarce, so you're better off hitching a lift, squeezed in between a grinning nomad and his dog, or holding on for dear life in the back of a pickup.

Shuangpengxi (also known as Zhoepang) is, for now, the calm eye of a materialist storm that Chinese modernization has brought to many other areas of Tibet. It is set on a gentle incline, sloping toward yellow barley fields, with a swift, shallow river at its base. A wooden temple at the village heart punctuates low rooftops and brittle wooden racks where animal skins dry in the hot sun. On one side of the mountain face, watched over by brightly colored prayer flags, is a new middle school, whose brick walls, painted red, look unnaturally clean against the village's clay houses and twin stupas.

In the summer of 2007, fresh out of university, I was amazed to find myself in such a windswept, Lost Horizon location. I called it Song-pongshee, in my best monkey-hear imitation. Later, as I began to learn Chinese, I discovered that the name Shuangpengxi means "two friends in the west." I was there with five British friends. We were English teachers at a new school built in 2005 through the generosity of French donors who had studied Buddhism in Nepal. A hundred or so shy Tibetans between the ages of ten and eighteen were in our charge. Their numbers decreased steadily as "summer religious festivals" drew them back home. We soon realized that these holidays were almost entirely made up.

As the weeks went by, the floor of our dorm slowly filled up with dry bread buns, empty fruit beer bottles, and a carpet of multicolored paper scraps left over from various activities. We rose too early for our liking and taught through the morning, with sport, art, and drama options in the afternoon. In the evening, we walked into the village to eat dumplings with new local friends, or to buy vegetables to stir-fry ourselves. On days off, we explored the mountains on either side of the school. Sometimes young monks from a nearby monastery would come down to play basketball with the foreigners, dirtying their ankle-long robes.

When Tashi heard that there were foreign teachers in the school, he came by to introduce himself. He was dressed in flared jeans, a shirt, tie, and waistcoat, with a heavy sheepskin coat over it all. By turns shy and boastful, he invited us to his home for tea with yak butter, cheap cigarettes, and *tsampa,* a Tibetan staple food made out of barley. Later, we went to his girlfriend Lhamu's larger house, where we watched Michael Jackson videos on a crackly color TV.

Tashi and I became fast friends. When my classes ended, the two of us traveled to his best-loved grasslands in a neighboring province. As a picnic, we bought a rump of yak, the corresponding weight of bread buns and (at Tashi's insistence) twenty bottles of beer. Beer bottles in China flirt with the liter mark. Tibetans deserve their reputation as formidable drinkers, and Tashi is no exception. Taking huge power gulps and chugging through smoke after smoke, he began to really talk.

. . .

Tashi's father and mother were both fifteen when he was born in 1983. Fifteen years later, in one of life's symmetries, Tashi married, and a son was born. The marriage had been decided on by Tashi's grandfather a good many years before that. The bride's family was rich and held high status in the village. But neither Tashi nor his new wife was happy. "At that age," Tashi says, "you don't know anything—what is love, what is marriage, nothing. But there is no choice. Custom is more important."

The couple also shared a secret. The child was not Tashi's son at all. For the first two years of their marriage, Tashi slept in the same bed as his wife but they did not have sex. Only the boy's real father and some village elders knew the truth. Everyone else assumed that the child was Tashi's, and he raised him as his own.

Four years later, Tashi's grandfather died. Tashi's wife—none too discreetly—found another boyfriend. This time there was no secret. Everybody knew, everybody gossiped. Soon after, she left their home to move back in with her parents. Tashi tried to persuade her to come back. A month passed before he found out why she had left. She was pregnant again, and she insisted that the child was his. Three months into her pregnancy, against Tashi's wishes, she had an abortion. Tashi divorced her. He was not yet twenty.

To escape this sour episode, or perhaps out of simple wanderlust, Tashi took off. There was nothing to keep him in Shuangpengxi. Estranged from his mother and father, who had sent him to a monastery when he was three (he left at seven to go to school), he was close only to his grandmother. Young and ambitious, he felt he had more to see than what his village could show him.

Tashi studied Tibetan history and English for three years in Xining, then Chinese for a year in Beijing. He went home once a year to celebrate Losar, the Tibetan new year, with his grandmother. But his fifth year away, Tashi didn't make it back. He was busy in Sichuan to the south, rebuilding a pagoda, and in Shenzhen near Hong Kong, on a failed business venture. He taught English in Xining, and opened an art school in the nearby Kumbum monastery. He traveled to Lhasa and worked for a month as a scribe, tracing golden ink over fading letters in a monastery library.

When I first met Tashi in that summer of 2007, he was twenty-four and in Shuangpengxi for the first time in a long while. Back from the grasslands, and somewhat worse for wear, we retreated to his house on the outskirts of the village. The following morning, I asked Tashi to make good on a drunken promise from the day before and write me a poem.

Obliging, he sat cross-legged on the heated platform of his room, where a hard mattress formed his bed. Like a schoolboy, he had plastered posters on his walls, but instead of footballers, the blue Buddhist god Tara sat in the lotus position, framed by two fake stuffed birds and a miniature ram's head. To their left was a large landscape poster of Lhasa, with Potala Palace unmistakable at its center. The fourteenth Dalai Lama, its former resident, looked down from above it, framed by a white ceremonial scarf, or *khata*. The Dalai Lama is still a familiar face in Tibetan homes and the bolder monasteries, despite the Chinese ban on his image.

Scratching diligently on a sheet of paper with my fountain pen, Tashi wrote for thirty minutes, the crumpled spiders of his Tibetan characters hugging their lines from below, vowels hovering over every third or fourth consonant like halos. Later, I asked an ethnic Tibetan who teaches at Oxford University to translate the poem for me. It is called "Potala Palace":

Red prince of my heart
That quenches my thirst for the history of a thousand years,
In your presence sprouts the life force of knowledge
In the garden of my consciousness.
The eternal flame of the butter lamp that flickers in my eyes
Is stoked by my sweat and blood.

The land of snows has entrusted everything to you,
And you too
Fearlessly speak the word of truth
For the sake of our hopes and prayers.

Potala Palace!
The consciousness of my forefathers rests
On your high throne.
I forever
Will decorate your pillars with golden rings.

But the fierce wind from the East
Has many times racked with tongues of flame
Your tender form.

O great yogi, in whose heart swirls unadulterated compassion,
You forever
Like the blood moving in my body
Will rise to face the challenge of history.
Embodying the integrity of a nation,
Even though you are hurt you lick your wounds
And stand proud in all circumstances.
While the sharp fangs of a dark beast
A tailless dog pretending to be a lion
Utters empty threats from its cave.

Potala Palace!
The solitary hero, never changing.
I forever
Will serve under your blessing.

Potala Palace!
From the first time I welcomed the sun and the moon
Until when the circulation of my blood stops,
My loyalty to you in body, speech, and mind
Shall remain eternal.

As he handed it to me, Tashi smiled sheepishly and said, "There is some
. . . what is the English word? . . . *metaphor*."

• • •

China was worried about more than metaphor the following spring. In
March 2008, riots broke out in Lhasa and spread across ethnically
Tibetan regions, including Qinghai. Monks, workers, and the angry
unemployed joined the fray, some peacefully, others violently. Over a
dozen people died in Lhasa. Han immigrants were targeted by Tibetans
who felt that the Chinese were unfairly reaping the benefits of the area's
economic stimulus, which on paper was intended for Tibetans. As the
fire ebbed, ethnic tension was further stoked by the refusal of many
Chinese to understand that Tibetans had just cause for discontent.

The first signs of trouble that year were in Tongren in February,
during Losar. I returned to Tongren the following new year and

interviewed a monk at the topmost temple of Longwu monastery, a hot spot of the protests. His recollection of the events the year before more or less corresponded with what I had read in wire reports and other eyewitness accounts.

During that Losar of 2008, riots were sparked by the smallest of quarrels. According to the monk, a Hui Muslim was selling balloons, one of which caught the eye of a passing Tibetan child. As it changed hands, the balloon flew up and away. The father of the child refused to pay three yuan for it, and the merchant was angry. Police officers tried to break up the ensuing fracas, but by then a large Tibetan crowd had gathered. The crowd felt the police were being too harsh on the nomad father and formed a circle to protect him from being arrested. Blows were struck, and the nomad was taken in. But later that night, against the backdrop of new year fireworks, a larger crowd—including monks from Longwu—threw rocks and protested, as much against pervasive injustice toward Tibetans as about this specific case.

After that night and the arrests that followed, the monk told me, the police increased their presence in the monastery, searching rooms randomly and smashing portraits of the Dalai Lama, even stealing hoarded money. "It felt like 1959," he said, referring to the protests in Lhasa that culminated in the Dalai Lama fleeing to India. "Sure, I'm angry. But I can do nothing. What can I do?"

One year on, the festivities of 2009's Losar in Tongren were decidedly chilly. In remembrance of those who died in Lhasa, locals refused to celebrate the new year with fireworks. Instead, the police lit their own fireworks and bribed other Tibetans to follow suit in an attempt to create an air of normalcy. Meanwhile, just north of town, the foundations were being laid for a new barracks of the People's Armed Police. Control was tighter than ever. A short while before the night of the new year, Tashi introduced me to two monks who had been imprisoned for six months after having taken part in the Tongren riots. They were being tailed, they told me, and they couldn't agree to an interview. In fact, they continued, the dormitory we were in was probably bugged. Tashi and I left quickly.

Afterward, in his brother's office—his brother is a property developer, a lucrative business in expanding towns like Tongren—I asked Tashi what he thought of the riots of the year before. Up until that moment, we had never really talked about politics. "We all agree with the Dalai Lama," Tashi began, "that the world needs peace, not violence. But the Dalai Lama doesn't know about these things. . . . If you beat, beat, beat an animal, for a long time it can sit still. But it also becomes angry, and in the end it will fight you."

"This is kind of a joke," he went on, fired up, "but if I ever have power, I want to go to Obama or some other president, take a lot of new guns, fight the Chinese, and take my land again. Why can't I do this? In Tibet, the highest leader is always Chinese. I'm Tibetan, but I had to study Chinese law and language and history. I can't act like I'm Tibetan. I have to act like I'm Chinese, or I can't get my school graduation receipt. And if I don't know Chinese, I can't find a job in my land, my motherland. In my own motherland, I have to speak Chinese."

My natural sympathies were with Tashi—how could I side against such an underdog narrative?—but I couldn't help thinking of the benefits he reaped from this new world he protested against. Tashi's ex-wife's son attended a school bankrolled by the local Chinese government. And just days before, we had visited a sick friend of Tashi's at a refurbished hospital in Tongren. He was receiving far better medical attention than he would have were it not for the modernization that Chinese rule had brought with it.

Most of all, I thought of the school in Shuangpengxi where I had taught English a year and a half before, and of the kind of future my students now faced. When I was there, all classes were taught in Tibetan, and the children's Chinese was poor by comparison. It was clear that they should have been focusing on their Chinese, not their English, if they wanted to get ahead in life. Now the school is now under pressure to teach all its classes, except Tibetan- and English-language classes, in Chinese. It is not the only school in the area to feel such pressure. In October 2010, thousands of Tibetans took to the streets of Tongren again to protest this threat to their language and culture. But from a young age, the trade-off for Tibetans is between identity and opportunity.

After his outburst, I returned to Shuangpengxi with Tashi, camping on his floor the way I used to. I visited my old school and offered to teach a refresher English class for its students. Once so hospitable, the head teacher told me he must decline. My friends and I had been the last foreigners to teach there; after the 2008 riots, the local authorities had forbidden any more foreign teachers in Tibetan classrooms. The atmosphere was just as muted in the village itself. It was one day until Losar, and the residents all knew that their neighbors might be reporting on their behavior to the local police, whose presence was more noticeable and now included Han Chinese minders.

Instead of staying in the village, I resolved to climb the high mountain ridge beyond the school with my girlfriend, with whom I was traveling. The ridge cut an irresistible silhouette, with stegosaurus contours culminating in a jutting outcrop of rock. We had been hiking for several hours and were resting at the top when we spotted a black dot below, climbing up toward us. Half an hour later, the dot turned into a man. He gave us the occasional friendly wave, his shouts lost in the winter wind. Another half hour and a flushed local policeman was with us, the very picture of good cheer, chuckling at how hard we were to find and asking if we would kindly come down with him now so that we could all take a trip to the police station.

What was this? Were we at an illegal altitude? Together we picked our way down to the valley, where—conforming far too neatly to ethnic stereotype—a thoroughly nasty Han minder awaited his beaming Tibetan deputy. In a back room of Shuangpengxi's police station, the nasty minder sucked on a cigarette and rifled through the photos on my camera. Luckily, it contained the unoffensive one of my two memory cards. We were staying unregistered at Tashi's house, he explained, and should move to the hotel for foreigners in Tongren that night and leave for Xining within two days. "Why?" we asked. "For your own safety . . . *dangran*," of course.

Of course, we weren't the ones in trouble. Tashi told me later that he didn't get more than a slap on the wrist from the police, but suffered a lasting humiliation in the village when his neighbors misinterpreted the police car outside his home and assumed that he had stolen something. I felt terrible and asked if he knew who had told the police we were staying with him. I had assumed it was a neighbor, but the truth was worse. Tashi's own brother had informed on him. He had been in the room during Tashi's earlier tirade and disapproved of such a cavalier attitude with foreigners, no doubt among more self-serving motives. Not every Tibetan, it was evident, remains eternally loyal to Potala Palace.

. . .

That was the first of two betrayals of Tashi that winter. The second cut much deeper. Before leaving our police-approved hotel in Tongren, we snuck back into Shuangpengxi to say goodbye to Tashi. At that point, he was set to be married to his girlfriend Lhamu in just a few days—Losar being an auspicious time for unions. But two days later the call came in Xining. "She left me, brother. Please come quickly."

Lhamu (also a pseudonym) is an unassuming policewoman with a shy, low laugh. She was born into a relatively well-off family in Shuang-pengxi and is a bit shorter than Tashi, with the characteristically strong build of Tibetan women. She and Tashi had been together for two years, through which she was unwaveringly patient with his restless wandering and his roving eye for other women. They shared the same sense of humor, loved each other, and had been talking about marriage for some time.

There were initially two problems with this idea. Problem one: An obscure village law said that no man could remarry within the same village. Tashi's childhood wife was also from Shuangpengxi, so the elders of the village said he had to look further afield for a second bride.

Tashi came up with an ingenious solution for this. Knowing that the only thing village elders believe in more than tradition is religion, he went to get the blessing of the nearest incarnate lama. Incarnate lamas aren't to be found just anywhere, mind you. We had to drive a full forty minutes down the valley to a monastery where an octogenarian incarnate was supposedly in deep meditation. Together we performed the preliminaries—a full circuit of the monastery, turning every prayer wheel on every stupa in three clockwise circuits—before we came to the central temple and gave the door a rap. A monk came out. Tashi delivered his pitch. A brief exchange. The monk went in. Fifteen minutes later, he emerged with a piece of paper from the lama, not larger than a fortune cookie slip. Written on it, with the directness of someone in his eleventh life, was: "Pray to Buddha once in the morning, once in the afternoon, and once before sleep, and this marriage will be success-ful." It was good enough for the elders.

Problem number two was both more familiar and a tougher nut to crack: Lhamu's parents hated Tashi's guts. They thought he was a layabout. He rarely sticks with a job for longer than a few months. He never visits his mother and father, even if he is devoted to his grand-mother. He dresses like a Chinese yuppie. His long hair is often tinged with artificial red. And he is almost always away from Shuangpengxi, in Xining or further afield.

When visiting me in Beijing, Tashi would flirt left and right. In the American-style bars of the student district, he would try his luck with Western girls and text old flames. When I showed him how to bypass the "great firewall" of Internet censorship, he first asked me to look up Radio Free Asia, which he heard had reported truthfully about the 2008 riots. Next, he googled "American girl sex"—which he had heard was more experimental than Tibetan girl sex.

At the eleventh hour, Lhamu—who had agreed to the marriage against her family's wishes—caved into parental pressure and decided that Tashi would make a poor husband. He learned of her decision one day into the year of the ox, when he saw her walking hand in hand with another man.

The humiliation of this breakup was so great that Tashi did not feel he could show his face in Shuangpengxi. He moved back to Xining, and threw himself into a more Chinese pace of life. One new venture was a monastery being built in the south of Qinghai, funded by a Californian millionaire and born-again Buddhist. Another was the impractical idea of selling Tibetan yak and sheep wool direct to factories in southern China—a business that has long been the monopoly of Hui Muslims in the region.

Tashi once told me his role model was Gendun Choepel, a famous twentieth-century Tibetan monk whose face appears on mouse pads from Lhasa to Tongren. Like Tashi, Choepel was born in Shuangpengxi. The school where I taught is named after him—Gendun Choepel Middle School—and its gatekeeper claims to be his direct descendant.

Choepel is sometimes called a "rebel monk." In the 1920s, as a young man, he befriended a Christian missionary despite his family's warnings that his hair would turn blond and his eyes blue. As a monk, he was open about his drinking, smoking, and love of women. Later in life, he traveled to India, where he translated the Kama Sutra into Tibetan, writing that "if natural passions are banned, unnatural passions are grown in secrecy."

In Choepel's time, Tibet was tragically missing the opportunity to modernize. The death of the progressive thirteenth Dalai Lama returned power to reactionary elites. The 1930s could have been the moment in history when Tibet secured its lasting independence from China. But history went the other way. Vocal in his criticism of the status quo and a founding member of the Tibetan Revolutionary Party, Choepel was accused of being a communist spy, spent three years in a Lhasa prison, and died shortly after his release. He lived just long enough to see Chinese troops "liberate" Tibet in 1950.

Tashi is no rebel monk. He may drink and sleep around as much as Gendun Choepel did, but he lives in a very different Tibet. Choepel wanted to see Tibet change on its own terms. Sixty years after his death, it has changed on China's. It has more than its fair share of injustice and ethnic inequality. But it also has new hospitals and schools, a modernized infrastructure, and opportunities for success for Tibetans who play by China's rules. Tashi, along with so many of his generation, embraces those opportunities with the same breath that he protests against their inequalities.

It was a long time coming, but Tashi's mental journey away from his Tibetan heritage and toward a world of new possibilities in China or abroad was thrown into sharp relief after Lhamu left him. Sometimes we talk about Lhamu, and Tashi tells me that he wants a foreign girlfriend next. He used to say that he would take a Tibetan wife, or else he might lose his identity as a Tibetan. He used to say that he would always live in Qinghai—before he became alienated from his home village. Now he dreams of living in London or Paris, or of being a professor of Tibetan history, but in a Chinese or overseas university. In short, he wants to get out of Tibet.

. . .

It is summer, a year and a half after that tumultuous Losar of 2009, and Tashi and I are together in Shuangpengxi again. Leaving Tibet is no easy matter for him, and whenever I am there, I don't want to leave. I have finally climbed that high ridge—with no police interruptions— and command a sweeping view of the village. The scene looks much the same, with one addition: a new China Mobile tower rises high over the police station. Making use of full signal, I text Tashi that I'm coming down for tea.

Shuangpengxi is all but deserted at this time of year. Mid-June is high season for picking caterpillar fungus, called "winter worm, summer herb" in Chinese, which is highly valued as medicine. If you have a keen eye and the patience of a Buddha, the high plains of Qinghai are among the only places to find it sticking up a half inch from the brown earth. One season's harvest can be worth several times what a Tibetan farmer earns in a year. Every able-bodied man and woman in Shuangpengxi is away from home, caterpillar hunting. But that is not so drastic a change from the norm. In small villages across Tibet and the rest of China, droves of adults are leaving to work in big cities. Shuangpengxi is swift becoming a ghost village of children and the elderly.

It is dusk when I reach Tashi's house, which he built himself out of stone, sand, clay, mud, and wood. His grandmother, bent double like a crowbar by the weight of her seventy years, greets me with a toothless smile. I step through a small courtyard to the kitchen, where she puts a charred kettle on the fire and lays out a bag of roasted barley and three bowls. We each take a handful of barley, add warm water and a generous chunk of yak butter (I ask for extra sugar), then knead the mixture until it's about the size and consistency of a stress ball. *Tsampa*. Gulps of yak butter tea help it down.

After we have eaten, Tashi lights a cigarette, takes a terrifyingly long pull and exhales endlessly, then sucks the smoke back through his nose for another inhale. He grins at me and lifts a bag from a hidden nook. It clinks and sloshes with the sound of beer.

Six months later, when I am back in England, Tashi tells me on Skype that he has sold that house in Shuangpengxi. Now twenty-nine, he lives in Xining, where he works for a Chinese company that exports steel to Australia.

PART TWO

Past and Present

How do memories and stories about historical events shape contemporary experiences? This question is worth asking at any point in time and all over the world, because past and present are always intertwined. It is especially relevant, though, where contemporary China is concerned. One reason is that, since China's leaders never stand for election, the Communist Party relies heavily on people's trust in an official story of the past that gives it legitimacy as a ruling party. So textbooks glorify the 1949 Revolution, while televised historical sagas are shown repeatedly on major anniversaries, and state-funded big-budget movies focus on the past. Memories and beliefs about the past also have significance in China because of the speed with which many cities, Beijing among them, are being transformed. The process of development is challenging how people think about their identities. In chapter 4, we see this tension in a traditional Beijing neighborhood, flanked by massive construction projects, whose residents live in limbo. Many people who were highly influential in their own day are now scarcely remembered at all. In chapter 5, in the southwestern megacity of Chongqing, we meet a former Red Guard whose memories of the Cultural Revolution reflect the disconnect between what people know occurred and what is said—or left unsaid—in public. In chapter 6, we meet a monk in the Bronx who—because of his exile—is important to China's reinvention of its relationship to Buddhism. Such conflicts of memory and history are not unique to China, but there is certainly something unusual about the kinds of shadows from the past that hover over the country's present.

CHAPTER 4

Belonging to Old Beijing

HARRIET EVANS

Old Lady Gao is the oldest "Old Beijinger" I know. She is eighty-nine and has lived on a *hutong* near the Guanyin temple off Dashanlanr's West Street for seven decades. She used to be quite tall and imposing, but when I meet her now, she is hunched, painfully thin, and can no longer walk. Her thin gray hair is tied back in a bun, revealing a broad face and eyes dimmed by age, but she is alert and her memory is sharp. Occasional smiles light up her face when she greets visitors or shares a joke, but most of the time she dozes, eyes closed, wrapped up in her own thoughts,

As the Beijing government accelerated the demolition of the capital's old neighborhoods in the run-up to the 2008 Olympics, the loss of Old Beijing became international headline news. International human rights organizations and heritage associations joined the clamor to halt what they saw as the wanton destruction of the capital's picturesque court-yard houses. The Old Beijing neighborhoods around Houhai and the Drum Tower were overrun by designer boutiques, elegant restaurants and bars, and their modernized courtyard houses were sold at astro-nomical prices, often to wealthy foreigners eager to savor the capital's disappearing architectural tradition.

But Old Lady Gao never shared in this reimagining of a picturesque history. Her Old Beijing is fraught with poverty, deprivation, and strat-egies of survival. She has lived in Old Beijing all her life, and it is the physical, social, and spatial center of her sense of self as a person. Its transformation is thus not about the destruction of traditional court-yards, but a denial of recognition of her as a person.

I have been collecting Old Beijingers' personal histories since 2005 as part of an oral history of everyday life over the past half century in a neighborhood of the capital's "south city." The people I meet are angry about the loss of their neighborhood. Their understanding of the world has been almost entirely shaped by the lanes and alleys of their homes in Dashanlanr, and their sense of belonging to the neighborhood is profound. Although the neighborhood has undergone relentless, if patchy, demolition and reconstruction since the late 1990s, their con-tinuing description of themselves as Old Beijingers is a kind of demand for recognition based on their privileged relationship with a place over time.

Old Lady Gao's neighborhood in central Beijing is one of the few old areas of the capital that has not been entirely demolished. Dashan-lanr is situated on the east-west axis at the southwestern corner of Tiananmen Square. It is a popular commercial district celebrated by tourist web sites as the essence of Old Beijing, with gray courtyard houses, tiny alleys and lanes, and small eateries selling delicacies such as tripe and steamed dumplings. Its hub is a paved walkway running west of Qianmen Street with vibrantly colored shop fronts displaying medicines, silks, teas, embroidered shoes and gowns, and local knick-knackery. Painted plaster statues of bearded Old Beijingers playing chess at a small table, stone lions, big red paper lanterns, and monu-mental pillars interrupt the otherwise straight gray façades of early Republican-style buildings. Due west is a smaller pedestrian lane, Dashanlanr West Street, also known as Guanyin Temple Street, where small restaurants and unspectacular shops sell bags, clothes, sweets, Buddhist trinkets, and calligraphy items. The *hutong* where Old Lady Gao lives is just two minutes from here.

· · ·

Not long ago, the scene in Dashanlanr was very different. In 2005, public access through Dashanlanr East Street to Qianmen Street was blocked by billboards that announced its 600-year-old commercial history with cartoon figures of "Old Beijingers" and displayed digitized panoramas of the "Old Beijing" of the future. Adjacent lanes were full of piles of rubbish and rubble, potholes, trashed furniture, and broken cables. Courtyards were boarded up, often designated for demolition by the now famous white character *chai* (demolish), and warning notes threatened penalties for anyone trying to enter. Dashanlanr West Street remained open, however, and it echoed with the sounds of street vendors crying their wares, bikes and rickshaw pullers shouting to pedestrians to get out of the way, and restaurateurs booming Old Beijing–style cries of welcome to their customers.

Many young people who were born and brought up in Dashanlanr moved out some time ago, by marrying into "modern" parts of the city or by renting apartments in the newly built blocks beyond the outer ring road. There has been a massive increase of migrants into Dashanlanr over the past two decades, and many locals rent out their small courtyard rooms to finance their relocation. With few exceptions, the locals who remain are too poor to move. Elderly or unemployed, they pick up short-term jobs as garbage collectors, restaurant cleaners, or illegal rickshaw cyclists. Most of the people I know in Dashanlanr are on local government welfare. They live in cramped and dilapidated conditions, without hot water or toilets, in the small rooms of what are known as *dazayuan,* old courtyards filled in with single or two-room dwellings. Those who own the leaseholds to their properties are eligible for local government compensation to support relocation, but compensation is allocated on the basis of property size and is woefully inadequate to pay rent elsewhere.

Over the past two decades, Dashanlanr's district government has issued numerous "cultural protection" orders and regulations. Indeed, Dashanlanr was first designated one of many culturally protected areas in 1980 under the Cultural Asset Protection Law, which controlled the height and design of new urban buildings. However, local officials are replaced every few years. District and municipal government interests produce a never-ending stream of commercially driven construction projects, and existing cultural protection plans become obsolete. Small plaques on the wooden doors of a few remaining courtyards in neighborhoods adjacent to Dashanlanr announce their protected status. Few of the plaques, however, prevent destruction of the spaces hidden behind them. In the summer of 2007, I followed up on a local newspaper report about a successful case against the local government's demolition order on a lane near Old Lady Gao's home. Inside the courtyard were enormous piles of rubble, broken doors, and glass. Like many of the nearby courtyards, this one had long before become a "compound courtyard," and at least two of its dilapidated interior dwellings were still occupied by long-term tenants who refused to leave. The only inner courtyard that had been "protected" was behind a locked gate.

. . .

Old Lady Gao's home consists of two rooms of a crowded *dazayuan*. The main room holds a double bed, a TV on a big dresser, a fridge and a microwave, a small table where the family eats, one small armchair, and a few stools. An outside extension by the door to this room is a tiny kitchen with a small stove top and a cold-water sink. Inside, at the back, is a smaller bedroom with a big wardrobe and a double bed, under which are boxes of the family's extra bed linen and clothes. The place is warm and full of bits and pieces, including a few family photographs, a framed picture of the Buddha at the side of the TV, a few decorative soft toys, and sauce and wine bottles. The bed linen is worn and gray-looking. As in all such courtyard homes I have visited, the floor is bare concrete. Its dilapidated walls and peeling green paint are the first signs that Old Lady Gao's home is badly in need of repair.

Old Lady Gao is now bedridden. She spends her days lying back against a pillow on the big bed in the front room, knees raised in front of her, sometimes watching television, but mostly dozing or just looking around. She keeps a small wooden box at her side with her immediate necessities: cigarettes, lighter, and tissues, and the family's small dog often sleeps at her side. Her daughter-in-law does the cooking and cleaning early in the morning before she goes to work and later in the afternoon when she returns. Until recently, Old Lady Gao passed most of her days in the company of her unemployed son, Young Gao, whose main pastime was drinking. When his wife was out at work, he helped his mother use her bedpan and do anything else she needed.

Old Lady Gao's story is one of childhood hardships, constant shortages of food and fuel, the births and sicknesses of her four children, and the work she did to make ends meet before and during the Mao years. The youngest of four, she says was born with a "bad fate," because her father fell sick during a storm and died at the time of her birth. She lived with her mother and siblings in a tiny room near Deshengmen in the north of Beijing. Without a husband and without any resources of her own, her mother picked up whatever work she could: cleaning, gathering fuel left on the streets, and making shoes for people in the "east city" where they lived. At the age of five, Old Lady Gao was sold as a child bride (*tongyangxi*) to a local household and their two sons, where she collected coal, washed clothes, and generally served the family. Time and again she ran back to her mother and married older sister, and time and again her mother returned her to her in-laws. "I didn't know where I would eat next," she explained.

Old Lady Gao finally managed to leave her in-laws when she was ten and went to live with her older sister, where she earned a bit of money doing odd jobs for neighbors. At thirteen, since neither her mother nor her sister could support her, she decided to find work at the nearby East Winds market. She lived in the house of a local vendor, collected bits of coal off the street, and cleaned. But this did not last for long. Her older sister angrily insisted that she return home; a young girl working away from home brought shame on the family. It gave public evidence of their poverty and broke the rules of propriety and filiality. Gao returned home to her mother.

Gao's older brother then disappeared, and she and her mother spent three days searching for him in and around Dashanlanr's Guanyin Temple, known as an important center where local people gathered to find work. They eventually discovered him in a household near the temple, where he was learning to make shoes. Through his new connections, Old Lady Gao, then seventeen, was introduced to the man who became her second husband.

In 1937, when Old Lady Gao married into Dashanlanr, she lived in one room allocated to her husband through his work for the local police. With a long history as a popular commercial center of the outer "south city," Dashanlanr was one of the most densely populated and poorest areas of Beijing, with a diverse mix of Han, Hui Muslims, and Manchus, including a large floating population. Before the fall of the Qing dynasty in 1911, it was occupied by the officials, entrepreneurs, and merchants who moved away from the imperial palace under the early Qing government's segregationist ban of all non-Manchus from within the inner walls. It was the place where aspiring officials and their entourages stayed in their provincial associations, often for months at a time, as they prepared to sit the arduous metropolitan civil service exams. Its brothels, opera houses, and eateries also offered many popular pleasures.

By the 1930s, when Old Lady Gao arrived in the neighborhood, Dashanlanr's winding alleys were home to large numbers of rural migrants displaced by decades of war and hardship. Its warren of tiny lanes also offered petty thieves and vagabonds ready escape routes as they attempted to evade the watchful eyes of the local police. Like many other areas of Beijing, it was overcrowded and unable to cope with the rapid population growth of the post-"liberation" years. Most of its dwellings, like Old Lady Gao's, were single-story courtyard houses, some dating back to the seventeenth century, but many courtyards had been filled with adjoining single or two-room structures that were rented out. Services were dismal, disease was rampant, and food was always in short supply. Local archives reveal that by the famine years of the late 1950s, residents repeatedly complained to local officials about poor welfare facilities and inadequate food supplies. The government's 1950s campaigns to eradicate prostitution, speculation, and corruption, together with its nationalization of private enterprise and industry, especially affected the neighborhood, given its entrepreneurial and recreational character. Property was confiscated from many families, and many local residents were labeled capitalists and denied access to gainful employment.

. . .

Some time in the early 1950s, Old Lady Gao, her husband, and their three children moved out of their single room into the two rooms of the adjacent courtyard compound where she still lives and where Young Gao was born. The 1950s was a time when gaunt Stalinist-style structures of several stories appeared in many areas of the city, planned and managed by different government departments, ministries, and bureaus. These *danwei* (work units) combined office, factory floor, apartment blocks and dormitories, and welfare and recreational services. They rapidly became the dominant type of building that shaped the work, family lives, and social networks of Beijing's population. The main spatial and architectural character of Dashanlanr remained more or less untouched, however. Dashanlanr was close to the seat of political power, and its district government, still known as Beijing's poorest, had limited resources to deal with population density and faced severe economic constraints. By 1959, as famine began to affect Beijing's population and destitute peasants flooded into the city, *dazayuan* courtyards such as Old Lady Gao's were crammed with shack-like constructions to increase residential capacity.

Between 1937 and the 1950s, Old Lady Gao's life revolved around her home and the nearby lanes in Danshanlanr. She had little food for her four children; corn dumplings were the staple, with noodles at New Year and when relatives came to visit. Meat was a rarity. In the 1960s, under the coordination of the local neighborhood committee, Gao made shoes and clothes, stuck matchboxes together, and folded paper into pages for Mao's "little red books" of quotations. She was illiterate and without any skills that would give her employment in a *danwei;* instead, her neighborhood "sisters" took their shoes and paper to her back room, where they enjoyed cigarettes and exchanged local gossip as they worked. "This was all someone like me could do," Old Lady Gao said.

When I first visited Dashanlanr in 2004, many of the adjacent lanes and buildings were boarded up and closed off as reconstruction of the neighborhood got under way. Thousands of residents had already been dislocated from Meishi Street, running south from Qianmen. Ou Ning's moving 2006 documentary about the widening of Meishi Street gave early evidence of locals' rage and despair at Beijing's transformation. The reconstruction of some of the lanes between Dashanlanr and Qianmen Street was also already under way, and piles of rubble, mud, and trash, boards surrounding demolition sites, doors painted with big white circles enclosing the character *chai,* bamboo scaffolding, and corrugated iron now became features of everyday life. Many dilapidated walls displayed silhouette profiles of heads overwritten with "AK 47." They were painted by Zhang Dali, a Beijing artist who became famous for these murals, as powerful symbols of local responses to the urban planners' vision. As other wealthier and more strategically placed parts of Old Beijing were rebuilt, often with investment from private property developers taking advantage of the commercialization of urban housing in the late 1980s, Dashanlanr's reconstruction seemed much patchier and messier. New shops were set up, their wares spilling onto the street, and a new army of migrant street vendors and rickshaw cyclists added to the crowded bustle of Dashanlanr's West Street. But it was only in 2007 that reconstruction around Old Lady Gao's home seriously took off. Shop owners on West Street were ordered to take their wares off the street and to refurbish their shop fronts with new signage and fresh gray paint. Street vendors and rickshaw pullers were no longer permitted to continue their trade and were cleared from the lanes as the city prepared for the Olympics. Excavation of the street began in the winter of 2007, and migrant workers labored through the night to lay new pipelines in preparation for a widened street surface. West Street's makeover was finally completed in time for the sixtieth anniversary celebrations of the founding of the People's Republic.

I first met Old Lady Gao in early 2007. Gloom clouded the atmosphere. She had just spent two weeks in the hospital with pneumonia, and the doctors had told her family to prepare for the worst. Her elder daughter and son-in-law and younger daughter-in-law took turns looking after her while she was hospitalized; neither Gao nor her family had the resources or desire to employ a nurse. Her younger son could not care for his mother because his arm had been broken in a collision with a rickshaw cyclist. Finances were clearly on everyone's minds, and the family was anxious about the old lady's health. But Young Gao had more on his mind than bills and his mother.

Young Gao had a job at a local vegetable depot, but was laid off when he was hospitalized with tuberculosis. When I first met him in 2007, he had just been fired from another job as a night watchman after arguing with his boss about drinking during working hours. Young Gao also had a chronic lung condition that made him unfit for regular employment, and he received 300 yuan per month (about US$46) from the local government as a basic welfare payment (*dibao*). But he largely depended on his wife's income as a pedicab driver until she and many other locals were officially ordered off the streets in 2008. His anxieties about his mother revealed his anxieties about his own future. Sick and unable to work, Young Gao had long felt that he was unable to be the husband and son he would like to be.

Old Lady Gao was again hospitalized for a brief period two years later. When I visited her home one morning in June 2009, her condition had clearly deteriorated. Young Gao was in quiet despair. He had lost a lot of weight and looked depressed; there was a lot of noise around from the local demolition work. Only he and his wife were at home. His elder sister was sick and rarely around to help. Though it was only 10 A.M., he had already started drinking strong sorghum spirits. "My mother was in the hospital and we couldn't go on," he said. "We had to find a caregiver. Elder sister was also sick and she wanted the 'boss' [Young Gao's wife] to go and look after her again . . ."

His words trailed off, and he was silent for a while. The conversation turned to a neighbor, a middle-aged woman whom he and his mother knew well. This woman had a troubled personal history. Old Lady Gao had opened her home to her and given her food and emotional support, and, once, a loan of two hundred yuan (less than US$30). For her part, the younger woman often helped around the house, washing clothes and doing other small chores. With a quick mind and infectious laugh, she was a powerful presence. Old Lady Gao and her son developed an affectionate bond with her. But she became angry when the Gaos asked her to repay the loan. Old Lady Gao was clearly sad. "My children are really filial. They always look after me. But she doesn't come any more. I treated her like one of my own [*bushi ba ta dang wairen*]. I still miss her."

Spanning the anti-Japanese and civil wars of the 1930s and 1940s, the Mao era between the 1950s and the 1970s, and China's embrace of global capitalism since the 1980s, Old Lady Gao's memories of life in Dashanlanr move back and forth between different moments and, except for the famine years, have little to do with key twentieth-century political events. Despite her sharp memory for the names of neighbors on the lane, the numbers of the houses where they lived, and when their children married, she has few memories—few, at least, that she cares to discuss—of the Cultural Revolution. Red Guards were extremely active in Danshanlanr between 1966 and 1967; they ransacked the homes of "capitalists" and demanded food and accommodation from residents. They destroyed the Bodhisattva Temple, although local residents still refer to its remaining two walls as an important landmark, and its name is prominently displayed on the wrought-iron archway over the entrance of West Street. Unlike some others in the neighborhood, Gao has little nostalgia for the Mao years. Like many elderly people, she instead dwells on her childhood and youth. Her memories of suffering and her mother's destitution often bring tears to her eyes. She does not have much good to say about the changes of the past three decades, despite reminders from her daughter-in-law that there was no welfare or old age pension in the past. True to her Old Beijinger status, her stories are repeatedly framed by references to the comings and goings of family, friends, and neighbors, family quarrels and celebrations in the lanes and alleys of Danshanlanr. Since she married her second husband, Old Lady Gao has only ever left the neighborhood to go back to the Beijing district where she was born on one occasion. Her entire life—her sense of social being in the world—is rooted in and shaped by the spatial and social character of Dashanlanr. Or as her son once put it, "Once the buildings go, the people go as well."

· · ·

Everyday activities for families like Old Lady Gao's therefore revolve around their homes, from the walls of their *dazayuan* to the narrow lanes connecting them to others nearby. Engagements and marriages, family quarrels, financial difficulties, teenage mishaps, and run-ins with the local police are the staples of local conversations on the *hutong*. Indeed, the overlapping boundaries between the dwellings of the *dazayuan* courtyards are a hotbed of gossip, and residents often come into conflict. For many, the arrival of market competition and migrants has exacerbated local tensions. The sense of home and neighborhood that they ascribe to Old Beijing has long since given way to untrusting competitiveness created by the struggle for market success. "We may have more to eat and a bit more money, but we do not feel at peace," a 54-year-old man from the neighborhood said.

For Old Lady Gao and her son, the everyday evidence of Old Beijing's destruction—the noise, the bulldozers, the dirt, rubble and garbage, the quarrels, fights, and arrests—is evidence of the state's disregard for the lives that have been molded by it. "We are just the bottom rung of society [*diceng shehui*], trash [*laji*], and no one has ever cared about us," Young Gao said. Through decades of political campaigns and social turmoil that have brought them few benefits, my acquaintances in Dashalanr are fully aware of the fact that they live in a political system that does not offer them much human recognition. One resident is vociferous in his resentment against a system that, in his view, permits regular violation of ordinary people's human rights, his own included. All of them are aware that as members of Beijing *diceng shehui,* they are the commonly disdained by other Beijingers, as well as by the government. Indeed, among its many associations, Dashalanr has long been equated with Beijing's low life.

I have often tried to talk with my local acquaintances about how they imagine their futures. Some, like Old Lady Gao's son, just shrugged their shoulders in response, as though offering silent acknowledgement of their powerlessness in the face of urban planners. Others asked, "What do you expect us to do? All we can do is wait and see what they say." The radical transformation of the neighborhood has involved coercive evictions, relocations as well as voluntary departures. Plans and information concerning refurbishments and demolitions are circulated with little warning and involve no consultation with local residents. For most of them, the eventual demolition of their own homes is only a matter of time. With no information about government plans, all they can do is wait for a future they cannot or do not want to imagine.

October 1, 2009, marked the sixtieth anniversary of the founding of the People's Republic of China. The makeover of Dashanlanr's West Street had just been completed, and its public opening was timed to coincide with the national holiday. A local friend of mine took a clandestine video that shows the street unusually tidy, its shop fronts newly repainted gray and decorated with small flowerpots of orange geraniums. The music and gun salutes from the celebrations in Tiananmen are clearly audible, but the street is completely empty except for a small dog. My friend's camera moved up the side of the buildings adjacent to the restaurant to focus on people standing on rooftops looking toward Tiananmen. The local government had issued a directive to each household that local people were not allowed out of their houses while the celebrations were under way. The prohibition likely came as little surprise to Dashanlanr's residents; for weeks in the run-up to the Olympics, they had not been allowed access to the nearest subway station at Qianmen. But the irony of this particular prohibition was not lost on my friend, whose video contrasted the emptiness of his neighborhood with the reminders of the state power echoing from the nearby heart of the capital.

. . .

When I visited Old Lady Gao in July 2010, it was clear that, despite her frailty, she remained the emotional mainstay and head of her household. Her family was extremely respectful and attentive to her, and though she found it difficult to talk, they always turned to her for her opinions about neighborhood comings and goings. They also frequently celebrated her "big fate" (*da ming*) to have lived so long and sustained a filial and supportive family through decades of hardship and deprivation. Their respect for her was born of her generosity. She often offered her home as a haven to neighborhood acquaintances down on their luck.

However, none of her past achievements could hide her son's anxieties about his uncertain future. Young Gao wanted to stay on in his mother's house after her death, but planning was difficult. Just before I last saw him, the local government announced the imminent demolition of the lane where his mother is living out the end of her life. "How can we think about the future when all we can do is think about getting by today?" he asked.

Young Gao's father passed away not long before I met the Gao family. At the time, Young Gao was sick himself, but waited to get treatment so that he could look after his father. Eventually, Young Gao had to go back into the hospital for an operation, and his father died before he was well enough to visit him again. "So I couldn't make it in time for my father's passing away," Young Gao said. "What regret. I cried, I really cried. Aiya!"

On October 29, 2010, I received an e-mail from a friend in Dashanlanr saying that Young Gao had died the day before. He had suddenly been admitted to hospital with severe chest pains, which turned out to be fatal lung cancer. Family and neighborhood friends attended his cremation, a solemn affair with military guards and musicians accompanying the coffin. His bedridden mother was unable to attend, but photographs reveal her face racked by grief. She cried for days, "Where is my son? Come back, my dear son."

The family returned from the crematorium to a local Dashanlanr restaurant, where they had a funeral banquet. As the place where Young Gao had been born and brought up, this was fitting acknowledgement of a life shaped by the neighborhood. But this acknowledgement could not have been much comfort to Old Lady Gao. She knows that her son, an unrecognized Old Beijinger, also felt that he was unable to give his parents the recognition they deserved.

The last time I saw Old Lady Gao was in July 2011, more than half a year since the death of her son. She wept as I sat on her bed and asked why it was her son who had died and not her. But her distress concealed a deep anxiety, which I only understood when her daughter-in-law later talked with me while Old Lady Gao dozed. Although they had long anticipated the demolition of their lane and relocation to some other part of Beijing, in early July they had been informed of the date when they had to leave: August 9. They were told that the district government would rehouse them in an apartment in the southern suburbs of Beijing. The apartment block would take three years to build however, and in the meantime, they were to move into rented accommodation, which they had to find for themselves. Old Lady Gao's daughter-in-law was clearly concerned about how she was going to move her frail mother-in-law, but had already decided that little of their sparse furniture was worth keeping.

But the bitter uncertainties Old Lady Gao had faced throughout her life were not at an end. August 9 came and went, and they still had not moved.

CHAPTER 5

Another Swimmer

XUJUN EBERLEIN

When I first met He Shu, he wanted to know how my sister Ruo-Dan had died. He was painstakingly collecting historical facts and stories about the pitched battles between rival factions during the Cultural Revolution era in China, and he thought that my sister must have been killed in one such skirmish.

I was visiting my hometown, the booming riverfront metropolis of Chongqing, in August 2006. He Shu was a scholarly man in his late fifties and was working on a book about the city in the late 1960s. We sat at a plastic table at a teahouse downtown—well, not really a teahouse at all, though that was what it called itself, but a café, which served Coca Cola and Sprite, with their names translated into Chinese. It was a far cry from the traditional teahouses I so fondly remember from my youth: square bamboo tables, teapots sporting foot-long spouts that could be poured across a table with never a drop spilled, penny-a-cup "old cool tea," and chirping, chatty "tea guests" cracking sunflower seeds. Those were gone, replaced by soda shops, like the one where I met He, with prices out of range for the average Chongqing resident. Such a commercialized "teahouse" felt like an unfit place to talk about a tragedy forty years old.

I gave He Shu a copy of the Canadian magazine *Walrus* that contained an essay I had written about my sister's death. It was not bullets that killed Ruo-Dan. She drowned in July 1968 while commemorating the second anniversary of Chairman Mao's famous swim in the Yangtze.

Ruo-Dan went into the Jialing River without so much as elementary swimming training. She did not expect that the current would be so rapid. Today's young people might not understand why she did it, but at the time, it was an act of faith, a hearty response to Mao's calling on Chinese youth to be tempered in big rivers, to "learn how to swim by swimming."

Without question, the Cultural Revolution that roiled the country from 1966 through 1976 was one of the biggest disasters in modern China's history. And yet a question continues to bother me: How should I evaluate the role of its many well-meaning young participants, such as my sister? My first meeting with He Shu was a moment for personal and intellectual exploration of the two years of intense violence that engulfed my hometown during the height of the Cultural Revolution. The masses split into two competing factions, each of whom claimed that only they truly understood Mao's words and theories. They engaged in *wudou* (armed fights) that amounted to a civil war. Faction members included not only the student Red Guards but also workers and peasants who called themselves "Rebels," a proud name alluding to Mao's famous maxim "It is right to rebel."

These kinds of factional fights broke out nationwide, but the deadliest battles occurred in Chongqing, in part because it housed many munitions factories. Thousands of people were killed on each side. Both my sister's and my mother's diaries from the time are filled with pages describing the horrors they witnessed: buildings burning, bodies lying on streets, and the gruesome deaths of acquaintances. This period is the subject of the book He Shu was working on when I met him.

. . .

He Shu was born in 1948, three years before Ruo-Dan. Though a native of Chongqing, he was not in town during the conflict, thanks to the Anti-Rightist campaign of 1957 when his father was designated a "rightist" for criticizing the Chinese Communist Party. As the son of a rightist, He was not allowed to attend high school and was instead sent to a temporary job at an oil field in the remote mountains of Sichuan Province. In the chaos of the Cultural Revolution, He Shu's oil field shut down and he was sent back to Chongqing, arriving home just as two years of violence in the city was ending. The distance gave him a literary sort of perspective; he saw the grandness of the Cultural Revolution as the perfect subject for an epic novel. To his delight, his father had collected and neatly bound nearly all of Chongqing's factional tabloids, which published everything from news and political commentaries to essays and poems. The tabloids ceased publication in late 1968, when Chairman Mao began disbanding all factional organizations and dispatching the student Red Guards from the cities to the countryside to be "reeducated" by poor peasants.

In 1970, Beijing launched a new nationwide campaign against "reactionaries," an elastic term, this time aimed at the ex-Rebels who had fought in Mao's name. Chongqing's authorities threatened to severely punish anyone in possession of faction tabloids. The pressure was so great that He's grandmother constantly cried and begged his father to get rid of their papers. He Shu reluctantly unbound the tabloids, picked out a few pages to hide and used the rest for cooking fuel. "It was very painful to see those hard-to-find-again tabloids turning into ashes," he told me.

In 1975, He wrote a screenplay about Chongqing's Cultural Revolution and mailed it to every film production company in China. Rejections and criticism were the only responses he got, the angriest from the E'mei Film Studio in nearby Chengdu, which demanded: "How dare you call Lin Biao 'comrade'!" The media had once hailed Communist Party Vice-Chairman Lin Biao as Mao's "most intimate comrade," but after his plane crashed in Mongolia on September 13, 1971, during an alleged attempt to defect, he could only be referred to as a "bandit." In a scene when Lin is still alive, a character in He Shu's screenplay uses "comrade Lin" instead of the official postmortem damnation, thus violating convention. (When He told me this, we both laughed hard at the absurdity of the rebuke.)

He Shu again started to collect artifacts of the Cultural Revolution in late 1976, after Mao had died and the country had begun to emerge from the chaos of the preceding decade. The deeper into his research he went, the more he realized that "the true historical contents and details are far more complex, exciting, surprising, and hard-to-imagine than fiction." Over time, his focus changed from fiction to history. In 1996, on the thirtieth anniversary of the Cultural Revolution, his article about foreigners in China (respectfully called "foreign experts") who participated in Rebel factions was published in the Hong Kong journal *21st Century*. Since then, he has been devoted to Cultural Revolution research and writing, both in his capacity as an editor of a Party history magazine—an unusual position for him to hold, because he is not even a Party member—and in his spare time.

In recent years, He Shu has helped many former leaders of Rebel factions write their memoirs to "rescue the folk history" of the era. He talks with urgency about these memoirs: those who remember are getting old and some have already passed away. The writings, without a publisher in mainland China, mostly circulate online among old comrades of the authors and researchers like me.

He Shu's effort is significant, especially because the Cultural Revolution research, limited as it is, has not given voices to the participants. Only when the mentality of the participants is adequately understood can another such "unprecedented great revolution," as it was called at the time, be avoided.

. . .

In that first meeting with He Shu, I mentioned a date: July 16. On that day in 1966, the 72-year-old Mao Zedong reportedly swam fifteen kilometers in the Yangtze. It was a show of strength to Mao's political enemies and signaled the violent high tide of the Cultural Revolution. It also sparked a thought for He.

"Do you know who still swims on July 16?" He Shu said.

I was surprised. "Who?"

"Zhou Rong."

To use a Chinese idiom, the name struck my ear like thunder. Zhou Rong was a household name when I was a child. His Red Guard group was known to have the most intrepid fighters in Chongqing. Every once in a while, we heard that Zhou had been killed in battle, but somehow he always managed to resurface. I wanted to meet Zhou, the other swimmer. His feelings might help me understand how my sister had felt on July 16.

He Shu said he could arrange a meeting. In Chongqing, the most interesting talks take place at the dining table, so three days later, I reserved a private room in a restaurant across the street from my hotel. I went early, worried that Zhou would not show up. He had been in jail for many years and might still be under police surveillance; meeting with an overseas writer was a sensitive matter.

But Zhou arrived exactly at noon, the agreed time. At his heels were He Shu and an older man, Li Musen, another prominent figure in Chongqing's Cultural Revolution, who had been a defense factory technician when the fighting began. Nowadays, Li is the self-appointed convener for Chongqing's old Rebel leaders; they meet annually and on significant birthdays, regardless of which faction they once fought for. Then, they were irreconcilable enemies, but now they are intimate friends, bound together by shared memories of their grand youth, however painful it was.

All three men wore short-sleeved dress shirts. He's had light-colored checks, Zhou's was textured white, and Li's was bright blue. Li was nearly seventy, the oldest of the group, with a white crew cut. He was the only one wearing shorts and looked fit for his age. My Chongqing accent surprised and pleased Li, who addressed me loudly and respectfully as "Teacher Xu," using my Chinese surname, then, with both hands, presented his business card. On the card were five titles, the first three from the Cultural Revolution era, the fourth his professional rank at retirement, and the last his post-retirement business title:

Vice Director, Chongqing City's Revolutionary Committee

Vice General Commander, Chongqing City People's Militia Headquarter

Director, the Mediation Committee of Chongqing Jiangling Machinery Factory

Senior Engineer, Chang'an Automobile Company

Vice General Manager, The 8th Village at Dashiba, North Bank (Rural Pleasure Resort)

Because of the first title, Li was stripped of his Party membership in 1986, a humiliating punishment at the time.

It was a hot August day in this "furnace city." Notwithstanding the restaurant's air conditioning, each of the men carried a paper fan and waved it in leisurely fashion. While they exchanged absurd political anecdotes from their youth and laughed, I ordered spicy Sichuan dishes and offered them Tsingtao beer. Zhou was the only one who accepted. "I can only drink half a bottle though," he said.

Zhou was a robust, short man with a down-to-earth face that made him look younger than his sixty-one years. His hair, still black, receded slightly at his forehead and his complexion was the peculiar brown of the Yangtze's muddy torrents. A scar about two inches long, a memento of his combative youth, crossed his right cheek.

"Did you go into the river this July?" He Shu asked him, apparently for my benefit.

Zhou replied lightly that his house faced the Jialing River and he swam there almost every day.

"I grew up by the Yangtze. It was a natural hobby," he explained to me. "I was called a 'water monkey.' Wherever I go, I swim."

"Especially on July 16," said He Shu.

"July 16 *and* August 31," Zhou corrected.

August 31 marks the formation of Zhou's Red Guard group, aptly called the "August 31" organization. On these occasions, he would swim for several hours, wrapping his clothes in plastic bags and dragging them behind him in the rapid water. Sometimes he was able to persuade a companion or two to join him, but more often he swam alone because it was too hard to find anyone who could keep up.

"Every year?" I asked.

"Every year."

I understood the personal significance of August 31, but I asked him why he still celebrated Mao's swim. Zhou chuckled, as if it were a funny question.

"This man, Mao Zedong, he was a great man," Zhou said after a pause. "Even though I disagree with many of his national policies." Zhou stressed that he wasn't a blind follower; he had been an independent thinker from a young age, and he was oppressed even before the Cultural Revolution. He was born in 1945 into an impoverished construction worker's family and was a 21-year-old cross-disciplinary student studying Fine Arts and Chinese Literature at the Southwest Normal College when the Cultural Revolution broke out in 1966. A bit older than his classmates, he had three years' experience as an apprentice at a natural-gas plant, where he had been both a "model worker" and a rebellious young man.

Zhou had lived through the anti-rightist campaigns of the late 1950s, experienced three years of famine from 1959 to 1962, and participated in the 1964–65 rural "Socialist Education Movement." These events had victimized innocent people whom he knew personally, which convinced Zhou that the local bureaucrats were doing something very wrong. Though he never doubted the Party as a whole, his thinking was unorthodox, and he constantly clashed with Party bosses, first at the factory and then at the university. Despite his best efforts, he was never allowed to join the Communist Youth League, let alone the Party. He Shu told me that among the leadership of the August 31 Red Guard group, Zhou was the lone "commoner," meaning that he had no Party affiliation.

"What the bureaucrats needed were thought slaves, not people who could think for themselves," Zhou said. "No matter how 'good' your family background, as long as you had your own thoughts, you were 'the other kind' in their eyes."

When Zhou thought about Mao, he was mostly impressed by the daring swim in the Yangtze. "I've read lots of biographies of great men in the world, and none dared to go down into a river at that old age. In his seventies Mao could still swim in the Yangtze, in the rapid currents at Wuhan no less!" Smiling, he added: "For one thing, swimming is my hobby. For another, I think his swim, his spirit, encouraged people's fitness practice nationwide."

"When Mao Zedong went into the water, how many safety measures had been deployed for him?" Li mocked good-naturedly.

"And you went all by yourself," He Shu chimed in.

"Mao's swim had a political agenda," I said as mildly as I could. "I don't think his purpose was to encourage people's fitness practice."

"There was the political motive at the time," Zhou agreed. And then he disagreed: "but from a very young age, Mao promoted the idea of a 'civilized spirit, barbarous body.'"

Zhou's words reminded me how, as a child, I had enthusiastically recited a poem Mao wrote in his twenties: "Confident of living for two hundred years/Will hit the water for three thousand miles." I wondered if my big sister had had those lines in mind when she stepped into the churning river and never looked back. I thought of how those well-meaning young people like my sister and Zhou had contributed to a great catastrophe despite their good intentions.

. . .

The Red Guards were never a uniform organization of Chinese youngsters. The majority of groups were self-organized and spontaneous. At the beginning, many had righteous motives. In Chongqing, the earliest Red Guard group was formed by Chongqing University students in the summer of 1966. The death of the university's well-respected president Zheng Siqun gave rise to the "August 15" faction. Threatened by Mao's enigmatic call to dig out "lurking capitalists" in their ranks, local Party leaders had denounced the 54-year-old Zheng, a senior revolutionary and devoted educator, as a "black gang element" in an attempt to protect themselves. In the early morning of August 2, 1966, while imprisoned on campus by a city council "work team," Zheng cut his own throat with a razor blade he had hidden in a volume of *The Selected Works of Mao Zedong*, one of the few things he had been allowed to bring with him into detention. Outraged students blamed the Party city council, which they suspected was complicit in Zheng's death. In response, the city council formed another faction called "Mao Zedong Thought's Red Guards," popularly dubbed "Thought Guards," a citywide organization composed of middle school and older children from families loyal to the Party. The two factions, referred to as "Rebels" and "Royalists," fought for months, with verbal debates turning into fistfights.

My big sister Ruo-Dan, a middle school student who grew up to "love the Party, love Chairman Mao," at first saw defending the city council as defending the Party, and became a firm Thought Guard. Little did she and her fellow Thought Guards know that their loyalty to the Party was actually getting in Mao's way. To destroy his political enemies and the ground from which they had sprung, the Great Leader planned to break the entire state apparatus. By January 1967, it became clear that Mao's Cultural Revolution headquarters in Beijing supported the Rebels, not the Royalists. The Thought Guard organizations disbanded, and their members miserably admitted their errors and changed sides.

This development befuddled and agonized my sister. For two months after her fifteenth birthday, Ruo-Dan's diary was filled with accounts of her inner struggles. She wrote about how she had painstakingly convinced herself that she had been on the wrong side, despite her whole-hearted wish to follow Chairman Mao's revolutionary line. On January 27, 1967, she joined the August 15 Rebellion at her middle school near Chongqing University. But the Rebels soon split into new factions, whose fights escalated into civil war.

At Southwestern Normal College, Thought Guards defended school officials, but denounced and beat teachers whom the Rebel students tried to protect. Zhou's August 31 group was formed to oppose the officials. Zhou said that his school's president, Xu Fangting, was notorious for labeling many students "rightists" in 1957 and sending them to labor camps. From the beginning, Zhou thought he understood Mao's purpose in launching the Cultural Revolution: to crush the old bureaucratic apparatus and construct a new, better governing body. That was exactly what Zhou wanted too. He believed that the Party bosses of Sichuan Province and Chongqing City were the principal culprits behind the famine and oppression he had witnessed, and that it was only serving justice to overthrow such authorities.

In January 1967, Chongqing's Rebels seized power. The two Rebel groups, August 31 and August 15, had been allies in the fight against old authorities and Thought Guards. But once power changed hands, the Rebel factions turned against each other. August 15 members took seats in the new power structure composed of Rebels, army representatives, and select Party cadres from the old government. August 31 labeled the whole thing a "capitalist comeback" that excluded true Rebels, and Zhou's group became the core of a new faction called the "Crushers." The conflicts became irreconcilable. Physical fights first broke out among students, and workers, and peasants soon joined in. The violence lasted two years.

Zhou led his group in several famous battles; his scar was the result of Chonqging's first large-scale "armed fight," which broke out on his campus. He still believes the conflicts were unavoidable given the historical circumstances. His only regrets are for friends who died or were injured because his faction was not better prepared for the many battles that followed. He regards those comrades as heroes, just like those who died fighting the Japanese or Nationalists in earlier times. This "revolutionary heroism," He Shu concludes in his book about Chongqing's armed struggles, was one pernicious consequence of the education system in the Mao era.

Zhou does not hide his fondness for weapons. The fighting gave him the opportunity to play with all kinds of guns, he told me. "What a great joy," he said. "It really hit the spot!" And he laughed as though he were twenty-one again—the only time I saw him let go completely during our five-hour conversation. "Joy? No matter that someone got killed by your gun?" I asked. He did not take offense. "No one was killed by my hand," he replied plainly. That, I suppose, does not count those who fought to the death in the battles he led.

Zhou fought for a little over a year. In October, 1970, two years after the fighting had stopped, he was arrested without explanation. At the time, he was an art editor at *Yibin Daily,* a newspaper in a small city up the Yangtze from Chongqing. He received a call at work that his mother was sick. A filial son, he immediately went home to Chongqing where plainclothes police handcuffed him on arrival. On the second day of his arrest, a severe beating by prison staff left him with a broken arm. He had "shouldered everything from ancient torture instruments to a modern yoke" in five different prisons, he told us, chortling. Zhou treated most subjects with jests. "I can write a whole book about China's prison system," he said with a chuckle.

Just as he was jailed without charge, Zhou was released without explanation six years later, after Mao's death on September 9, 1976.

But he was prohibited from returning to his old battleground, Chongqing. *Yibin Daily* took him back again as an art editor. He was good at what he did and repeatedly won awards for the paper. They valued him. He had his own studio, darkroom, and even a yearly vacation, which was rare at the time. But Zhou had changed. One day in 1984, during a business trip to Chengdu, he came across a Chinese translation of Alvin Toffler's 1980 book *The Third Wave,* where he encountered the concept of the "information age." On his return to Yibin, Zhou sent in his resignation. In 1985, at the age of forty, he violated the prohibition on going back to Chongqing to start an advertising and interior-decoration business there, based on Toffler's concept. For the next five years, as an illegal resident of his own hometown, he had frequent run-ins with the authorities who saw him as a political criminal.

Chongqing's Personnel Bureau ordered him to return to Yibin and criticized him for "anarchism." Zhou recalled one conversation this way:

"Anarchism?" Zhou replied with his usual sarcasm. "Then to which government is it that my business taxes have been going?"

"We wouldn't want you to get into trouble again."

"What trouble? Aren't I following our Party's call to develop a private business?"

"Who are you to say 'our Party'!"

"My mistake. Make it *your* Party then."

Tired of the repeated summonses, Zhou wrote a four-line poem in the classic seven-syllable quatrain form ridiculing the government's prohibition of his resident registration. He mailed the poem to the then Party chief of Chongqing, Liao Bokang. About a month later, the local police station summoned him again. He prepared for another arrest. The police reproved him for writing a "reactionary poem," but this time, they permitted his resident registration. There was an instruction from "above," the police said. Zhou's illegal resident status had finally ended, and he was able to run his business and make enough money to feed his wife and three young daughters.

. . .

In April 2011, I visited 87-year-old Liao Bokang at his Chengdu residence to find out why a Party chief would have given a former Red Guard a break. Liao's own history with the Party is ambivalent. In 1963, he was persecuted and sent to do labor reform because he had secretively reported Sichuan's severe famine to Beijing, contradicting the province's official report. It was two decades before Liao returned to office. I asked if he remembered dealing with Zhou's resident status. Liao, whose mind was still surprisingly sharp, said he knew the name, but the particular incident did not ring a bell. However, if Zhou's letter had been addressed to him, he would most certainly have read it. "I read every letter myself then," he told me. I wondered whether Liao's own experience as a victim of Party bureaucrats had made him more liberal or inspired him with sympathy for the Rebels. When I asked Liao what he thought of the Red Guards, he said, "They were just being young and ignorant, like the Boxers [during the 1898–1901 Boxer Rebellion]."

Zhou was lucky. Many old Rebels came out of prison without job prospects. Some were even prohibited from being employed. The government's lack of "procedural justice," a term often used by Chinese scholars today, reaffirmed Zhou's belief that he had done nothing wrong as a Red Guard. In his view, both his rebellion against the Party bureaucrats and using weapons to defend his beliefs were not only justified, but noble. Zhou still thinks it was Mao who provided him the opportunity to rebel. There are others who feel the same way. In April 2010, about twenty old Rebels gathered at Chongqing's Red Guard cemetery, the only cemetery in China dedicated to people killed in "armed fights" during the Cultural Revolution. He Shu watched their nostalgic speeches and songs. "Their thinking is stuck in the 1960s," he told me when we met again. "They are the products of Communist education." The romanticization of heroism in the Mao era encouraged—even honored—violence, and indoctrination put ideology above law.

When I visited Liao, I also asked whether he thought there might be a repetition of the Cultural Revolution, which he had said candidly should be totally repudiated. "No," he said, "just as the planned economy won't happen again." His optimism surprised me.

It's a common refrain in China that Chinese people cannot afford to let another Cultural Revolution happen because they have too much to lose now. But He Shu thinks differently: "The exact whole situation probably won't repeat," he said to me a week after I met Liao. "But partial repetition is already happening."

As of this writing, Chongqing's current Party boss, Bo Xilai, is pursuing a "red song" campaign, demanding that every work unit sing songs in praise of the Party and the People's Republic of China.

Bo Xilai was born in 1949 into the same generation as Zhou and He, and he was once a Red Guard himself in Beijing. Some of the "red song" singing is spontaneous, but much of it is organized by work units; some even pay their workers to participate. Though singing such songs is not a new phenomenon itself, pushing it as a mass campaign—with government financing—certainly has not been seen in recent decades and is reminiscent of the Cultural Revolution.

The legacy of the Cultural Revolution, at least part of it, lives on. He Shu, now retired with a modest pension, engages in his research ever more diligently. He has become a walking encyclopedia of Chongqing's Cultural Revolution. Day after day, he is busy editing the e-journal *Remembrance,* which the renowned Swedish China scholar Michael Schoenhals describes as the first journal dedicated exclusively to academic research on the Cultural Revolution. "I have no other hobby or indulgence," He told me. In late 2010, his book *Wei Mao zhuxi er zhan* (Combating for Chairman Mao: A Factual History of Chongqing's Large-Scale Armed Fights), was finally published in Hong Kong. He had not bothered to look for a mainland publisher.

CHAPTER 6

Looking for Lok To

JAMES CARTER

Perhaps the statue caught my eye because of the weeks I'd spent chasing calories.

Guoqing Temple, nestled at the base of Tiantai Mountain in Zhejiang Province, was an idyllic setting. The midsummer heat, or perhaps the doctrine, encouraged everyone to move slowly, giving the impression that it was impossible to be either early or late. The exception to this serenity came at mealtimes. Monks' daily schedules are long and full. Rising before 5 A.M., they spend their days moving among prayer, meditation, and chores, with little time to rest. Meals are one of the only unstructured times of the day, and monks eat their bowls of rice, tofu, and vegetables at dizzying speed, in the hope of getting a few additional minutes to nap or otherwise spend as they like. The pace of these meals and the low-calorie vegetarian fare left me constantly hungry.

So maybe this state of chronic hunger is what led me to notice, among the temple museum's many artifacts, the statue of an emaciated Buddha sitting cross-legged in meditation. The figure soon revealed itself to be important as more than just a representation of hunger: a label identified it as a gift of Master Lok To. I reached into my bag to look at the photo I carried: Lok To and I standing in front of an altar in a rowhouse temple in New York City.

· · ·

Lok To was born in 1923, in Anhui Province in eastern China, and his career as a Buddhist monk began when he was a child. When he was six years old, he became seriously ill, and his parents turned in desperation to a local temple for help. When he recovered—and the monks said he had died five times before getting better—they pledged that their son would become a monk. At age ten, eight years before the normal age for entering a monastery, Lok To was enrolled in a monastery in rural central China. At eighteen, he moved to Zhanshan Temple in Qingdao, Shandong Province, a Yellow Sea port city on China's northern coast. Zhanshan, one of the largest monasteries in north China, was then just a few years old. It was run by its founder, Master Tanxu, a prominent monk who had traveled up and down the coast for years, building and renovating Buddhist temples. Usually, Tanxu founded temples in colonies or former colonies, where they served the local Chinese community—religiously, socially, and politically—in the context of foreign influence.

Qingdao fit this pattern perfectly. Imperial Germany had used the city as the center for its colonization of the Shandong peninsula in the 1890s, and a brewery the Germans had helped found remains the purveyor of China's most popular beer, marketed under the British postal spelling "Tsingtao." When Lok To first arrived there in 1941, Qingdao was under Japanese occupation. The temple served mainly the local Chinese, and had few interactions with the Japanese occupiers. When the war turned against Japan, food in the city ran short, and the temple grew vegetables to feed both its monks and the Chinese community. After Japan surrendered, Nationalist Chinese troops and U.S. Marines tried to maintain order amid an intensifying civil war. Surrounded by U.S. troops and evidence of America's rising importance in the world, Lok To—now in his twenties—decided to learn English so that he could travel to America and spread the Buddha's teachings.

Hong Kong was the best place for Lok To to learn the language, but his first visit there, in 1948, was brief. He found the British colony not only chaotic but alien, because the locals spoke Cantonese. Frustrated, he returned to Qingdao after a few months to discuss his plans with Tanxu. His future, though, did not wait to be planned: the tide in China's Civil War had turned, and Communist armies were advancing on Qingdao. The impending Communist victory threatened Tanxu both because of the Communists' ideological opposition to religion of any kind and because Tanxu's work in Japanese-occupied territory would raise suspicions about his loyalty. Although he insisted that he had worked under the Japanese to fulfill his religious mission and serve the Chinese community, anyone who had not actively resisted the occupation was likely to be labeled a collaborator. As a result, as soon as Lok To arrived in Qingdao, he was sent back to Hong Kong to find an escape route for Tanxu and other monks. Tanxu flew out of Qingdao in a 21-passenger U.S. military DC-3 just months before the Communist victory. He arrived in Hong Kong on April 4, 1949, where Lok To greeted him at Kai Tak Airport.

Lok To stayed in Hong Kong with Tanxu for fourteen years, helping him to establish a temple and a Buddhist library to collect and preserve Buddhist texts from the mainland, before finally leaving for North America. Three months after Lok To arrived in America, however, Tanxu died, and he had to go back to Hong Kong again for his teacher's funeral. After the funeral, he returned to North America, where he translated and lectured on Buddhist texts in San Francisco, Toronto, and, finally, New York. This is where I met him forty-five years later at the house in the Bronx where we posed for the photograph that served as my "passport" into temples and monasteries across coastal China.

• • •

Lok To first came to my attention as the translator of one of Tanxu's treatises while I was researching a book on Tanxu's life and career and the role of Buddhism in Chinese nationalism. To my surprise, I learned not only that this translator, Tanxu's closest student and aide, was still alive, but that he was living just an hour's drive from my New Jersey home! So, in the winter of 2005, I drove to Davidson Avenue, near Fordham University in the Bronx, where Lok To's temple sits. A block away, the elevated subway line carries Lexington Avenue Express No. 4 trains above Jerome Avenue, a few stops north of Yankee Stadium. Davidson Avenue is typical of streets in New York's outer boroughs. Neither the enormous Kingsbridge Armory at the end of the street, nor the storefront Pentecostal churches nor the frenetic street corners with cheap restaurants of any cuisine suggest a Buddhist temple nearby. The temple itself, where Lok To and one or two other monks also lived, blends in with the neighborhood, identifiable only by the words "Young Men's Buddhist Association" in small letters on the door.

When we first met, Lok To was in excellent health for a man in his eighties, especially one who had lived through generations of war and thousands of miles of dislocation. He smiled frequently, especially when speaking about his former teacher. The reverence and joy with which he spoke about Tanxu was striking given that the Buddhist doctrine he preached emphasized the need to from break worldly attachments, including relationships with loved ones, as a means of achieving enlightenment. Even forty years after Tanxu's death, Lok To showed devotion and love for his master through the stories he told of their lives together. These stories became even more important to him as time passed. Although his physical health remained excellent, his short-term memory deteriorated, leaving the recent past inaccessible, while older recollections remained.

While Lok To was working with Chinese communities abroad, the People's Republic of China became increasingly hostile toward religion of any kind. This hostility peaked in the 1966–76 Cultural Revolution, which closed most religious institutions for twenty years or more. By the 1980s, however, the Chinese Communist Party had largely rejected its ideological foundations and sought to rehabilitate certain aspects of Chinese tradition, including Buddhism. Monks like Lok To became crucial to this project. Few remaining in China had the knowledge of Buddhism and the credentials to oversee the temples that the Party was now trying to revive. Throughout his travels, Lok To had remained the abbot of a temple in Hong Kong, and he was among the most senior Chinese Buddhist monks anywhere in the world. When Lok To returned to Qingdao in 2002 to take part in a ceremony at the temple he had fled as a young man, his role was complex and unclear. Although he had been away for five decades, his stature helped legitimate the temple's reopening. As the dharma heir to the temple's founder and a patriarch of the Tiantai sect, he was an insider—profoundly so. Yet he had not set foot in the temple, or Qingdao—or anywhere else in China for that matter—for half a century.

. . .

Questions of authenticity, participation, and observation shaped my own attempts to follow the paths of Lok To and Tanxu. Six months after meeting Lok To, I landed in Hong Kong, my first stop along that path, on a rainy night. The hot, misty darkness gave the illuminated skyscrapers an otherworldly quality: earth and sky seemed to constantly swap places amid steep cliffs and low clouds. After a 45-minute taxi-ride from the airport, I arrived in near-total darkness at Chamshan Monastery, the site of Tanxu's earthly remains, where Lok To was still the abbot, at least in name.

The monastery, overlooking the South China Sea in the Clearwater Bay section of the New Territories, was as serene as other parts of Hong Kong are frenzied. The dawn calls to worship prompted a steady stream of women to cross an iron bridge from an adjacent retirement home to the main Buddha hall. A nun, the only resident of this part of the complex, led services. I was the only Westerner and the only male in the building, so I kept my distance, observing but worrying that my presence might be a distraction.

Moving from the peaks and jungle of Clearwater Bay to the urban sections of Kowloon and Hong Kong Island, I found Buddhism in Hong Kong to be a vibrant, dynamic religion that occupied a central place in the lives of many, and an important, though peripheral part in the lives of many more. I moved from the quiet, often empty halls of Chamshan Monastery to the impressive, crowded monuments of Western Monastery in Kowloon to Happy Valley high-rises, where lobbies with mailboxes and elevators gave way to elaborate Buddhist sanctuaries, sometimes filled with monks and lay devotees, sometimes home to a solitary monk. My visits to these temples were brief, but the sense of kinship among the sangha, the community of Buddhist believers, was clear. And although I am not a Buddhist myself, the photo of me with Lok To and the relationships it represented gave me intimate access. The monks who lived and worked there were part of Hong Kong's Buddhist elite. Many of them had accompanied Lok To when he came to the territory in 1949, but they said little about him. As is so often the case, his absence from Greater China for so long had given him stature within the community but also distanced him from it. He represented a moment that had passed long ago but continued to echo through Hong Kong Buddhists' lives.

The next day, I boarded a Dragonair flight that took me further back along Lok To's path, to Qingdao, where he had first met Tanxu and enrolled in his monastery. Today, like many coastal Chinese cities, Qingdao is boldly international. McDonald's, Starbucks, Carrefour, and Ajisen Ramen compete for business on the main street, Hong Kong Road. The old downtown retains much of its colonial architecture and frequently resembles nineteenth-century Germany. Most of my time in Qingdao—like Lok To's six decades earlier—was spent away from these emblems of globalization, at Zhanshan Temple, overlooking the city from the surrounding hills. Closed during the Cultural Revolution, Zhanshan Temple reopened in the 1980s, and in recent years, has been promoted as a tourist site.

I wondered what Lok To thought of the transformation of the temple grounds into a tourist attraction when he returned in 2002: his own temple in the Bronx was simple, with little ornamentation, and although it looked like a typical New York rowhouse, it possessed an air of dignity and reverence. Zhanshan Temple, with its expansive pavilions perched on a hill amid pine trees, is among the most beautiful in China; but its beauty is compromised by its present role. To begin with, all visitors to the Qingdao temple are, by definition, "tourists." Unlike the Hong Kong temples I visited, Zhanshan Temple charged an admission fee and sometimes required additional tickets for particular pavilions. The Temple is peppered with snack carts and souvenir shops, where visitors can buy incense to burn in trough-like censers located throughout the grounds. Older visitors—usually women—approached this task with reverence, bowing gently while murmuring to themselves before placing a smoking stick in the censer. Many younger visitors purchased enormous packs of incense sticks and lit them all simultaneously, while making exaggerated bowing motions. Then, laughing and posing for photos, they tossed the smoking bunch of sticks into the trough, earning derisive glares from the old women.

While in Qingdao, I was often accompanied by young monks curious about Western perceptions of Buddhism, as though they were trying to understand their own relationship to the religion based on its appeal to others. I was rarely left alone. Many monks and lay believers—especially in Hong Kong—describe mainland monks as undisciplined dilettantes or worse, as poorly disguised state-security personnel. But my impression was that they are, for the most part, sincere, if not overly sophisticated, students of Buddhism.

The international tourists, mainly from South Korea and Japan, who arrive in busloads at mainland monasteries, especially famous ones like Guoqing Temple in Tiantai, are yet another contrast with the scenes in New York or Hong Kong. These visitors seemed desperate to engage with the tradition and practice with roots inside Chinese temple walls, bringing to mind the devotion on display among Lok To's followers in New York. Many in China see Buddhism, and especially the ancient Buddhist temples throughout the Yangtze River Delta, as an important aspect of the country's cultural legacy. They are eager to celebrate this evidence of China's long history as a great civilization as it regains this status through economic and political power. At the same time, many in China perceive Buddhism as superstition, part of a stagnant traditional culture that led to China's decline as a world power. My impression, as I worked or lived in a dozen temples throughout China, was that many Chinese visited Buddhist temples as monuments to China's past, but didn't take the religion very seriously as a part of today's China.

As I moved toward the historical centers of Chinese Buddhism, I collected more and more questions about what it meant to be a Buddhist. Monks and nuns everywhere I went—in Hong Kong, Qingdao, Linhai in Zhejiang Province, and Tiantai Mountain—were helpful and friendly, answering questions and arranging logistics. Their lifestyles, though, varied widely. In Hong Kong, the isolation of Chamshan Monastery contributed to simple, meditation-filled days. There were no conveniences to speak of, and running water only occasionally. Monks spent much of their time maintaining the grounds and preparing meals. Once the sun set, the only lights were the dim fluorescent bulbs that illuminated the monks' dormitory, and the only sound was the din of insects and frogs that filled the jungle.

In Linhai, the local monks were also helpful and kind, leading me to local points of interest and explaining the history and function of their 700-year-old Longxing Temple. But, when darkness fell, I was surrounded by the sounds of a small city: music and conversation, cars, motor scooters, and food carts on the street below. The sounds of televisions sets—the soccer World Cup, specifically—emanated from the quarters of the monks and other staff of the temple, something inconceivable in Hong Kong or Lok To's Davidson Avenue temple in the Bronx.

My last destination took me back to the beginnings of Tiantai Buddhism. The Guoqing Temple is where the sect was founded more than 1,500 years ago. Both Lok To and Tanxu are Tiantai patriarchs. Eleven thousand miles from home, in a remote mountainous region, I held Lok To's photo while looking at the statue of an emaciated Buddha on the cusp of enlightenment that Lok To had presented as a gift.

In the courtyards of Guoqing, I found moments to take notes, write in my journal, or just contemplate my environment. It was in these quiet times that I was approached by monks, most of whom appeared to be in their twenties. When they discovered that I could speak Chinese (none of them spoke English), they engaged me on many topics. Most wanted to know why I was there and were eager to hear my attitudes toward Buddhism. One young monk took my journal from my hands, and wrote a passage from the Lotus Sutra: "Chu wuni er bu ran, ru qingshui er bu zhan" (Emerging from filthy mud, yet not dirty; entering clear water, yet not wet). I was eager to learn more about his take on Buddhism, but even more about his personal story.

Before we could talk further, two other monks joined our conversation. Neither wanted to continue the discussion of Buddhism we had begun. They first wanted my opinion on comparative economic development, particularly among the United States, Canada, and South America. Before I could decide how (or if) to respond, the third monk stridently asked whether I was familiar with Falun Gong, and if I knew how evil it was. He did not seem interested in my answers, but rather in making a policy statement, ensuring that I understood the dangers of this sect, which its followers often describe as a mixture of Buddhist and Daoist teachings.

This line of questioning caught me off guard and dispersed the other monks. It was hard to decide what to make of the exchange. The anti–Falun Gong monk echoed government "documentaries" I had seen on television, depicting corpses of former Falun Gong members, alleged to have been murdered by "cult" leaders when they tried to leave the movement. I suspect he was a representative of the Public Security Bureau posing as a monk to monitor "subversive" activity, but he may have been a zealous Buddhist, who feared that Falun Gong was presenting a false impression of his religion to foreigners. Or perhaps he was trying to find out information that he was unable to get normally. I hoped to continue the conversations I had begun with the monks I met in Guoqing, but I never came across them again.

Conflicts over a temple's proper role were not a new phenomenon. Different constituencies tried to balance sanctity with accessibility, disagreeing on whether a temple is primarily a place from which to spread the Buddha's teachings, or a place where monks can pursue enlightenment in isolation from the outside world. I encountered this in my research on Tanxu: when he was working on renovating a temple in the 1920s, he argued with donors who wanted a tearoom with public lectures rather than a monastery for reclusive monks.

Of course, not all monks were interested in engaging the outside world, nor were all laymen sincere. The contrast was vivid in contemporary Tiantai. In a mountain hermitage a short walk from Guoqing Temple, a solitary monk lived alone, meditating, without running water or electricity (apparently by choice, since a hotel visible from his doorway had a large satellite TV receiver on its roof). Just a few miles away sits the "City of Buddhist Art," a museum, not yet open when I saw it, created to house replicas of important (which seemed to be defined as "big") Buddhist statues from across Asia.

The line dividing "tourists" from "practitioners" is not a sharp one. Most evenings during my stay at Guoqing Temple, I sat in the courtyard of the guesthouse, overlooking the small river valley where an 1,100-year-old stupa stood watch over the temple and the rice paddies and tourist hotels that flanked the entrance to the national park. As my laundry dried alongside the pants and shirts of pilgrims from Korea, Japan, and other parts of China, I spent a few hours writing in my journal and talking with the other residents. A young student joined me one evening. Originally from Zhejiang Province, she had emigrated to the United States and become an acupuncturist. After becoming interested in Buddhism in Los Angeles, she had come to Tiantai Mountain—in her home province—to meet with a friend who is a monk at the temple. He was instructing her in Buddhist texts and meditation techniques and was also helping her visit other temples where she could explore other sects and teachings. She shared with me her observations about the importance of meditation. The next day, she said, she would move on to another monastery, further up into the mountains, where a teacher would instruct her in Chan (the Chinese pronunciation of Zen) meditation.

Lok To's Bronx temple pointed me toward the roots of his tradition in China. I saw Chinese Buddhism from abroad, from its edges in Hong Kong, and its historical center in the Yangtze River Delta. Each place contributed something different. Like the emaciated Buddha that Lok To had presented to Guoqing Temple, Chinese Buddhism is hampered by its material body. Freed from sensual pleasures, the Buddha found himself closer to Enlightenment. Liberated from the architectural links to the past and the political and social agenda of the present, Chinese Buddhism might find fuller expression abroad. Still, the pull of the monuments and markers that comprise Buddhist tradition in China is strong.

. . .

When I first met Lok To, it seemed clear that traveling to China was the way to find the authentic roots of Chinese Buddhism. Sitting at his funeral, six years later on the tenth anniversary of the 9/11 attacks on New York City, I was surrounded by hundreds of mourners who had come from Hong Kong, China, and across North America to take part. Honoring Lok To's life and work had to take place in New York.

We chanted the Diamond Sutra to help speed his soul on its journey forward from this life to the next. Lok To had worked in America for sixty years, but the service was conducted entirely in Chinese, and many of the participants spoke no other language. Most of the mourners were members of the local Buddhist community, but several of the monks present had worked with Lok To and Tanxu in the 1950s and 1960s.

Just as the service was beginning, while mourners filed in and the scriptures that would be read were distributed, I heard what sounded like a disagreement, in whispers, between two women seated a few rows behind me. One said to the other that this service was about the Buddha, not about China. The details of their disagreement were unclear, but it seemed that the they were discussing who would preside over the ceremony and the roles that were to be played by the various monks from different parts of the world: mainland China, Hong Kong, New York, and Toronto.

When the service ended, any divisions that might have existed had broken down. Mourners filed past the open casket, bowing before Lok To's body and then out into the lobby of the funeral home, where monks, nuns, lay Buddhists, and friends mingled together. Volunteers handed out bottles of water (welcome after ninety minutes of chanting). Standing next to someone, I had no way of knowing where they were from, or in what language to address them, regardless of what they were wearing. The mix of languages, traditions, and backgrounds encapsulated Lok To's life: Buddhism in China could not have survived without the emigration of its followers and practitioners. In a Chinese-immigrant community in Queens, at a time of mourning for both Lok To and his adopted homeland, any attempt to categorize the mourners seemed to miss the point.

The last time I looked upon Lok To's face, gaunt in death, it reminded me of the emaciated Buddha statue in the treasury in Guoqing Temple. The resemblance made plain the connection: Chinese Buddhism abroad relied upon its roots in China, but those roots could only flourish because of the branches that had spread around the world. Lok To, in life and death, connected them.

PART THREE

Hustlers and Entrepreneurs

Several contributors to this volume have stressed in previous writings the parallels between today's China and the United States of the late 1800s and early 1900s. Like America in the past, China is a place where cities are expanding rapidly due to the influx of migrants. In China's case, these newcomers tend to come from other parts of the country rather than from across an ocean. But they too experience culture shock when they discover that their new homes come with new cultures and ways of life. China is now, as the United States was then, a place where rags-to-riches tales are popular. But it is also a place where people do not only struggle to get ahead, but fight to simply keep their heads above water. Chinese workers and entrepreneurs today often find themselves doing things that their parents never did—or imagined doing. This is the case with all three of the characters profiled in this section: the job-hopping country boy who made good in the city but keeps connected to the village of his birth; the bravado-filled businessman who jumped into the car-rental business just as China's love affair with the automobile kicked in; and the painter who does not think of her work in artistic terms.

CHAPTER 7

The Ever-Floating Floater

MICHELLE DAMMON LOYALKA

Zhang Erhua sleeps in a cardboard-lined metal box perched above a mountain of old newspaper. When he wakes up in the morning, he leaps from his bed and slides surfer-style down the towering mound of scrap paper. His ten-second commute finished, his boss hands him a steaming bowl of noodles, which he slurps down with loud, lip-smacking enthusiasm. Then he rakes his fingers through his wildly tousled hair, tucks a cigarette behind each ear, and pronounces himself ready for work.

There's not all that much to do just yet though, so to pass the time, the 28-year-old Zhang hurls himself into the paper heap and rummages for something to read. He stumbles upon his electric razor, which he quickly zigzags over his chin. Then, with a cigarette burning in one hand and the razor whirring in the other, he throws his arms around his co-worker and roommate up in the box, 58-year-old Wei Laifu, dragging the older man backward until they both collapse into the newspapers laughing. Their boss, 31-year-old Liang Hongxia, sniggers at them as she cleans her nails with a jagged shard of glass.

Things aren't always so relaxed in this open-air recycling operation, but Liang's husband has gone back to their village for a few days, and everyone's motivation seems to have gone with him. Eventually, business picks up as men on three-wheeled bicycles start rolling in, looking to exchange whatever recyclables they've scavenged for cash. After they balance their paper, cardboard, glass, plastic, iron, or copper on the recycling center's severely undersized scale, Zhang swings into action, dragging the goods to their proper piles around the 150-square-meter enclosure in which he and his co-workers live, work, and play.

Though logging long hours in grimy conditions is not his dream job, Zhang didn't leave his village for the glamour of city life, but to earn more than he could back home. Zhang is a member of the country's ballooning population of rural migrants, more than 150 million strong, who collectively form a key component of China's double-digit economic growth. It's not just that they provide cheap labor, but that they do so with extraordinary tenacity, resilience, and grit. In Chinese, this strength of character is called *chiku,* or literally *eating bitterness*—a term that means roughly to endure hardships, overcome difficulties, and press ahead, all in one.

Although *chiku* has long been considered a virtue in China, the tumultuous past six decades have forced the country's rural population to hone this ability to a new degree of perfection. These days, peasants flood China's urban areas in an ever-increasing stream, snapping up all manner of dangerous and distasteful jobs and helping catapult the country ahead, while they themselves remain largely on the outskirts of society, unable to enjoy the fruits of their labor or fully integrate into urban life.

When Zhang first left his village and made the six-hour trek here back in 1993, this area, called Gan Jia Zhai, was still essentially a farming village on the outskirts of Xi'an, the capital of Shaanxi Province. Today, Gan Jia Zhai bulges with tens of thousands of rural migrants, living and working in places like this dilapidated recycling center. Meanwhile, a glitzy new high-tech zone has grown up around the area, putting Zhang and his counterparts in the shadow of one of the premier locations in all of western China. "I don't think there's anything good or bad about it for people like us," Zhang explains. "There's no advantage or disadvantage. Mainly it's just good for them." He waves a hand toward towering luxury apartment buildings that loom behind the recycling center. "It is bringing glory to the ancient city of Xi'an."

The recycling crew have been working for about an hour when their star collector rides in, his three-wheeler piled high with empty shoeboxes and milk jugs. On good days, he brings in up to 50 yuan's worth of recyclables per hour. He'd be making a killing if it weren't for the fact that he and the other bicyclers have to pay for most of what they collect: with so many of them out hunting for recyclables, people don't just give the stuff away—at least not in any substantial quantity. To score this load, he paid out nearly thirty-five yuan, and now Liang hands him just forty-five yuan for his goods, a profit of less than US$2. The collector squirrels the bills into his wallet and rides off, already scouring the alleyway for more castoffs.

"China is very poor," observes Liang's mother, who recently came from their village to help her daughter for a while. "China is very poor and we are very poor."

Wei nods in agreement while Liang takes a quick survey of the cash left in her fanny pack. "In this country, all we talk about now is money," she says dryly. "We don't talk about anything else."

Zhang—who has scurried up the paper mound and catapulted himself into the box he and Wei call home—lights a cigarette and listens with amusement to the conversation below. He's been all over the country and worked all kinds of jobs, and no matter where he goes, everyone seems to thrive on talk of how poor they are. It's pervasive enough to be an unofficial migrant mantra of sorts.

On the one hand, it is understandable. Migrants in China have all left their families behind in pursuit of a better life. But even so it seems to Zhang that people need to let themselves think beyond money sometimes. People need to have time to move and laugh and live a little— otherwise, what's it all for? "You can't live without money, but as long as you've got some that's enough," he says. He pauses and holds his cigarette thoughtfully, before concluding: "Too much money makes it easy for a person to turn bad."

· · ·

China has no formal recycling program. The only thing even close to curbside pickup is the legion of recyclers who patrol street corners on hot summer days asking beverage-toting pedestrians to surrender their nearly empty bottles. In recent years, many cities have installed bins to keep recyclable and nonrecyclable materials separate, but so far few people differentiate between the two. Undaunted, recyclers pick their way through trash cans and garbage dumps.

It's no surprise, then, that recyclables arrive at Liang's place pretty dirty. They get even dirtier while piled up behind walls that are so cheap and slipshod that whole sections are simply stacked bricks without any mortar at all. A thin plastic awning arches high above the paper and cardboard mountains to protect them from the elements, but it's hardly adequate. By the time Liang accumulates a big enough load to haul off to the plant where everything is actually recycled, she invariably gets fined for turning in goods that are deemed too dirty.

While the recyclables might not be clean enough for the folks at the recycling plant, Liang and her crew have no qualms about using them. During this afternoon's post-lunch lull Wei lounges on a stack of cardboard, Liang sprawls out on half a lawn chair, and her mother balances on an overturned paint can. Zhang stretches out in his usual roost amid the newspapers, eyeing a rusty barrel that arrived this morning. It's the industrial-use kind that likely stored chemicals before savvy street vendors reincarnated it into a stove for baking sweet potatoes. Zhang picks himself out of the papers and rushes toward it, leaping into the air and delivering a kung fu-style kick that knocks it over with a loud thud. A cloud of powdery white ash rises up out of the old stove and engulfs him. He doubles over and coughs so theatrically that soon everyone is laughing.

Zhang is, to put it mildly, a bit rash and impetuous. Several times a day, for no apparent reason, he wraps his arms around someone's neck and pulls them into one of the recycling piles, hooting and hollering all the while. He'd be an intolerable oddity in more stoic Chinese circles, but here, his shenanigans are usually a welcome way to make the day go by more quickly. Despite his antics—or perhaps because of them—he's the best employee Liang and her husband have ever had. Zhang has worked here four times already, each time for just a couple of months to help them out of a bind. Liang would love to have him to stay on indefinitely, but that has proven impossible. It's not just that few people—Zhang included—are willing to work day after day in this filthy environment and sleep night after night suspended above it. The real problem is that, although all migrants are members of what is commonly referred to as China's floating population, for Zhang the term is almost a literal description.

Though the word sounds fairly innocuous in English, in Chinese *liudong,* or *floating,* connotes itinerant, unstable, shiftless and even dangerous. Back in the 1950s the government instituted the *hukou,* or household registration system, which designated every citizen as either urban or rural. In recent years, restrictions have eased and migration has skyrocketed, but the *hukou* system itself still remains. And though it no longer prevents peasants from heading cityward, it does keep them from accessing a host of city services and ensures that all but the most successful are forever seen as outsiders temporarily floating amid the true, legal urbanites.

Despite the label and its associated stereotypes, however, not all members of the floating population are interminably transient. Some, like Liang and her husband, find what could be called a career path and stay in the city for years or even decades, and yet are still considered floaters because their *hukou* is registered back in their village. Others, like the three-wheeling recyclers, go back to the countryside several times a year to help with planting and harvesting, but generally stick to the same line of work each time they return to the city. Still others, like Wei, come just once to fulfill some special financial need—in this case, his son's upcoming wedding—and then resume their agrarian lifestyles.

Then there are those like Zhang, who embody the term *liudong* to the fullest, floating from place to place and job to job with no apparent pattern. Over the past nine years, he has had more jobs in more cities around China than he can remember—running the spectrum from welding bed frames to assembling electronics to crafting ramen noodles. In the past year alone, he's worked in a leather factory in southern China, remodeled houses in central China, and has now been shepherding recyclables here in the west for about a month. "I don't like to work outside my village for too long," explains Zhang. "If I do it for too long, my heart gets tired."

Whenever Zhang misses home, he simply quits his job and hightails it back to the countryside. He spends a few days or weeks or months there helping his parents in the fields, riding around on his motorcycle, and playing with the farm dogs. Then, when he runs out of money or gets bored, he starts looking for work in a city again.

How long he stays at a given job depends on how well he gets along with the boss and how long he can stand the conditions. Usually, he does not stay long; whereas other migrants seem to have no problem throwing themselves into anything that makes money, Zhang is searching for something he can really put his heart into. He has yet to find a suitable vocation and so he keeps wandering, floating back and forth and contributing to the economy and his own personal prosperity in whatever way he can, whenever he feels like it.

Though some people might think he is lazy, unmotivated, and short-sighted, Zhang doesn't see himself as any of these things. He is just as willing and able to eat bitterness as the next guy; he's just not willing to focus his life exclusively on the pursuit of wealth. "I'm not in it just for money like most people are," he says. "Money isn't all powerful. You've got to live comfortably, too."

When the dust from the old barrel finally settles, Zhang knocks out the brick and coal chunks and starts pummeling it with a sledgehammer. Then he shovels the ashes into a wheelbarrow, singing an old folk song as he works on his heap of trash. While his way of life is far from what is typically considered living comfortably, real comfort for Zhang is choosing what he wants to do when he wants to do it rather than letting financial concerns dictate his every move.

. . .

There's a reason Zhang so dislikes the money-at-all-costs spirit infecting Chinese society: not only does it cause people to lose sight of the world around them, but too often it gives rise to a petty ruthlessness in which one's quest for getting ahead is put above moral considerations—including the health, safety, and livelihoods of others. In recent years, tainted milk, pet food, and drywall, and a host of other product-safety issues, have highlighted the dangerous extremes of a money-first mind-set.

In the recycling universe, such greed manifests itself most frequently as simple attempts to cheat the system. Some collectors hide rocks and sand in their recyclables to bolster their incomes. Owners of mom-and-pop recycling outfits employ similar tactics by watering their cardboard to make it heavier when they sell it to the recycling plant. Liang and her husband weren't initially inclined to cheat in this way, but the practice ultimately became so prevalent that the recycling plant started fining everyone, regardless of whether their cardboard was actually wet. After that, hosing down the cardboard became standard operating procedure.

And so each afternoon Zhang and Wei spend a couple of hours turning the cardboard heap into a slippery, soggy mess. Today, Wei scrambles to the top of the pile and starts dousing it with water while Zhang searches the recycling pit for stray cardboard. He spots the shoe boxes the star recycler brought in earlier and drags them over to the cardboard mountain, punting them in the air and erupting into a victory cheer each time one hits its mark.

If Zhang had grown up in another time and place, he might have very well been diagnosed with attention deficit disorder, but in rural China, he was just considered intolerably naughty. He never could sit still long enough to like school: he didn't start first grade until he was nine, and he quit after sixth grade at fourteen. When he couldn't sit still at home, his family found him a job finishing home interiors in Gan Jia Zhai, a six-hour train ride away from their village.

Zhang made the equivalent of a mere $12 plus room and board per month. For a boy who had never had money of his own, it seemed like a fortune—a fortune he spent on visiting local tourist sites, hanging out downtown, and playing cards with his buddies. "At that time I was so young, I only knew how to play. I never even thought about saving money," he says. Though he enjoyed his downtime, the work itself was anything but fun. A typical day lasted at least eleven intense hours and frequently dragged on well into the night.

It was during this time that Zhang and his new friends tried giving each other tattoos, and the botched attempts still decorate his forearms. His only legible tattoo is the character for "endure" imprinted on his wrist. Zhang took it as a sign and tried to bear with his job, but it wasn't easy for such a rambunctious teen. He had no particular problem with his boss or his work; he was simply too restless to be restrained by someone else's salary, schedule, and expectations.

And so, with a year-long, cursory introduction to the industry under his belt, Zhang quit his job at fifteen and went into business for himself. He rounded up two employees, aged sixteen and seventeen, and because they had significantly more experience than he did, promised them a full three hundred yuan a month. Then he rented a room for the three of them to live in and started drumming up business. "It didn't matter to me whether I did well or not. I just didn't want to work for someone else," he says. "Working for yourself is definitely still tiring, but it feels different. You feel that it's all yours."

His enterprise started off surprisingly well. It was 1993 and construction of the high-tech zone had just begun. With it came a corresponding house-building boom in Gan Jia Zhai, which made finding contracting jobs easy even for an inexperienced teenager. Collecting money after he finished a job, however, turned out to be far more difficult. Over time, the outstanding payments started adding up and eventually, with more than ten thousand yuan still owed him, he no longer had the cash flow to pay his employees. After several months of unsuccessfully trying to recover his money, Zhang borrowed some cash to cover his employees' salaries and then closed his doors for good. "No matter how things worked out, I definitely had to pay them," he says.

Maintaining such integrity was quite an accomplishment for an inexperienced youngster who was getting stiffed by many of the adults he worked for. Part of the reason he had such a hard time getting paid was that he was young, timid, and afraid to confront people. But he had also entered an emerging man-eat-man capitalist culture that condoned stepping on others to get ahead. "A lot of business people started small and grew big quickly, but that's not me. A bunch of people from our village did that, and now some of them even have millions. But they made their money by not paying their workers. If they were honest, they couldn't have taken off that fast," Zhang says. "There are so many big bosses around now who have black hearts."

In total, Zhang's enterprise lasted three years, making his teenage foray into entrepreneurship his longest-standing work experience to date. In 1996, he left for northern China to help his brother, who ran a stall in a wholesale market in Tianjin. He worked there for two years—his second-longest job ever—and would have remained even longer if his girlfriend hadn't suddenly broken up with him. He has been floating ever since, never able to find something worthy of his extended attention again. Even here in Liang's recycling pit, Zhang is so restless that he can't sit near the newspaper pile without rummaging through it like a madman, or douse down the cardboard mountain without turning it into punting practice.

. . .

Strangers are always drifting in and out of the recycling pit, meandering in to size up the metal scraps, weigh themselves on the scale, browse through old newspapers, or even just lounge around on the ever-changing array of makeshift furniture. Zhang and crew don't seem mind—it's difficult, after all, to have a closed-door mentality when living and working in an open-air setting. And so, when a passerby wanders in one morning and lets his toddler loose in the iron pile, none of them even blink. A few minutes later Zhang pulls himself out of his paper pile nest and starts playing with the little girl, who has already collected a handful of nails. He playfully directs her to throw them at Liang, and Liang reciprocates by showing the child how to slap Zhang's hand.

Zhang was not too keen on joining the recycling business in the first place, but Liang's husband is a hometown mate *(laoxiang)* of his and an old childhood friend, so Zhang couldn't refuse. Hometown connections are precious resources that need to be carefully preserved for villagers who head to the city. Though Zhang has none of the money-in-the-bank stability of most urbanites, thanks to the extensive network of hometown mates he's cultivated over the years, at the very least, he can almost always find a job when he wants one. More often than not, some *laoxiang* offers him a job before he's even ready to start working again.

Given the sometimes brutal environment permeating migrant life in places like Gan Jia Zhai, where a mishmash of people from every corner of the country take refuge, seeking hometown mates is more than an egocentric or parochial tendency: it's a survival instinct. Informal *laoxiang* networks help employers feel that they are getting reliable workers, while those seeking jobs feel more confident that they will be treated well and paid regularly. In lieu of strictly and consistently enforced labor laws governing migrant work, the *laoxiang* network serves as a sort of makeshift safety net where everyone looks out for their own.

The system has become so integral to the inner workings of China's cities that entire markets are often run by entrepreneurs from a single village, entire streets are canvassed by peddlers from a single county, and entire industries are sometimes dominated by people from a single province. In Gan Jia Zhai, there are sixteen recycling outfits like Liang's, and all of them are run by people from their same corner of Henan Province. The result of all this *laoxiang* back-scratching, Liang says, is that their hometown is now thriving financially. "Now the villagers all have a lot of money. They all have cell phones, motorcycles, vehicles—everything," she says. "In our area, anything under a hundred thousand yuan [about US$13,000 in 2007] is small potatoes now."

It's true that conditions in some parts of the countryside are changing rapidly, thanks in large part to the influx of cash sent back home by those who've already left. But the ironic thing for Zhang is that for all the focus on money, for all the conniving and wheedling to get ahead, he doesn't see many migrants attaining a significantly better life. Living conditions for migrants in places like Gan Jia Zhai are often much worse than they were in the country. Most peasants now enjoy a host of modern conveniences, but in the city migrants' living spaces are too cramped and their stays too uncertain for such luxuries.

Liang is a perfect example: she has lived in Xi'an for nearly a decade and has never been downtown, much less to see the Terra Cotta Soldiers or any other local historic sites. Sometimes months can pass without her stepping out of Gan Jia Zhai, even though the high-tech zone is just half a block away. And in all this time she has never hired anyone who was not a hometown mate, nor has she befriended anyone outside her network.

. . .

A truckload of scrap wood arrives later that afternoon, but the recycling pit is so packed that there is nowhere to put it. Zhang and Wei decide to clear some space by moving a sack of miscellaneous junk up onto a wall behind the cardboard mountain. Liang urges them to be careful; there are two parallel walls and she doesn't want the junk to get stuck in between them. As Wei balances the big bag up on the ledge, Zhang pokes it with a stick and, sure enough, it falls into the narrow opening.

Wei shimmies in between the walls to dislodge the sack while Zhang neatly stacks a heap of tires to make more room for the scrap wood. He inadvertently piles the tires in front of the passageway between the two walls, trapping Wei in the crawl space. Rather than moving the tires, Zhang scales the cardboard mountain and spends the next five minutes trying to heave his roommate up and over the wall. Liang tries to look stern as she watches from her broken swivel chair, but she can't help laughing at her two bumbling employees.

Though Zhang doesn't love working here or sleeping in the cold, drafty box, he does appreciate having a boss who usually shrugs off his escapades. With other bosses, goof-ups much smaller than this have led to serious problems, which is one reason why he would like to work for himself again.

His most recent entrepreneurial attempt came last summer, when he opened a small restaurant in Tianjin. The location seemed perfect, next to a school, a military base, and a construction site. But after opening the restaurant in July, he realized that students weren't in school and people weren't allowed off the military base—which made construction workers his only remaining customers. In August, the construction manager ran off with the investment money and the site closed down. The construction workers ended up going home unpaid and empty-handed, and a few weeks later, with no business left to sustain him, so did Zhang.

. . .

A few days later, Liang's husband returns from the village along with Wei's youngest son, who has decided to find a job in the city for a few months. The 19-year-old has never done anything other than farm work in his life, but that doesn't seem to daunt him. His attitude sums up the quintessential floater mentality: "I came to play and I came to work. I'm only staying until Spring Festival, so any old job I can find is OK." With so many of their *laoxiang* living in Gan Jia Zhai, he's fairly confident he'll have a job by the afternoon.

Now that her husband is back, Liang takes an uncharacteristic leave of absence to run some errands. With this changing of the guard, the place takes on a new tone. Zhang and Wei move outside behind the recycling pit to work on the part of the operation that Liang's husband oversees: bagging beer bottles. Three eight-foot-high stacks of bagged bottles line the brick wall, and there is still an enormous pile of bottles left for them to deal with before Liang's husband hauls the entire load away.

From inside the recycling center, the rubbish heaps, the box bed, and the parade of nameless wanderers all seem perfectly natural. From out here, however, with the gleaming new high-tech zone dominating the skyline, it is clear just how rapidly the rest of China is changing. But the real change that Zhang has noticed—the change that is affecting everyone—is the change taking place in people's hearts.

"Before people were better than they are now. Before people here treated others extremely well," says Zhang, recalling how, when he first came to Gan Jai Zhai as an out-of-his-element 14-year-old, it was the kindness of the local people that helped him survive. It might also have been their greed that caused his first business to fail, but even so the place was much better back then than it is today, he says. "We were so young and out working already, and the people here treated us like their sons. But no one cares about these types of kids anymore. Now people don't have any feelings. Now they only have feelings for money."

As he talks, Zhang absently crushes pieces of broken glass beneath his foot. He's not just referring to those who do anything to get ahead—he's talking about an entire shift in culture and country that's sweeping everyone into its vortex. "Now everywhere has changed to be very complex. Now it's so hard to understand what people are thinking. Beijing, Tianjin—everywhere was different before. Everywhere was better."

Zhang has already saved enough to launch another diner, but in such an unstable environment, who knows if and when fate will ever be on his side? For now, he's trying to be rational, biding his time at temporary jobs until just the right opportunity presents itself. And yet, even if someone offers him a better job than working at the recycling center, he won't take it. Instead, he will take the advice of his only legible tattoo and endure. He promised Liang and her husband that he would stay until the upcoming Spring Festival, and, if nothing else, he is a man of his word. Though China is changing around him, though people may not be as warm or as welcoming as before, for Zhang, the floater extraordinaire, a person has to draw the line somewhere. Otherwise, he will become just another anonymous "black heart" joining the country's crazy chase after money.

CHAPTER 8

King of the Road

MEGAN SHANK

At a bus stop near Beijing's Dashanzi Art District, shoppers swayed with bulging bags. Coughing, a middle-aged man lit a second cigarette from a still-burning butt. "Soon, soon," cooed a young woman to her boyfriend, who stamped his feet impatiently. Horns swelled. Trucks rumbled. Saturday. Six o'clock. Stuck.

Beside me, my friend, 27-year-old Wang Shuyue, murmured in the lyrical Mandarin of the capital city, "The traffic in Beijing is really over the top." She kicked a pile of ashy fallen leaves. It was November 2010. The days had grown short. We waited in the dark.

"You want a picture of how many private cars there are in Beijing now?" a cab driver had asked me earlier that day. "Just look at the license plates. All Beijing plates start with *jing*, of course. All *jing* B plates are cabs and all *jing* O plates are official cars. Most other letters are private cars. After the first letter there is an additional five-character number. For example, *jing* A 12345, understand?"

"What happens after *jing* Z 99999?"

"It's already happened! Look at that plate. It's *jing* Q H8025. That means it has already gone through Q A, Q B, and all the numbers."

"What letter and number are we up to now?"

"Z QZZ?"

She shrugged.

The cabbie wasn't completely right about the complex Beijing license plate system, but the point she wanted to illustrate doesn't require fabrication: the number of cars in the city is astonishing. In 2010, Beijing, once the kingdom of bicycles, added two thousand new cars to its streets every day, contributing to the nearly five million vehicles in the city. If the trend continues, the city will have seven million vehicles by 2015. Nationwide, Chinese consumers bought seventeen million passenger cars in 2010, about five million more than Americans. Although only 36 percent of Beijing households own a vehicle—few in comparison with 65 percent among Washington, D.C., households or the 90 percent ownership among American households overall—the flood of new private vehicles in Beijing and other Chinese cities is congesting roads and darkening skies. The environmental and social repercussions don't dissuade hopeful buyers. More than half of respondents to a 2010 nationwide survey by *China Youth Daily* said they planned to buy a car—a growing reality thanks to increased personal wealth and lowered automobile tariffs, compliments of China's 2001 entry into the World Trade Organization.

Wang counted herself among the potential buyers. Our bus arrived, and we packed in among fierce elderly women with razor-sharp elbows. "I really need a car," she grunted as a squat woman in a padded jacket boxed her out. "You'd still be stuck in traffic," I said, surveying the grim landscape outside the window. Cabbies gulped tea from cloudy glass jars. Bus drivers scowled. "On the weekends, I'm stuck on the bus like this. On the weekdays, I leave my apartment at seven in the morning, stuff myself into a crowded subway and arrive exhausted before I even start work," Wang said. A stray piece of hair escaped her ponytail. She was too wedged in to brush it off her face. "At least if I had a car I could have a little more space, a little more freedom."

Her frustrations and desires—common to upwardly mobile young Chinese—inspired Zhang Ruiping (Ray Zhang), a 47-year-old entrepreneur and Shanghai native, to found eHi Car Rental in 2006. Zhang sought to play it green while building off a Chinese car culture in overdrive.

"Chinese people have been underserved in terms of personal convenience and privacy, but they're starting to value these things. They're starting to value freedom. We started eHi because we believe Chinese people can have these things without owning a car," Zhang told me in his Shanghai office. "It would be a catastrophe if China continued to follow the American model of car ownership."

"With eHi, you drive when you really need to drive, not just because you own a car. Our figures demonstrate that among Chinese car owners, one family drives one vehicle 6,200 to 9,320 miles a year. At eHi, multiple families use one car, which has an annual average mileage of 25,000 to 31,000 miles. If we deliver good service with sufficient convenience at a good price, why would anyone want to own a car? We hope to deter many Chinese families from buying their second, third, or—if we're lucky enough—first car."

Unlike traditional car rental agencies that primarily target out-of-towners, eHi caters to local customers and would-be car owners who want to take weekend trips or run errands like taking mom to the doctor. These local customers are the majority of eHi's rental client base. The company also offers chauffeurs and a Zipcar-inspired car-sharing service called FastCar for customers who only need a vehicle for a few hours. FastCar piloted in Shanghai in late 2009, and was scheduled to expand to several cities soon afterward.

From eHi's founding in 2006 to 2010, when I met Zhang, the company had raised $95 million in three rounds of equity financing and zoomed to the front pack of a highly fragmented Chinese car rental market. There are 40,000-plus car rental companies in China, according to Zhang, but most are local mom-and-pop shops. Foreign car rentals such as Hertz and Avis arrived in China earlier, but have faced the constraints of partnerships with state-owned enterprises. Hertz and Avis also can't rely on their international customer base because most of the foreigners working or traveling in China can't rent cars because China does not recognize International Driver's Permits. There are ways around this—converting a license into a Chinese license or applying for a temporary license—but these are often complicated and time-consuming. To Chinese consumers, car rental branding is still in its infancy, so it's anyone's game. Another national franchise, Beijing-based state-owned Legend Holdings, has had some success, but eHi is the first independent nationwide chain and the first car rental company in China to adopt a green focus. In 2010, Zhang told me his 1,400-employee company had 150 outlets nationwide, 500,000 rental-service members. and 4,000 business clients who used eHi chauffeurs.

Because there are so many players, no car rental company has yet won a majority share of the market. "But this industry is going to consolidate. It's going to become very centralized and dominated by a few leaders," Zhang said. In several Western media outlets, he made this plug: "The largest car rental industry will be in China . . . and the largest car rental company will be in China." By that, he meant his company. In seeking to lead the industry Zhang has positioned himself as a central figure in the development of the Chinese relationship with the car. That means taking on car culture and the complex forces that have given rise to it.

. . .

U.S. politicians and business elites have long encouraged China to embrace American ideals. In the case of car ownership, they got what they thought they wanted—perhaps to the world's detriment. It is hard to imagine why a rising China would follow the addled and archaic American car-dependent formula, where suburban sprawl sucks the lifeblood out of once-vibrant cities and the government subjects its national policies to the whims of oil-rich pariah regimes, but history has played a role in this trajectory. Early in the twentieth century, Detroit pushed American automobiles into China. American engineers and Chinese returnees from Western nations led efforts to raze city walls to make room for modern roads from Guiyang to Nanjing. In 1989, China had 168 miles of highway. At the end of 2010, China's minister of transport, Li Shenglin, announced that the country had almost 46,000 miles of highways, almost as many as the American Interstate System.

Chinese leaders have expressed ambitions to build 53,000 miles of national expressway by 2020. It is a feasible goal considering that 20,500 of China's 46,000 miles were built in the past five years. The government is also aggressively expanding its road network in rural areas. In addition to roads, China's major cities are building subway lines and high-speed trains. Just in time for its 2008 Summer Olympics, Beijing introduced three new lines. And since winning the bid in 2002 to host the 2010 World Expo, Shanghai has launched several new lines and extended old ones. Its magnetic levitation (maglev) train, already under construction at the time of the bid, opened in 2004. During the Expo, it whisked guests from the airport to its suburban subway stop at speeds exceeding 260 mph.

But alleged corruption, technical problems, and accidents have plagued efforts to create sustainable mass transit. Hundreds of Shanghai residents concerned about radiation turned out to protest the maglev's extension in 2008, which led to suspension of the project. A fatal crash involving two high-speed trains outside of Wenzhou in July 2011 led to widespread distrust in the trains' safety. And even as mass transit options expand and roads increase, in the past two decades, the number of vehicles in China has grown three times faster than road capacity.

This may have something to do with how Chinese cities are being built—suburbs require cars.

Around the nation, as traditional housing in urban centers falls to commercial development, large-scale high-density suburban projects blossom. There, car ownership has become the norm. Access to a personal vehicle is transforming how middle-class Chinese live, socialize, and shop. During an autumn 2010 trip to Shanghai, I stayed in the spare bedroom of friends' spacious apartment in the far-flung suburb of Pudong Xinqu. Like most people living in the suburban apartment compound, 34-year-old Gu Xiaoming and 29-year-old Xue Xiaowen own a vehicle, a Buick Excelle. They bought a car so that they could easily visit their parents in their hometowns, nearby Suzhou and Yangzhou, and take short holidays to Hangzhou and other popular local spots.

"It wasn't convenient to live in this neighborhood without a car," Gu said. "The commute was aggravating. We bought a car so that I could drive to work, pick my wife up somewhere along her way home, and grab dinner before we headed back." Gu and Xue enjoy living in the suburb because it is quieter, more affordable, and more spacious than the city center. The air is better. From their window, they can see a small park where willow trees dance and grandmas coddle babies. A brief drive down the road, the French mega-mart Carrefour does a brisk trade. Chinese shoppers pile carts high with vegetables, toys, and electronics. Roomy homes and double-door fridges make weekly shopping trips the new norm.

But there are few amenities in their neighborhood within walking distance: a chain gym, a couple of fast-food restaurants, and convenience stores. A Sichuanese woman in their complex opened an underground restaurant from her home and sends out her own china to residents who lament a lack of good eateries. On their way to attractions outside the neighborhood, residents barrel cars around the residential drive at 40 mph. Adolescent guards wave them through the gate like track marshals with racing flags. During my week-plus stay, I noticed only a handful of people leave by foot.

Less than a year and a half after Gu bought his Buick, a cab driver T-boned him. His car was in the shop for nearly two months. The Buick repair shop was backed up, he told me wryly. That the accident had happened on the day prior to the start of the week-long National Day holiday added to the delay. Going back to using cabs and public transportation, he said, was a personal hell.

On a warm day that fall, Zhang sent a driver to pick me up in Pudong Xinqu. The eHi chauffeur was in his late twenties, with a thin neck and a generous round head. He liked working for eHi because the company had an attractive profit-sharing program and there wasn't the same pressure to make money by fare. "That's why these guys drive so aggressively," he said, motioning to a cab driver attempting to squeeze between two lanes of traffic on the highway. "Most of us drivers don't have any *benling* [skills]. That's how we wind up doing this," he said. "But some gigs are better than others."

The office high rise where eHi rented three floors was around the corner from St. Ignatius Cathedral in Xujiahui, one of Shanghai's busiest commercial areas. Men drove mopeds through thickets of fruit sellers carrying baskets on poles. Buses blazed past neon billboards. A Dairy Queen pumped out ice cream cones, many of which fell, bled, and bloomed on the sidewalk. Women tottered over the sticky mess in stilettos. The traffic lurched, as did my stomach. I learned that opening a window was not the solution—the exhaust fumes were a KO punch for the carsick.

eHi's offices buzzed with more than 400 employees rubbing shoulders and sweating in front of monitors accessorized with stuffed animals and mini clip-on electric fans. Zits and experimental hair colors betrayed the staff's youth—mid-twenties on average. "They sometimes call me uncle," Zhang said. He admitted one of the reasons his business model worked was because of low labor costs. "I'm not really proud of this," he said.

He wore a crisply tailored blue pinstripe shirt and gray pants that revealed a trim waistline. When I pointed out he hadn't acquired the typical Chinese businessman's girth, he grinned and said he assigned drinking dinners to a wingman. He wanted to run his business differently, he explained. He wanted to avoid the pitfalls of modern Chinese business culture. "There are so many big failures in China, and it usually has to do with being too aggressive, focusing too much on short-term results. Many businessmen can't contain their egos. They're afraid the competition will take the lead. They don't view the long road. I'm not in this for the quick flip. I want to build a sustainable business."

Zhang's rhetoric sometimes sounded canned, but his ideas were admirable, and he exhibited passion for his convictions. He often talked himself into a frenzy.

"China doesn't need another web-game company addicting teenagers, another rice wine or tobacco company, or another real estate tycoon with an associated official in jail on bribery charges. China needs a different value system," he said, leaning forward on a black couch. Even from his office on the twenty-third floor, car horns could be heard sounding nonstop. "If our civilization is not moving forward, what will become of it? Owning the biggest cars, buying ten Louis Vuitton bags in one shot—it doesn't fit with our country's new economic status. It's ugly rich. Car-sharing, resource-sharing: in China this could be a revolution. A cultural revolution!"

He laughed and smoothed his California-style shag. After graduating from Fudan University in 1985, Zhang traveled to the United States to study computer science at Cal State, Sacramento. His father, Zhang Jialin, a Sino–American relations scholar, was a visiting scholar at the University of California in Berkeley in the early 1980s. While in California, the elder Zhang met a friend to sponsor his son's stint in America. As a student in Sacramento, Zhang Ruiping bought his first car—a used Toyota Corolla—for $800. He learned how to drive stick shift in an empty parking lot at night. In the early 1990s, he worked on a theoretical project that led to the development of software for fleet management. With a partner, he launched Aleph, Inc., a logistics software company that provides livery outlets with software, system integration, online reservations, scheduling, and billing services, and enhanced communications among drivers, dispatchers, and customers in the United States. At its height, Aleph owned about 10 percent of the U.S. market for e-commerce solutions for ground transportation services, according to Zhang.

But then the invincible, vigorous America that Zhang had known for fifteen years dissipated. The dot-com bubble burst, and 9/11 dampened the nation's spirit. Zhang turned his attention back to China. While he'd been away, his home country had liberalized its economy and fattened its pockets. In 2002, Zhang returned to scout business opportunities for Aleph. "But China didn't even have a fleet, so forget about fleet management," he recalled. "At that time I asked myself a question, one that seemed quite natural: What could I do for my own country?" He returned to Shanghai to study for an MBA at the China Europe International Business School and mapped out his plan to launch eHi.

In recent years, young Chinese not yet able to afford their own cars have embraced alternatives. That has given rise to carpooling web sites such as Pinchela.com and Ganji.com. Zhang's model also soared. In 2009, eHi had about $15 million in revenue. Zhang projected that the company would have about $30 million in 2010 and expected similar growth in 2011. In October 2010, he told me that he planned to take eHi public by 2012. Soon afterward, he stopped disclosing eHi's financial figures to me.

The last round of financing—$70 million from a Goldman Sachs–led consortium in 2010—and efforts to increase eHi's FastCar service came at the end of a particularly snarled summer in China. A traffic jam between Beijing and Inner Mongolia that was over sixty miles long made world headlines for ten days. Beijing has attempted to curb clogged roads and smoggy skies with a series of driving restrictions, including efforts to remove a fifth of private cars from the roads. But if China persists in its automobile boom, it is on track to accumulate more than a billion cars, said Zhang. It's a number that keeps him up at night.

"Look at our cities now! A mess! Shanghai, Beijing . . . how many Shanghais and Beijings are we going to have in China? This is going to be a disaster, not just for Chinese people, but for all mankind. We're not going to see the sun again."

In the eHi office, he led me into a room where a young man in a hooded sweatshirt monitored an electronic map of Shanghai. Countless dots squiggled across it.

"We know where our cars are at any given moment," Zhang said. "This GPS technology helps us track our assets. This is one of the biggest challenges of the business."

"You even track the personal rentals?"

"Yes," Zhang said. "We can see and manage any of our cities from here. It helps us better respond to our clients' needs."

The young dispatcher flashed shots of Beijing, Nanjing, and Hangzhou on the screen. Then he returned to Shanghai and scrolled through it.

"Here's the Inner Ring Road," the dispatcher said. "And connected to it there is the Nanpu Bridge—the first built across the Huangpu River in Shanghai's city limits."

Efforts to bring together Shanghai's two halves, Puxi and Pudong—or "west of the Huangpu" and "east of the Huangpu"—arguably began with the construction of the Puxi section of an Inner Ring Road and two bridges, first the Nanpu and then the Yangpu—all completed in the first half of the 1990s. Later, and in some cases ongoing, construction of the Outer Ring Road, the Pudong section of the Inner Ring Road, and the Middle Ring Road, among other major expressways and roads, extended the city's vast boundaries and transformed the Huangpu River into Shanghai's heart rather than its extremity.

These developments were part of a massive push to build road infrastructure that began in 1984, when the central government loosened financing restrictions and approved toll roads. That year, the nation's first expressways broke ground. In 1988, the Shanghai-Jiading Expressway (also known as the Hujia Expressway) opened. It was eleven and a half miles long.

During the next three decades, developers connected poor inland provinces to the wealthy coast and laced modern cities with highways—but not without forcing countless families from their homes. Construction of a single two-mile section of Shanghai's Inner Ring Road displaced twelve thousand people. In some instances, Shanghai city officials could have spared millions of dollars and much heartbreak by choosing tunnels rather than bridges, but tunnels didn't make the same statement. A bridge to the future was sexier than a tunnel to the future.

By the time the Shanghai World Expo opened in 2010, eight bridges, six subway lines, and more than a dozen tunnels traversed the Huangpu, making it one of the most crossed waterways in the world. On both sides of the river, the inaugural Nanpu Bridge and the Lupu Bridge, an arch bridge with a record-breaking span and clean lines, sandwiched the World Expo grounds. Looking up from the scene of Shanghai's coming-out party, the symbolism was difficult to ignore: China had arrived, it seemed, by car.

eHi's success does not require all Chinese to change their thinking about car ownership, Zhang told me. 10 percent of aspirational buyers is enough, he said. Financially, this may be true, but for eHi to make the broad social and environmental impact it claims it is after, it needs to do better—or another like-minded company has to step up. Shaving 10 percent off a billion potential car owners still leaves nine hundred million new cars. Somehow, car sharing needs to outshine car ownership. Providing good service, adding hybrids—these are great benefits to potential eHi customers, but not as thrilling as showing off your new Mini Cooper. Uprooting the aspirational object, replacing it with a new green culture: these are greater challenges. In China, car ownership announces personal status. It represents security. In many cases, it has become an expected part of the marriage contract.

These ugly realities hit home with a 2009 video on Youku.com that quickly generated seven million views. In it, a couple argues in a Buick showroom.

"This car doesn't suit you," says the man.

"This car does suit me; it does suit me!" the woman screams.

"You do this every time we go shopping! But it doesn't suit you."

"It does! It does!"

The woman slams the driver-side door shut. She revs the engine four times and peels forward as other shoppers scramble to get out of the way. "Stop the car! Stop the car!" the man and the sales agent shout, running alongside and tapping the windows. She backs up the Buick and then drives it forward again. Then she repeats the process. Finally, the man relents. "OK, OK, OK! Stop the car! I'll buy it! I'll buy it!" He takes out his credit card and waves it in front of the windshield and hands it to the sales agent.

In addition to status, car ownership also gives young Chinese a new outlet for creativity and adventure, and, in a nation of only children, where religious, civic, and political affiliation opportunities remain limited, it provides a ready-made tribe of like-minded friends.

In Nanjing, Xue Peng, a 36-year-old e-commerce entrepreneur, pumped electropop by Ke$ha as we barreled toward the western part of the city in his Mitsubishi Lancer EX. A bundle of sweet osmanthus flowers dangled from the rearview mirror, filling the car with a heady scent. We arrived at a wide eight-lane road split by an island.

"The racing happens here," he said.

Across the country, racers and fans organize online and meet in the middle of the night in suburbs like this one. Sometimes racing involves gambling, but mostly it is just a way to let off steam and test the limits of new toys. For spectators, it is raw performance—very different from the choreographed shows on television.

"Racing became cool with movies like *The Fast and the Furious* series and video games," said Xue Peng. "Many drivers modify their cars to go faster, switching out engines and stuff. I don't race, but I installed an air-charger so my car would purr louder and I'd have more control. It makes other cars respect mine—that's a big part of driving in China."

In Wuhan, another example of blood-pumping car exhibitionism took place when eight women members of the Shijia brand car club wearing different colored stockings performed an all-legs dance through their sunroofs. The effect was akin to water ballet combined with PG pole dancing. Regional car clubs such as the Wuhan Shijia group—usually banded by make and model, a brand manager's dream—organize outings or choreograph performances. Sometimes they even act like gangs. In 2007 on the Ningbo to Lianyungang Expressway outside of Nanjing, a convoy of Mazda driver club members, equipped with fake police sirens and CB radios, surrounded a Hummer on all four sides and forced it to slow down to 18 mph for several minutes.

To keep up with the car-owner clubs, eHi organizes out-of-town rental packages to the countryside to eat crab or view ancient cities. "Of course, access to a car can make your life better and broaden your horizons, but we maintain you don't have to own a car to enjoy the benefits," Zhang said.

When I asked Zhang whether eHi's growth contradicts its environmental goals—the more successful it becomes, the more cars it adds to the road—he tensed. "We should instead ask, 'Without eHi how many more cars would be on the road?' If our aim is to eliminate automobiles, then we, along with automobile manufacturers, shouldn't even be in business."

While eHi continues to expand locations and increase membership, it spends little on marketing or advertising. Zhang told me he doesn't think the company can handle a higher growth rate. Word-of-mouth suffices.

. . .

In January 2011, two months after we hung out in Beijing, Wang Shuyue put her name in the new municipal license plate lottery. Beijing had begun restricting issue to 20,000 a month, reserving 17,600 for private buyers. Wang scored her plate the same month she entered, and she bought a Volkswagen in March. She didn't end up driving to work. The gridlock proved too daunting. Instead, she parks her car from Monday to Friday and takes it to her parents' nearby house on the weekends.

In Shanghai, after his Buick finally emerged from the shop, Gu Xiaoming picked his wife up on her way home from work again. And just in time, for Xue Xiaowen was pregnant. Their son, nicknamed Duoduo, was born in July 2011. He will grow up believing car ownership is a normal part of Chinese life.

Xue Peng had a similar stroke of luck: he got married less than a year after we cruised Nanjing's streets, and now his wife occupied the passenger side of their car, buckling her seatbelt under the growing expanse of a pregnant belly. Navigating the traffic, Xue Peng worried about the safety of his wife and unborn child. He revved his engine, but it was getting harder and harder to hear it.

The traffic is just too loud.

CHAPTER 9

Painting the Outside World

PETER HESSLER

In the countryside southwest of the city of Lishui, where the Da River crosses a sixth-century stone weir, the local government announced, four years ago, that it was founding a Chinese version of the Barbizon. The original French Barbizon School developed during the first half of the nineteenth century, in response to the Romantic movement, among painters working at the edge of the Fontainebleau Forest. Back then, the French artists celebrated rural scenes and peasant subjects. This wasn't exactly the mood in Lishui: like most cities in eastern China's Zhejiang Province, the place was focused on urban growth; there was a new factory district, and the export economy was then booming. But the local Communist Party cadres wanted the city to become even more outward-looking, and they liked the foreign cachet of the Barbizon. They also figured that it would be good business: art doesn't require much raw material, and it's popular overseas. They referred to their project as Lishui's *Babisong*, and they gave it the official name of the Ancient Weir Art Village. One Party slogan described it as "A Village of Art, a Capital of Romance, a Place for Idleness."

In order to attract artists, the government offered free rent in some old riverside buildings for the first year, with additional subsidies to follow. Painters arrived immediately; soon, the village had nearly a dozen private galleries. Most people came from China's far south, where there was already a flourishing industry of art for the foreign market. Buyers wanted cheap oil paintings, many of which were destined for tourist shops, restaurants, and hotels in distant countries. For some reason, the majority of artists who settled Lishui's Barbizon specialized in cityscapes of Venice. The manager of Hongye, the largest of the new galleries, told me that it had a staff of thirty painters, and that its main customer was a European-based importer with an insatiable appetite for Venetian scenes. Every month, he wanted a thousand Chinese paintings of the Italian city.

Another small gallery, Bomia, had been opened by a woman named Chen Meizi and her boyfriend, Hu Jianhui. The first time I met Chen, she had just finished a scene of Venice, and now she was painting a Dutch street scene from what looked like the eighteenth century. A Russian customer had sent a postcard and asked her to copy it. The painting was 20 inches by 24, and Chen told me that she would sell it for about 25 dollars. Like most people in the Ancient Weir Art Village, she described Venice as Shui Cheng, "Water City," and referred to Dutch scenes as Helan Jie, "Holland Street." She said that over the past half year she had painted this particular Holland Street as many as 30 times. "All the pictures have that big tower in it," she said.

I told her that it was a church—the steeple rose in the distance, at the end of a road bordered by brick houses with red tile roofs.

"I thought it might be a church, but I wasn't sure," she said. "I knew it was important because whenever I make a mistake they send it back."

Through trial and error, she had learned to recognize some of the landmark buildings. She had no idea of the names of St. Mark's Basilica and the Doge's Palace, but she knew these places mattered, because even the tiniest mistake resulted in rejection. She worked faster on less iconic scenes, because customers didn't notice slight errors. On average, she could finish a painting in under two days.

Chen was in her early twenties, and she had grown up on a farm near Lishui; as a teenager, she learned to paint at an art school. She still had a peasant's directness—she spoke in a raspy voice and laughed at many of my questions. I asked her which of her pictures she liked the most, and she said, "I don't like any of them." She didn't have a favorite painter; there wasn't any particular artistic period that had influenced her. "That kind of art has no connection at all with what we do," she said. The Barbizon concept didn't impress her much. The government had commissioned some European-style paintings of local scenery, but Chen had no use for any of it. Like many young Chinese from the countryside, she had already had her fill of bucolic surroundings. She stayed in the Ancient Weir Art Village strictly because of the free rent, and she missed the busy city of Guangzhou, where she had previously lived. In the meantime, she looked the part of an urban convert. She had long curly hair; she dressed in striking colors; she seemed to wear high heels whenever she was awake. On workdays, she tottered on stilettos in front of her easel, painting gondolas and churches.

Hu Jianhui, Chen's boyfriend, was a soft-spoken man with glasses and a faint crooked mustache that crossed his lip like a calligrapher's slip. Once a month, he rolled up all their finished paintings and took a train down to Guangzhou, where there was a big art market. That was how they encountered customers; none of the buyers ever came to the Ancient Weir Art Village. For the most part, foreigners wanted Holland Streets and the Water City, but occasionally they sent photographs of other scenes to be converted into art. Hu kept a sample book in which a customer could pick out a picture, give an ID number, and order a full-size oil painting on canvas. HF-3127 was the Eiffel Tower. HF-3087 was a clipper ship on stormy seas. HF-3199 was a circle of Native Americans smoking a peace pipe. Chen and Hu could rarely identify the foreign scenes that they painted, but they had acquired some ideas about national art tastes from their commissions.

"Americans prefer brighter pictures," Hu told me. "They like scenes to be lighter. Russians like bright colors, too. Koreans like them to be more subdued, and Germans like things that are grayer. The French are like that, too."

Chen flipped to HF-3075: a snow-covered house with glowing lights. "Chinese people like this kind of picture," she said. "Ugly! And they like this one." HF-3068: palm trees on a beach. "It's stupid, something a child would like. Chinese people have no taste. French people have the best taste, followed by Russians, and then the other Europeans." I asked her how Americans stacked up. "Americans are after that," she said. "We'll do a painting and the European customer won't buy it, and then we'll show it to a Chinese person, and he'll say, 'Great!'"

Lishui is a third-tier Chinese factory town, with a central population of around two hundred and fifty thousand, and, in a place like that, the outside world is both everywhere and nowhere at all. In the new development zone, assembly lines produce goods for export, but there isn't much direct foreign investment. There aren't any Nike factories, or Intel plants, or signs that say DuPont; important brands base themselves in bigger cities. Lishui companies make pieces of things: zippers, copper wiring, electric-outlet covers. The products are so obscure that you can't tell much from the signs that hang outside factory gates: Jinchao Industry Co., Ltd.; Huadu Leather Base Cloth Co., Ltd. At the Lishui Sanxing Power Machinery Co., Ltd., the owners have posted their sign in English, but they did so from right to left, the way Chinese traditionally do with characters:

DTL ,.OC YRENIHCAM REWOP GNIXNAS IUHSIL

It's rare to see a foreign face in Lishui. Over a period of three years, I visited the city repeatedly, talking to people in the export industry, but I never met a foreign buyer. Products are sent elsewhere for final assembly, some passing through two or three levels of middlemen before they go abroad; there isn't any reason for a European or an American businessman to visit. But despite the absence of foreigners, the city has been shaped almost entirely by globalization, and traces of the outside world can be seen everywhere. When Lishui's first gym opened, it was called the Scent of a Woman, for the Al Pacino movie. Once I met a demolition-crew worker who had a homemade tattoo on his left arm that said "KENT." He told me he'd done it himself as a kid, after noticing that American movie gangsters have tattoos. I asked why he'd chosen that particular word, and he said, "It's from the ciga-rette brand in your country." Another time, I interviewed a young factory boss who wore a diamond earring in the shape of the letter "K." His girlfriend had an "O": whenever they were together, and the letters lined up, everything was all right.

The degree of detail often impressed me. The outside world might be distant, but it wasn't necessarily blurred; people caught discrete glimpses of things from overseas. In many cases, these images seemed slightly askew—they were focused and refracted, like light bent around a corner. Probably it had something to do with all the specialization. Lishui residents learned to see the world in parts, and these parts had a strange clarity, even when they weren't fully understood. One factory technician who had never formally studied English showed me a list of terms he had memorized:

Padomide Br. Yellow E-8GMX

Sellanyl Yellow N-5GL

Padocid Violet NWL

Sellan Bordeaux G-P

Padocid Turquoise Blue N-3GL

Padomide Rhodamine

In the labyrinth of the foreign language, he'd skipped all the usual entrances—the simple greetings, the basic vocabulary—to go straight to the single row of words that mattered to him. His specialty was dyeing nylon; he mixed chemicals and made colors. His name was Long Chunming, and his co-workers called him Xiao Long, or Little Long. He would consult his notebook and figure out the perfect mixture of chemicals necessary to make Sellanyl Yellow or Padocid Turquoise Blue.

He had grown up on a farm in Guizhou, one of the poorest provinces in China. His parents raised tea, tobacco, and vegetables, and Little Long, like both of his siblings, left home after dropping out of middle school. It's a common path in China, where an estimated 130 million rural migrants have gone to the cities in search of work. In the factory town, Little Long had become relatively successful, earning a good wage of 300 dollars a month. But he was determined to further improve himself, and he studied self-help books with foreign themes. In his mind, this endeavor was completely separate from his work. He had no pretensions about what he did; as far as he was concerned, the skills he had gained were strictly and narrowly technical. "I'm not mature enough," he told me once, and he collected books that supposedly improved moral character. One was "The New Harvard MBA Comprehensive Volume of How to Conduct Yourself in Society." Another book was called "Be an Upright Person, Handle Situations Correctly, Become a Boss." In the introduction, the author describes the divides of the worker's environment: "For a person to live on earth, he has to face two worlds: the boundless world of the outside, and the world that exists inside a person."

Little Long had full lips and high cheekbones. He was slightly vain, especially with regard to his hair, which was shoulder-length. At local beauty parlors, he had it dyed a shade of red so exotic it was best described in professional terms: Sellan Bordeaux. But he was intensely serious about his books. They followed a formula that's common in the self-help literature of Chinese factory towns: short, simple chapters that feature some famous foreigner and conclude with a moral. In a volume called "A Collection of the Classics," the section on effective use of leisure time gave the example of Charles Darwin. (The book explained that Darwin's biology studies began as a hobby.) Another chapter told the story of how a waiter once became angry at John D. Rockefeller after the oil baron left a measly one-dollar tip. ("Because of such thinking, you're only a waiter," Rockefeller shot back, according to the Chinese book, which praised his thrift.)

Little Long particularly liked "A Collection of the Classics" because it introduced foreign religions. He was interested in Christianity, and when we talked about the subject he referred me to a chapter that featured a parable about Jesus. In this tale, a humble doorkeeper works at a church with a statue of the Crucifixion. Every day, the doorkeeper prays to be allowed to serve as a substitute, to ease the pain for the Son of God. To the man's surprise, Jesus finally speaks and accepts the offer, under one condition: If the doorkeeper ascends the cross, he can't say a word.

The agreement is made, and soon a wealthy merchant comes to pray. He accidentally drops a money purse; the doorkeeper almost says something but remembers his promise. The next supplicant is a poor man. He prays fervently, opens his eyes, and sees the purse: overjoyed, he thanks Jesus. Again, the doorkeeper keeps silent. Then comes a young traveler preparing to embark on a long sea journey. While he is praying, the merchant returns and accuses the traveler of taking his purse. An argument ensues; the traveler fears he'll miss the boat. At last, the doorkeeper speaks out—with a few words, he resolves the dispute. The traveler heads off on his journey, and the merchant finds the poor man and retrieves his money.

But Jesus angrily calls the doorkeeper down from the cross for breaking the promise. When the man protests ("I just told the truth!"), Jesus criticizes him: "What do you understand? That rich merchant isn't short of money, and he'll use that cash to hire prostitutes, whereas the poor man needs it. But the most wretched is the young traveler. If the merchant had delayed the traveler's departure, he would have saved his life, but right now his boat is sinking in the ocean."

When I flipped through Little Long's books, and looked at his chemical-color vocabulary lists, I sometimes felt a kind of vertigo. In Lishui, that was a common sensation; I couldn't imagine how people created a coherent worldview out of such strange and scattered contacts with the outside. But I was coming from the other direction, and the gaps impressed me more than the glimpses. For Little Long, the pieces themselves seemed to be enough; they didn't necessarily have to all fit together in perfect fashion. He told me that, after reading about Darwin's use of leisure time, he decided to stop complaining about being too busy with work, and now he felt calmer. John D. Rockefeller convinced Little Long that he should change cigarette brands. In the past, he smoked Profitable Crowd, a popular cigarette among middle-class men, but after reading about the American oil baron and the waiter, he switched to a cheaper brand called Hibiscus. Hibiscuses were terrible smokes; they cost about a cent each, and the label immediately identified the bearer as a cheapskate. But Little Long was determined to rise above such petty thinking, just like Rockefeller.

Jesus' lesson was easiest of all: Don't try to change the world. It was essentially Taoist, reinforcing the classical Chinese phrase "Wu wei er wu bu wei" (By doing nothing everything will be done). In Little Long's book, the parable of the Crucifixion concludes with a moral: "We often think about the best way to act, but reality and our desires are at odds, so we can't fulfill our intentions. We must believe that what we already have is best for us."

One month, the Bomia gallery received a commission to create paintings from photographs of a small American town. A middleman in southern China sent the pictures, and he requested a 24-inch-by-20-inch oil reproduction of each photo. He emphasized that the quality had to be first-rate, because the scenes were destined for the foreign market. Other than that, he gave no details. Middlemen tended to be secretive about orders, as a way of protecting their profit.

When I visited later that month, Chen Meizi and Hu Jianhui had finished most of the commission. Chen was about to start work on one of the final snapshots: a big white barn with two silos. I asked her what she thought it was.

"A development zone," she said.

I told her that it was a farm. "So big just for a farm?" she said. "What are those for?"

I said that the silos were used for grain.

"Those big things are for grain?" she said, laughing. "I thought they were for storing chemicals!"

Now she studied the scene with new eyes. "I can't believe how big it is," she said. "Where's the rest of the village?"

I explained that American farmers usually live miles outside town.

"Where are their neighbors?" she asked.

"They're probably far away, too."

"Aren't they lonely?"

"It doesn't bother them," I said. "That's how farming is in America."

I knew that if I hadn't been asking questions Chen probably wouldn't have thought twice about the scene. As far as she was concerned, it was pointless to speculate about things that she didn't need to know; she felt no need to develop a deeper connection with the outside. In that sense, she was different from Little Long. He was a searcher—in

Lishui, I often met such individuals who hoped to go beyond their niche industry and learn something else about the world. But it was even more common to encounter pragmatists like Chen Meizi. She had her skill, and she did her work; it made no difference what she painted.

From my outsider's perspective, her niche was so specific and detailed that it made me curious. I often studied her paintings, trying to figure out where they came from, and the American commission struck me as particularly odd. Apart from the farm, most portraits featured what appeared to be a main street in a small town. There were pretty shop fronts and well-kept sidewalks; the place seemed prosperous. Of all the commissioned paintings, the most beautiful one featured a distinctive red brick building. It had a peaked roof, tall old-fashioned windows, and a white railed porch. An American flag hung from a pole, and a sign on the second story said "Miers Hospital 1904."

The building had an air of importance, but there weren't any other clues or details. On the wall of the Chinese gallery, the scene was completely flat: neither Chen nor I had any idea what she had just spent two days painting. I asked to see the original photograph, and I noticed that the sign should have read "Miners Hospital." Other finished paintings also had misspelled signs, because Chen and Hu didn't speak English. One shop called Overland had a sign that said "Fine Sheepskin and Leather Since 1973"; the artists had turned it into "Fine Sheepskim Leather Sine 1773." A "Bar" was now a "Dah." There was a "Hope Nuseum," a shop that sold "Amiques," and a "Residentlal Bboker." In a few cases, I preferred the new versions—who wouldn't want to drink at a place called Dah? But I helped the artists make corrections, and afterward everything looked perfect. I told Chen that she'd done an excellent job on the Miners Hospital, but she waved off my praise.

Once, not long after we met, I asked her how she first became interested in oil painting.

"Because I was a terrible student," she said. "I had bad grades, and I couldn't get into high school. It's easier to get accepted to an art school than to a technical school, so that's what I did."

"Did you like to draw when you were little?"

"No."

"But you had natural talent, right?"

"Absolutely none at all!" she said, laughing. "When I started, I couldn't even hold a brush!"

"Did you study well?"

"No. I was the worst in the class."

"But did you enjoy it?"

"No. I didn't like it one bit."

Her responses were typical of migrants from the countryside, where there's a strong tradition of humility as well as pragmatism. In the factory town, people usually described themselves as ignorant and inept, even when they seemed quite skilled. That was another reason that Chen took so little interest in the scenes she painted: it wasn't her place to speculate, and she scoffed at anything that might seem pretentious. As part of the Barbizon project, the cadres had distributed a promotional DVD about Lishui, emphasizing the town's supposed links to world art. But Chen refused to watch the video. ("I'm sure it's stupid!") Instead, she hung the DVD on a nail beside her easel, and she used the shiny side as a mirror while working. She held up the disk and compared her paintings to the originals; by seeing things backward, it was easier to spot mistakes. "They taught us how to do this in art school," she said.

Together with her boyfriend, Chen earned about a thousand dollars every month, which is excellent in a small city. To me, her story was amazing: I couldn't imagine coming from a poor Chinese farm, learning to paint, and finding success with scenes that were entirely foreign. But Chen took no particular pride in her accomplishment. These endeavors were so technical and specific that, at least for the workers involved, they essentially had no larger context. People who had grown up without any link to the outside world suddenly developed an extremely specialized role in the export economy; it was like taking their first view of another country through a microscope.

The Lishui experience seemed to contradict one of the supposed benefits of globalization: the notion that economic exchanges naturally lead to greater understanding. But Lishui also contradicted the critics who believe that globalized links are disorienting and damaging to the workers at the far end of the chain. The more time I spent in the city, the more I was impressed with how comfortable people were with their jobs. They didn't worry about who consumed their products, and very little of their self-worth seemed to be tied up in these trades. There were no illusions of control—in a place like Lishui, which combined remoteness with the immediacy of world-market demands, people accepted an element of irrationality. If a job disappeared or an opportunity dried up, workers didn't waste time wondering why, and they moved on. Their humility helped, because they never perceived themselves as being the center of the world. When Chen Meizi had chosen her specialty, she didn't expect to find a job that matched her abilities; she expected to find new abilities that matched the available jobs. The fact that her vocation was completely removed from her personality and her past was no more disorienting than the scenes she painted—if anything, it simplified things. She couldn't tell the difference between a foreign factory and a farm, but it didn't matter. The mirror's reflection allowed her to focus on details; she never lost herself in the larger scene.

Whenever I went to Lishui, I moved from one self-contained world to another, visiting the people I knew. I'd spend a couple of hours surrounded by paintings of Venice, then by manhole covers, then by cheap cotton gloves. Once, walking through a vacant lot, I saw a pile of bright-red high heels that had been dumped in the weeds. They must have been factory rejects; no shoes, just dozens of unattached heels. In the empty lot, the heels looked stubby and sad, like the detritus of some failed party. They made me think of hangovers, spilled ashtrays, and conversations gone on too long.

The associations were different when you came from the outside. There were many products I had never spent a minute thinking about, like pleather—synthetic leather—that in Lishui suddenly acquired a disproportionate significance. More than 20 big factories made the stuff; it was shipped in bulk to other parts of China, where it was fashioned into car seats, purses, and countless other goods. In the city, pleather was so ubiquitous that it had developed a distinct local lore. Workers believed that the product involved dangerous chemicals, and they thought it was bad for the liver. They said that a woman who planned to have children should not work on the assembly line.

These ideas were absolutely standard; even teenagers fresh from the farm seemed to pick them up the moment they arrived in the city. But it was impossible to tell where the rumors came from. There weren't any warnings posted on factories, and I never saw a Lishui newspaper article about pleather; assembly-line workers rarely read the papers anyway. They didn't know people who had become ill, and they couldn't tell me whether there had been any scientific studies of the risks. They referred to the supposedly harmful chemical as *du*, a general term that means "poison." Nevertheless, these beliefs ran so deep that they shaped that particular industry. Virtually no young women worked on pleather assembly lines, and companies had to offer relatively high wages in order to attract anybody. At those plants, you saw many older men—the kind of people who can't get jobs at most Chinese factories.

The flow of information was a mystery to me. Few people had much formal education, and assembly-line workers rarely had time to use the Internet. They didn't follow the news; they had no interest in politics. They were the least patriotic people I ever met in China—they saw no connection between the affairs of state and their own lives. They accepted the fact that nobody else cared about them; in a small city like Lishui, there weren't any NGOs or prominent organizations that served workers. They depended strictly on themselves, and their range of contacts seemed narrow, but somehow it wasn't a closed world. Ideas arrived from the outside, and people acted decisively on what seemed to be the vaguest rumor or the most trivial story. That was key: information might be limited, but people were mobile, and they had confidence that their choices mattered. It gave them a kind of agency, although from a foreigner's perspective it contributed to the strangeness of the place. I was accustomed to the opposite—a world where people preferred to be stable, and where they felt most comfortable if they had large amounts of data at their disposal, as well as the luxury of time to make a decision.

In Lishui, people moved incredibly fast with regard to new opportunities. This quality lay at the heart of the city's relationship with the outside world: Lishui was home to a great number of pragmatists, and there were quite a few searchers as well, but everybody was an opportunist in the purest sense. The market taught them that factory workers changed jobs frequently, and entrepreneurs could shift their product line at the drop of a hat. There was one outlying community called Shifan, where people seemed to find a different income source every month. It was a new town; residents had been resettled there from Beishan, a village in the mountains where the government was building a new hydroelectric dam to help power the factories. In Shifan, there was no significant industry, but small-time jobs began to appear from the moment the place was founded. Generally, these tasks consisted of piecework commissioned by some factory in the city.

Once a month, I visited a family named the Wus, and virtually every time they introduced me to some new and obscure trade. For a while, they joined their neighbors in sewing colored beads onto the uppers of children's shoes; then there was a period during which they attached decorative strips to hair bands. After that, they assembled tiny light bulbs. For a six-week stretch, they made cotton gloves on a makeshift assembly line.

On one visit to Shifan, I discovered that the Wus' son, Wu Zengrong, and his friends had purchased five secondhand computers, set up a broadband connection, and become professional players of a video game called World of Warcraft. It was one of the most popular online games in the world, with more than 7 million subscribers. Players developed characters, accumulating skills, equipment, and treasure. Online markets had sprung up in which people could buy and sell virtual treasure, and some Chinese had started doing this as a full-time job; it had recently spread to Lishui. The practice is known as "gold farming."

Wu Zengrong hadn't had any prior interest in video games. He hardly ever went online; his family had never had an Internet connection before. He had been trained as a cook, and would take jobs in small restaurants that served nearby factory towns. Occasionally, he did low-level assembly-line work. But his brother-in-law, a cook in the city of Ningbo, learned about World of Warcraft, and he realized that the game paid better than standing over a wok. He called his buddies, and three of them quit their jobs, pooled their money, and set up shop in Shifan. Others joined them; they played around the clock in twelve-hour shifts. All of them had time off on Wednesdays. For World of Warcraft, that was a special day: the European servers closed for regular maintenance from 5 A.M. until 8 A.M. Paris time. Whenever I visited Shifan on a Wednesday, Wu Zengrong and his friends were smoking cigarettes and hanging out, enjoying their weekend as established by World of Warcraft.

They became deadly serious when they played. They had to worry about getting caught, because Blizzard Entertainment, which owns World of Warcraft, had decided that gold farming threatened the game's integrity. Blizzard monitored the community, shutting down any account whose play pattern showed signs of commercial activity. Wu Zengrong originally played the American version, but after getting caught a few times he jumped over to the German one. On a good day, he made the equivalent of about twenty-five dollars. If an account got shut down, he lost a nearly forty-dollar investment. He sold his points online to a middleman in Fujian Province.

One Saturday, I spent an afternoon watching Wu Zengrong play. He was a very skinny man with a nervous air; his long, thin fingers flashed across the keyboard. Periodically, his wife, Lili, entered the room to watch. She wore a gold-colored ring on her right hand that had been made from a euro coin. That had become a fashion in south-ern Zhejiang, where shops specialized in melting down the coins and turning them into jewelry. It was another ingenious local industry: a way to get a ring that was both legitimately foreign and cheaply made in Zhejiang.

Wu Zengrong worked on two computers, jumping back and forth between three accounts. His characters traveled in places with names like Kalimdor, Tanaris, and Dreadmaul Rock; he fought Firegut Ogres and Sandfury Hideskinners. Periodically, a message flashed across the screen: "You loot 7 silver, 75 copper." Wu couldn't understand any of it; his ex-cook brother-in-law had taught him to play the game strictly by memorizing shapes and icons. At one point, Wu's character encoun-tered piles of dead Sandfury Axe Throwers and Hideskinners, and he said to me, "There's another player around here. I bet he's Chinese, too. You can tell because he's killing everybody just to get the treasure."

After a while, we saw the other player, whose character was a dwarf. I typed in a message: "How are you doing?" Wu didn't want me to write in Chinese, for fear that administrators would spot him as a gold farmer.

Initially, there was no response; I tried again. At last, the dwarf spoke: "???"

I typed, "Where are you from?"

This time he wrote, "Sorry." From teaching English in China, I knew that's how all students respond to any question they can't answer. And that was it; the dwarf resumed his methodical slaughter in silence. "You see?" Wu said, laughing. "I told you he's Chinese!"

Two months later, when I visited Shifan again, three of the comput-ers had been sold, and Wu was preparing to get rid of the others. He and his friends had decided that playing in Germany was no longer profitable enough; Blizzard kept shutting them down. Wu showed me the most recent e-mail message he had received from the company: "Greetings, We are writing to inform you that we have, unfortunately, had to cancel your World of Warcraft account. . . . It is with regret that we take this type of action, however, it is in the best interest of the World of Warcraft community as a whole."

The message appeared in four different languages, none of which was spoken by Wu Zengrong. It didn't matter: after spending his twen-ties bouncing from job to job in factory towns, and having his family relocated for a major dam project, he felt limited trauma at being expelled from the World of Warcraft community. The next time I saw him, he was applying for a passport. He had some relatives in Italy; he had heard that there was money to be made there. When I asked where he planned to go, he said, "Maybe Rome, or maybe the Water City." I stood with him in the passport-application line at the county government office, where I noticed that his papers said "Wu Zengxiong." He explained that a clerk had miswritten his given name on an earlier application, so now it was simpler to just use that title. He was becoming somebody else, on his way to a country he'd never seen, preparing to do something completely new. When I asked what kind of work he hoped to find and what the pay might be, he said, "How can I tell? I haven't been there yet." Next to us in line, a friend in his early twenties told me that he planned to go to Azerbaijan, where he had a relative who might help him do business. I asked the young man if Azerbaijan was an Islamic country, and he said, "I don't know. I haven't been there yet."

After I returned to the United States, I talked with a cousin who played World of Warcraft. He told me that he could usually recognize Chinese gold farmers from their virtual appearance, because they stood out as being extremely ill-equipped. If they gained valuable gear or weapons, they sold them immediately; their characters were essentially empty-handed. I liked that image—even online, Chinese traveled light. Around the same time, I did some research on pleather and learned that it's made with a solvent called dimethylformamide, or DMF. In the United States, studies have shown that people who work with DMF are at risk of liver damage. There's some evidence that female workers may have increased problems with stillbirths. In laboratory tests with rabbits, significant exposure to DMF has been proved to cause developmental defects. In other words, virtually everything I had heard from the Lishui migrant workers in the form of unsubstantiated rumor turned out to be true.

It was another efficiency of the third-tier factory town. People manufactured tiny parts of things, and their knowledge was also fragmented and sparse. But they knew enough to be mobile and decisive, and their judgment was surprisingly good. An assembly-line worker sensed the risks of DMF; a painter learned to recognize the buildings that mattered; a nylon dyer could pick out Sellanyl Yellow. Even the misinformation was often useful—if Christ became more relevant as a Taoist sage, that was how He appeared. The workers knew what they needed to know.

After I moved back to the United States, I became curious about the small town that Chen Meizi and Hu Jianhui had spent so much time painting. At Ancient Weir Art Village, I had photographed the artists in front of their work, and now I researched the misspelled signs. All of them seemed to come from Park City, Utah. I lived nearby, in southwestern Colorado, so I made the trip.

I was still in touch with many of the people I had known in Lishui. Occasionally, Chen sent an e-mail, and when I talked with her on the phone, she said that she was still painting mostly the Water City. The economic downturn hadn't affected her too much; apparently, the market for Chinese-produced paintings of Venice is nearly recession-proof. Others hadn't been so lucky. During the second half of 2008, as demand for Chinese exports dropped, millions of factory workers lost their jobs. Little Long left his plant after the bosses slashed the technicians' salaries and laid off half the assembly-line staff.

But most people I talked to in Lishui seemed to take these events in stride. They didn't have mortgages or stock portfolios, and they had long ago learned to be resourceful. They were accustomed to switching jobs—many laid-off workers simply went back to their home villages to wait for better times. In any case, they had never had any reason to believe that the international economy was rational and predictable. If people suddenly bought less pleather, that was no more strange than the fact that they had wanted the stuff in the first place. As 2009 progressed, the Chinese economy regained its strength, and workers made their way back onto the assembly lines.

In Park City, it was easy to find the places that the artists had painted. Most of the shops were situated on Main Street, and I talked with owners, showing them photos. Nobody had any idea where the commission had come from, and people responded in different ways when they saw that their shops were being painted by artists in an obscure Chinese city 6,000 miles away. At Overland ("Fine Sheepskim Leather Sine 1773"), the manager appeared nervous. "You'll have to contact our corporate headquarters," she said. "I can't comment on that." Another shop owner asked me if I thought that Mormon missionaries might be involved. One woman told a story about a suspicious Arab man who had visited local art galleries not long ago, offering to sell cut-rate portraits. Some people worried about competition. "That's just what we need," one artist said sarcastically, when she learned the price of the Chinese paintings. Others felt pity when they saw Chen Meizi, who, like many rural Chinese, didn't generally smile in photographs. One woman, gazing at a somber Chen next to her portrait of the Miners Hospital, said, "It's kind of sad."

Everybody had something to say about that particular picture. The building brought up countless memories; all at once, the painting lost its flatness. The hospital had been constructed to serve the silver miners who first settled Park City, and later it became the town library. In 1979, authorities moved the building across town to make way for a ski resort, and the community pitched in to transfer the books. "We formed a human chain and passed the books down," an older woman remembered. When I showed the painting to a restaurant manager, he smiled and said that a critical scene from *Dumb and Dumber* had been filmed inside the Miners Hospital. "You know the part where they go to that benefit dinner for the owls, and they're wearing those crazy suits, and the one guy has a cane and he whacks the other guy on the leg—you know what I'm talking about?"

I admitted that I did.

"They filmed that scene right inside that building!"

When I visited, the Park City mayor kept his office on the first floor of the Miners Hospital. His name was Dana Williams, and he was thrilled to see the photo of Chen Meizi with her work. "That's so cool!" he said. "I can't believe somebody in China painted our building! And she did such a great job!"

Like everybody else I talked to in Park City, Mayor Williams couldn't tell me why the building had been commissioned for a portrait overseas. It was a kind of symmetry between the Chinese Barbizon and Park City: the people who painted the scenes, and the people who actually lived within the frames, were equally mystified as to the purpose of this art.

Mayor Williams poured me a cup of green tea, and we chatted. He had an easy smile and a youthful air; he played guitar in a local rock band. "It's the yang to being mayor," he explained. He was interested in China, and he sprinkled his conversation with Chinese terms. "You mei you pijiu?" he said. "Do you have any beer?" He remembered that phrase from a trip to Beijing in 2007, when he'd accompanied a local school group on an exchange. A scroll of calligraphy hung beside his desk; the characters read "Unity, Culture, Virtue." He told me that he had first thought about China back in the 1960s, after hearing Angela Davis lecture on Communism at UCLA. There was a copy of the "Little Red Book" in his office library. When the Park City newspaper found out, it ran a story implying that the mayor's decisions were influenced by Mao Zedong. Mayor Williams found that hilarious; he told me that he just picked out the useful parts of the book and ignored the bad stuff. "Serve the people," he said, when I asked what he had learned from Mao. "You have an obligation to serve the people. One of the reasons I'm here is from reading 'The Little Red Book' as a teenager. And being in government is about being in balance. I guess that has to do with the Tao."

PART FOUR

Rebels and Reformers

The Nobel Laureate Liu Xiaobo, who was one of the many prominent Chinese who called for an end to one-party rule in the famous online petition "Charter 08," and the artist-activist Ai Weiwei, who routinely criticizes China's government for corruption and human rights violations, are well known to the Western world. Both have been arrested for their dissidence—Liu in 2008 and Ai in 2011—and their persecution is often cited by Western news media as exemplifying the Chinese Communist Party's wrongdoings.

What is often overlooked is the importance of a much larger group of people who are also working for change in China but would not think of themselves as dissidents. These scholars and activists do not necessarily face the same kind of persecution as the most outspoken of China's rebels, though they are frequently harassed and sometimes put behind bars. Instead of calling for comprehensive transformation of the state, they often focus on single issues, and they feel that they can do the most good by trying to stay under the Party's radar if possible. They do their best not to cross lines that the government has drawn in the sand. The crusading academics whose experiences figure centrally in the first and third chapters of Part Four and the environmentalist of the second chapter all belong to this often overlooked category of Chinese reformers.

CHAPTER 10

The Road to a Better Life

ANANTH KRISHNAN

When Alim first attended a lecture by the economist Ilham Tohti, he was stunned. Alim had spent most of his student life in sterile, cloistered classrooms where the lessons were, without exception, stale and uninteresting, infused with the unappealing political rhetoric of Communist Party propaganda. The 26-year-old student never took his lessons seriously; he gave them just enough attention to ensure that he got good enough grades.

But Tohti's lectures were different. Alim listened with rapt attention from beginning to end, absorbing every word and furiously noting the smallest details. Indeed, everything about Tohti was new. Even his appearance was in striking contrast to the staid instructors Alim was used to back home. Tohti was a charismatic, forceful young teacher. He spoke with emotion, and his lectures were almost like sermons: he would punch his hands into the air to make a point, and his eyes would grow wide to match the import of his words. And, most important, in Alim's eyes, he spoke the truth.

Alim traveled a long way, almost three thousand miles, to listen to Tohti. It was a journey that took him away from his family and far from his home, a quiet village that sits amid corn fields in Xinjiang, the rugged desert region that stretches across much of China's western frontier. He was one of only three dozen students from Xinjiang granted admission to Beijing's Minzu University, a school with a focus on ethnic studies, set up by the government for students from China's fifty-five minority ethnic groups, whose name translates as University of the Minorities. Alim's cohort from Xinjiang were all Uyghur, members of the largest Turkic ethnic group native to the western region. They had all sacrificed much to get to Beijing. When they finally arrived in the university, they stuck together.

In the Chinese capital, the Uyghur students quickly found themselves to be strangers in an unfamiliar land, surrounded by people with whom they had little in common. Since their native language was Uyghur, communicating with Mandarin speakers was a strain. They also ate differently, with rules and restrictions their Chinese classmates found strange and amusing. Cosmopolitan Minzu University was a world away from their small-town homes. The university is a unique—and somewhat anomalous—bubble of diversity at the heart of China's capital. Even a walk through its quiet campus presents a fascinating snapshot of China's variety of people and cultures. Here, Uyghurs study and live together with Tibetans, Huis, and Mongolians. Separated by language, religion, and diverse cultural histories, their lives are unexpectedly brought together by their common goal of education and advancement.

. . .

Alim (a pseudonym) was the first in his large family to leave home. He was the only one among his seven siblings to finish high school. He comes from a dusty village in the southern county of Kizilsu. His village is home to fewer than a hundred families, most of whom scrape together a living from growing cotton and corn on their small plots of land. When Alim was growing up, his village had no elementary school. Families who were determined enough to give their children a good education had to walk their young ones to a town over three miles away every morning. There were no buses—or paved roads, for that matter. Alim's two older brothers worked with their elderly father on the family's three-acre plot of land, which barely provided enough to feed the family. His younger sisters married young and moved to other towns.

Alim's grandfather, a native of the old Silk Road city of Kashgar, worked for the Nationalist Party during the Chinese Civil War in the 1940s but switched his allegiance to the Communist Party shortly after Xinjiang fell under its control in 1949. He could not, however, bury his past. During the Cultural Revolution, he was made to suffer for his prior allegiances. His family lost their property in Kashgar, and he was imprisoned for five years. He moved his family to the village in Kizilsu in the early 1980s to start anew. Still, like many others in his generation, he remained a staunch follower of Mao for the rest of his life. He brought up his two sons in this largely Muslim region as atheists, teaching them to follow the Communist Party. Alim's father even joined the police force.

When Alim's father retired from the police force, he tended his farmland with the help of his young children. Life in the village was simple. The children's days were spent at elementary school in the nearby town and their evenings on the farm. Alim's father was not religious, but his mother was deeply so. The children were sent to the local mosque for lessons from the imam every weekend. They never missed daily prayers. There were few marks of Han Chinese influence in the countryside aside from the Mandarin lessons that some students took in elementary school, starting between twelve and fourteen. During his childhood, Alim's hometown remained largely insulated from the changes sweeping across their homeland under Chinese rule. But as he grew older, the life he knew was fast nearing its end.

. . .

Xinjiang, a land of black deserts nestled between the towering mountain ranges of the Karakoram and the Tibetan plateau, sits uneasily at the confluence of different civilizations. Before the newly established People's Republic of China took control of Xinjiang in 1949, an independent republic set up with Soviet support briefly existed in northern parts of the region. Various Chinese kingdoms, from the Han dynasty in the second century B.C.E. to the later Tang and Qing rulers, sought to bring this frontier land under their control, with varying degrees of success.

Xinjiang has historically been China's cultural and commercial bridge to the west, providing links to India, Pakistan, Afghanistan, Tajikistan, Kyrgyzstan, Kazakhstan, Russia, and Mongolia. This history has bestowed a unique duality on Xinjiang's culture: it is deeply resilient, accustomed to withstanding myriad competing onslaughts, but it also bears the marks of a long history of syncretic engagement, absorbing elements of the many cultures that have passed through this land on the Silk Road. Today, Xinjiang is the site of yet another struggle, whose likely outcome is unclear.

China's ruling Communist Party proudly holds up Xinjiang as an example of how Beijing's rule has brought great benefits to undeveloped far-flung frontiers. Local apparatchiks reel off statistics like automatons: double-digit GDP growth every year, soaring investments in fixed assets and infrastructure, more schools and more hospitals. Chinese rule, they say, has brought development to Xinjiang's cities in the form of skyscrapers and shopping malls, highways and power plants. The evidence is there to see. Prosperity is easy to find on the wide boulevards of Xinjiang's capital city, Urümqi. New wealth inhabits the neon lights of Renmin Lu, the People's Street, that bear the labels of international luxury brands and the flashy cars driven by the city's Chinese elite.

The Chinese government's strategy has been clear: fast-paced development led by Chinese companies and enabled by increased migration. Much of the growth in Xinjiang has been led by state-run Chinese companies, many of whose sole focus is on tapping the region's vast energy and mineral resources. Behemoths like the China Petroleum & Chemical Corporation (Sinopec) often enjoy close relations with local Party chiefs and mayors and hold great influence on Xinjiang's politics. As early as the 1950s, Mao Zedong exhorted Chinese to migrate to Xinjiang to seek their fortunes and serve their motherland by helping develop this backward but vital frontier territory.

Early on, Mao had an urgent sense of the importance of strengthening China's grip on the region. In 1949, Han Chinese made up roughly 6 percent of Xinjiang's population. By the 2004 census, this had risen to 40 percent—more than other ethnic groups like the Kazakhs and Huis, and second only to the Uyghurs. For Uyghurs, the impact of this development has been profound. Radical demographic changes are fundamentally altering older ways of life. The changes are most evident in Xinjiang's prosperous centers, in cities like Urümqi, where Uyghurs are no longer in the majority.

The impact of these changes has been far-reaching, filtering down to the farms and small homes in villages. Incomes have risen, but the lives of farmers have fast become lives left behind. For people here, getting a piece of their land's new riches often means giving up on how they used to support themselves. With rising costs of living, families find they can no long simply rely on agriculture as a sustainable livelihood. Fathers and sons are heading to the towns and cities in search of work. But there are few well-paying jobs for Uyghur graduates who do not read or write Chinese. They are faced with three choices: attend bilingual government schools, usually located in bigger towns; settle for low-paying jobs that don't require language skills; or leave Xinjiang to find work in another part of the country.

For Alim there was no choice. He was the great hope of his parents, who invested heavily in his education and sent him to college, an opportunity not afforded any of his siblings. Even so, he was utterly unprepared to enter a Chinese university. Schools in smaller counties like Kizilsu offered only minimal language training. This left their graduates with little chance of finding jobs or securing admission to good schools, where they would not only be expected to take classes in Mandarin but also compete with Chinese students for grades.

After he graduated from high school, Alim's teachers advised his parents to send him to take a preparatory course in a university outside Xinjiang, where he would study Chinese along with other minority students for two years. Alim and his high-school classmates were dispatched to Lanzhou, the bustling, modern provincial capital of neighboring Gansu Province, on the banks of the Yellow River. For the Uyghur students, moving away from home was a wrenching process. It was their first, crucial step of assimilation into Chinese culture. The Uyghur students led isolated lives: they were all housed in the same dormitory with Tibetans and Huis from neighboring Ningxia, who were also wrestling with the challenges of integration. In Lanzhou, Alim and his classmates also experienced their first real engagement with young Chinese. There were few Han Chinese in Kizilsu, aside from scattered businessmen in the small towns, and none in the countryside. At first, the Han and minority students went out together for nights of karaoke—much loved by young Chinese—and trips to Lanzhou's famous night market, where they got rare tastes of home from street vendors who had also left their far-flung villages in search of opportunities. But the mixing had its limits: over time, students largely stuck with their ethnic groups. Alim and his classmates formed no real friendships with Han Chinese students. Language was often one impenetrable barrier. Their different eating habits were another: the Uyghur students would seek out Halal Muslim restaurants and would stay home when others went drinking.

For them, leaving home also meant leaving behind religious habits. In small towns and villages, Islam is, in some sense, at the center of everyday life. Every small village in Xinjiang has a mosque, whose imam is a towering presence. His importance extends beyond the realm of religion: he provides moral advice, educates young children, and in some instances, is even the arbiter of disputes. In schools in Xinjiang's small towns, religious studies are a central part of the curriculum, as are daily prayers. But in Lanzhou, the Uyghur students were shocked to find that their classes did not stop for prayers. The university did not even have a mosque.

The centrality of religious practice to the Uyghur way of life is at the heart of the tensions around this process of assimilation unleashed by Chinese rule. Over five decades, the Chinese government has clearly defined the limits of the autonomy that Xinjiang will be entitled to as a minority "autonomous region." In theory, the protection of ethnic groups' language, culture, and religion is guaranteed under the Chinese Constitution, which reads as a very progressive document. But in practice, things are different. Xinjiang's schools and mosques are closely controlled by the Communist Party and government departments. Xinjiang officially has eight hundred imams and twenty thousand mosques, but many more are not registered with the government's religious affairs bureau and can be shut down at any moment.

In 2010, the government put in place new policies calling for all religious texts, even those used in local schools, to be submitted for government approval. It has also expanded regular inspections of religious sites. "Religious teachers are strictly prohibited from using unapproved texts, and anyone engaging in religious activities outside of preapproved religious sites will face investigation as an unauthorized imam," one regulation states. The Party's moves to regulate the role of religion in mosques and religious schools have been unpopular. The government has also cracked down on informal schools and Quran study groups, long an important forum for religious education.

Communist Party members, who occupy most high positions in the government, universities, and even state-run companies, are strongly discouraged from practicing religion. Those who are found attending mosques are warned that they will likely lose their jobs. Advertisements for job positions in the government openly declare that they favor candidates without religious backgrounds. One classified advertisement for the education department said it sought a candidate "who did not believe in religion" and "did not participate in religious activities." Students in state-run schools are from an early age routinely encouraged to follow the Party's officially atheist line, though state policy suggests otherwise.

It is doubtful whether the government's efforts to regulate—and, in a sense, marginalize—religious practice have been successful; there are few signs that suggest that religiosity is on the decline. But it is clear that the central role of Islam in Uyghur life has been a persistent source of tension under the rule of the officially atheist Communist Party. The

Party appears to view the influence wielded by imams with much anxiety, increasingly seeking to regulate their appointments and shape the messages they deliver in sermons.

Government schools in Xinjiang, for their part, are phasing out religious education. Classes do not stop for prayers, which makes official bilingual educational programs unpopular compared to local schools. Jobs in the government, or in government-run companies and universities, often bar daily prayers and discourage employees from attending mosques. Uyghurs are, in essence, often forced to choose between their faith and their professions—a choice they say they should not have to make.

. . .

Given the Chinese government's sensitivity to minority issues, academic programs—and the staff—at Minzu University are carefully and strictly monitored. (This is hardly different from any other Chinese university. But Minzu is viewed by Party officials as being especially sensitive, considering the particular importance of Tibet and Xinjiang to stability.) It is, therefore, surprising that fierce debates often rage within Minzu's lecture halls. That they do owes much to the daring of its professors, who often push the boundaries at great risk.

Few are more daring than the Uyghur scholar Ilham Tohti, a towering figure in the university's academic life. An economist by training, he has emerged as an influential critic of the development model in Xinjiang. Through his powerful lectures, he has also emerged as a leading light for the university's some 300 Uyghur students.

Empty seats are hard to find in his lectures, which routinely venture into areas that sterile textbooks don't dare touch. Tohti has called for reform of bilingual education in Xinjiang and questioned the government's emphasis on promoting Mandarin at the expense of the Uyghur language. He has also strongly criticized the Chinese government's energy-focused, heavy industry–led development model, arguing that it has led to widening disparities between Han Chinese and Uyghurs and allowed big industry to strip the land of its resources at little cost. Tohti speaks passionately and animatedly, delivering his lectures in Chinese (often at high decibels). His audience is, by no means, limited to Uyghur students. Han Chinese students listen in, too, as do a smattering of foreign students.

The Uyghur professor is routinely called in for "cups of tea" with the university's resident Communist Party representatives and officials from the Public Security Bureau. He is given regular warnings to refrain from deviating from the official line. As passionate a lecturer as Tohti is, he is surprisingly calm and measured outside the classroom. When we meet, we talk over a walk through Minzu's green campus. Meeting in a café is too risky, he says. On one occasion, Tohti tells me he has just returned from a compulsory "weekend vacation" to the popular island holiday destination of Hainan with his wife and young son. He was sent away just before the 2010 Nobel Peace Prize was awarded in absentia to the jailed Chinese dissident Liu Xiaobo.

Tohti is surprised that he hasn't met the same fate as Liu, that he is still teaching after a decade of pushing the boundaries. Today, he expects a knock on the door at any moment. Perhaps his popularity provides him with some protection. A Uyghur friend of his with a lower profile has not been as fortunate. Gheyret Niyaz was jailed in 2011 for running a popular Uyghur web site that discussed social and economic issues and often featured Tohti's articles. Uyghur Online was widely read among students at Minzu and even had a following back in Xinjiang, before it was blocked by authorities. Its message resonated. Tohti's popularity underscores the serious credibility gap that the Chinese government has with Uyghurs. One sentence from him renders chapters of Party propaganda meaningless.

For Alim, Tohti's lectures were a revelation. He lapped up the freshness and ferocity of the ideas, which closely resonated with his own experience. "In Xinjiang, none of us believe what we read in our school textbooks," Alim tells me after one Tohti lecture. "We go through school learning nothing about our own culture. We only learn about how the Chinese look at us." Alim speaks slowly in Chinese, an alien language he has mastered after years of immense effort. His tones are flawless, though heavily accented. Awkward pauses hint that he isn't completely at ease. "Language," he tells me one evening, "is at the heart of all our problems. My language is a part of my identity. But for me, it will always be a disadvantage, a handicap. In university, I have to work so much harder just to keep up. If I want to work for a Chinese company, I will need to speak their language. If I work for the government, I will have to learn their language. They will never learn mine."

. . .

Having to adjust to the changes unfolding rapidly in today's Xinjiang has left deep anxieties among young Uyghurs. For many, the process of assimilation has engendered only growing fears that their identity is being eroded. For Alim, the process began when he left his village and was first exposed to life in the big city, where Chinese influence was entrenched. Nowhere is this assimilation more evident than in Urümqi.

The journey from Alim's village to Urümqi takes three days. It starts with a bus ride to Kashgar, an old Silk Road oasis town on Xinjiang's western frontier, and continues with a grueling day-long train ride across the northern boundaries of the Taklimakan desert. Alim's village and Urümqi are two faces of Xinjiang: far removed from the dusty roads and sparse fields of the southern Uyghur heartland, Urümqi is the grand center and symbol of the Chinese government's plans to develop the region. At the heart of the Urümqi oasis, Chinese construction cranes busily hover, day and night, adding an impressive new skyscraper to the skyline every other month. Sprawling shopping malls selling the wares of high-end Chinese designers line the city's downtown streets. On one main street stands a five-star Sheraton hotel, frequented by foreign tourists and Chinese government officials. Xinjiang's only Pizza Hut outlet sits just opposite.

A few months before he arrived in Beijing, Alim boarded a rickety bus in a crowded Urümqi suburb. His destination was an examination center at the heart of the city. Before him lay a three-hour test that would make or break his future. It would determine whether, after a decade of sacrifice from his family, he would fulfill his life's ambition to attend university in Beijing and set out on the road to a better life.

The subject of Alim's examination that afternoon was the often-repeated narrative of the region's long history of assimilation. In one essay, which he wrote in Mandarin Chinese, he described how the Han dynasty's rulers married their daughters to rebellious tribesmen in frontier lands to bring "harmony." Another essay questioned his sense of patriotism to the Chinese motherland. He wrote that the Chinese Communist Party had brought his backward homeland development and prosperity. In another answer, he described the good relations that Han Chinese enjoy with their Uyghur brothers and the country's other ethnic minorities. Alim passed the three-hour test. As he left the exam hall, he knew he had done well. He was delighted—even if he didn't believe a word of what he had written that afternoon.

While leaving the examination hall that evening and heading for the Urümqi's modern train station, Alim was told by a friend that hundreds of students from Xinjiang University had gathered at the heart of the city, in its grand and imposing People's Square. The students, he heard, were protesting the recent deaths of two Uyghurs in a factory brawl in southern China. Thousands of unemployed Uyghurs have moved to find work in factories in China's prosperous south. The government has encouraged this process of migration, viewing it as an easy way to address the rising unemployment problem without having to tinker with its development model in Xinjiang. In factories, Uyghurs often work side by side with Han Chinese, but their presence isn't always welcomed. This was particularly true after the 2009 financial crisis left thousands of factories closed in China's southern manufacturing heartland. In one such factory in Dongguan, Guangdong Province, rumors that a Han Chinese female employee had been raped by Uyghur workers sparked a massive brawl. The rumors, police official said later, were spread by a disgruntled Han employee who had been laid off and found to be untrue. Gruesome images of the attack by a Han mob on the dormitory where the Uyghur workers resided spread quickly on the Internet, and calls for an inquiry into the deaths grew more strident. The Chinese government's slow response, compounded by the clear lack of credibility it has with many in Xinjiang, led to the protest that afternoon.

Hours later, Urümqi was in flames. Little is known about what unfolded that afternoon on People's Square. By the evening of July 5, 2009, armed Uyghur mobs were seen rampaging on the streets, setting fire to Han Chinese–owned business and brutally attacking Chinese residents of the city, including women and children. The Chinese government said the mob violence was premeditated, organized by exile groups with links to terrorist organizations. Many Uyghurs have questioned that story, blaming heavy-handed policing of the protests for sparking the violence. Uyghur students who were present at the initial protest, which they said was organized by students at local universities, said rumors that a female student had been shot by police—this was never verified—enraged the gathering. The scale of the violence—official reports said that 197 people, mostly Han, had been killed and more than 1,700 injured—indicated that the government was grossly unprepared. For three days, the city was torn apart by mob violence. On July 6, organized mobs of Han Chinese attacked the city's Uyghur neighborhoods in revenge for the killings of the previous evening.

Two years on, calm has returned to the streets of Urümqi, but tensions between the two ethnic groups still linger. An already segregated city has been further divided. Han Chinese residents, who have long settled in old Uyghur neighborhoods surrounding the famous Erdaoqiao market where the riots began, are moving out. The riot has left deep scars on both communities, fueling distrust between them and anger at the government. Many Han migrants were encouraged by the government to leave their homes and families in poorer provinces like Sichuan and Gansu to seek their fortunes here, but instead found a land where opportunities were scarce and they were not welcome. A series of syringe attacks targeting the city's Han Chinese residents followed the riots, and Han Chinese in Urümqi staged a protest in front of the Communist Party's headquarters to demand greater security. Surprised by the anger of both communities, Beijing responded by first sacking the Communist Party chief in Urümqi, and later transferring Xinjiang's powerful and unpopular party boss, Wang Lequan.

Wang directed Xinjiang's policies for more than a decade, championing the bilingual education program and encouraging Chinese energy companies to set up shop. The events of July 5 laid bare the failure of his policies. In the shops of Erdaoqiao, many were shocked by the scale of the violence, but few were really surprised that the riots and attacks had occurred. Both Han and Uyghur pointed to the region's lopsided growth and rising unemployment as underlying causes.

Many of the rioters, locals said, were unemployed Uyghur migrants from Xinjiang's less developed south, from counties like Khotan and Kashgar. In the year 2000, the Chinese government unveiled a massive plan to accelerate development across Xinjiang and bridge internal disparities through a "Go West" development drive. A decade later, this campaign has had mixed results. Incomes are rising, and so is the region's GDP. But the policies also brought rising inflation and fuel shortages, prompting many locals, both Uyghur and Han, to increasingly question who was really benefitting from development.

Leaving behind the violence in Urümqi, Alim boarded a train to Kashgar. When he arrived in the old Silk Road town after a day-long journey, he found it locked down. Armed troops patrolled the streets. The grand 550-year-old Id Kah mosque, which sits at the center of the city, was shut down by the police. The local community was enraged and staged an impromptu protest to demand that the government allow prayers to take place. The protest was quickly dispersed by forewarned armed police, who nonetheless relented and opened the mosque.

The old mosque has been at the heart of Kashgar's life for centuries. On a summer's evening, the square in front of the Id Kah is a hub of activity. Young women in brightly colored headscarves stroll around it, children in tow. Old men, with tanned and weathered faces topped by intricately designed skullcaps unique to the region, sit side by side on a rickety wooden bench and silently watch life on the square. Outside the Id Kah, a newly posted sign from the local government proclaims: "All ethnic groups live together here in a friendly manner. They cooperate to build a beautiful homeland, heartily support the unity of the country, and oppose ethnic separatism and illegal religious activities."

Prayers finished, Alim boarded a bus at Kashgar's dilapidated station, a short drive from the Id Kah mosque. His destination: home. After a tiring journey on bumpy roads running through parched fields of corn, he arrived at his old house. He was relieved to find that here, at least in appearance, nothing had changed.

CHAPTER 11

Yong Yang's Odyssey

CHRISTINA LARSON

In January 2007, an independent geologist named Yong Yang set out from his home in Sichuan with five researchers, two SUVs, one set of clothes, and several trunks of equipment for measuring rainfall and water volume; a camping stove, a rice cooker, canned meat, and more than sixty bottles of locally made hot sauce; a digital camera, a deck of cards, and several CDs of Tibetan music; and as many canisters of fuel as his team could strap to the roofs of their vehicles. No roads cross the part of China to which Yong was traveling, so he also brought topographical charts and satellite photos of the region. His final destination, deep in China's wild western frontier region, was the unmarked place on the Tibetan plateau from which the Yangtze River springs.

For several weeks the two SUVs followed the Yangtze west. The river turned from running water to ice, and the thermometer became useless when the temperature dipped below the lowest reading on its scale. Occasionally, they spotted an antelope, and once wolves devoured their fresh yak meat. As they climbed in elevation, tracing the course the Yangtze cut through the Dangla Mountains many millennia ago, the air grew thinner and the wind fiercer. When the ground rose too steeply into the surrounding peaks for the SUVs to maneuver along the river-banks, they drove on the frozen river itself, though this approach was not without its perils. About a month into their trip, on the auspicious first day of the Lunar New Year, Yong heard a great crunching sound as his front and then back tires slid through the ice, trapping his vehicle midstream. Fortunately, it wasn't too far submerged, and the backseat passengers managed to clamber out and signal to the second SUV. With a rope tied to the rear bumper, they dragged the vehicle from the frozen river, with Yong still in the driver's seat, transmission in reverse.

Yong and his companions made it safely out of the river. But since then he's continued to travel, in many senses, on thin ice. A vital question propelled his journey up the Yangtze: the Chinese government has devised the most colossal water diversion project ever attempted, and Yong had taken it upon himself to discover whether it would work.

Water is an unevenly distributed resource in China. Historically, the south has been lush, while the north has been a land of dry tundra and frozen desert. In 1952, Mao Zedong conjured a solution to this inequity: "Southern water is plentiful, northern water scarce," he said. "Borrowing some water would be good." Ever since, China's leaders have dreamed of diverting water from one of the country's great rivers to the other—from the southern Yangtze River into the northern Yellow River. (To fathom the scale of this undertaking, imagine watering the American Southwest by diverting the Mississippi River into the Colorado.)

In recent years, water shortages in China's northern cities have become more and more dire, and this eccentric scheme has become increasingly appealing to the government. In 2002, China's highest executive body, the State Council, converted Mao's grandiose notion into a plan known as the South-to-North Water Transfer Project, which will divert water from the Yangtze in southwestern China to the north, across mountains that rise to 15,000 feet above sea level. The entire project will cost at least an estimated $60.4 billion, and it has aroused intense opposition, because it is expected to displace hundreds of thousands of people and devastate fragile ecosystems.

Between January and March 2007, Yong's team traveled more than sixteen thousand miles in the Yangtze River basin, threading every bend in the western reaches of the river. The previous summer, they had driven roughly the same route, so they could compare water levels in different seasons. On both trips they collected data on rainfall, geology, receding glaciers, and other factors that affect the volume of water in the river. Yong had learned from firsthand experience that for about four months each year, the upper Yangtze is a ribbon of ice; only an engineering miracle could transport the frozen water north. After he spent the summer and fall compiling data and circulating it among several dozen peer researchers for feedback, he found more reasons to be skeptical of the ability of the project to live up to the government's vision. The bounteous stream of Beijing's imagination became, in Yong's careful calculations, a trickle.

The fact that Yong is free to conduct such inquiries at all says much about the recent political evolution of China. Fifteen years ago, the government wouldn't have tolerated public questioning of large-scale infrastructure projects. But in recent years, criticism from independent scientists and environmental organizations has prompted it to postpone two planned western dam projects. Recently, officials even acknowledged (after the fact) that unsound planning for the controversial Three Gorges Dam project had created a potential "environmental catastrophe." This isn't a sign that China's Communist Party is throwing the country's political system open to full democratic participation. But China's leaders know that a rapidly deteriorating environment could stall the country's economic miracle and ignite political unrest, so they're experimenting with limited openness to help avert these hazards. It remains an open question just how much scrutiny the government will tolerate, however, and how much impact Yong will be permitted to have. His midwinter expedition was only the first stage of his odyssey into uncharted terrain.

On my first visit to Beijing in February 2007, I wheezed all the way from the airport to my hotel. The thick smog hid any hint of direct sunlight, and I didn't see my shadow for a week. When I returned in mid-October, the city seemed a changed place. I was surprised to see clear blue skies. Skyscrapers were visible from a distance, not shrouded in haze. There were other changes, too—swept sidewalks, a sudden absence of bootleg DVD hawkers, more policemen on the streets.

A week later, Beijing looked, sounded, and smelled like its familiar self again. The street vendors were back, along with the curbside cobblers and the men waving pirated DVDs. The skies were gray, the sun obscured, and cigarette butts and orange peel once again speckled the sidewalks.

The temporary makeover coincided—not accidentally—with the Seventeenth Communist Party Congress, the meeting of party bigwigs that happens once every five years and attracts numerous domestic and international visitors. During the Congress, the central government, eager to punctuate its new talk of environmental protection with some proof of its commitment, had directed its might toward cleaning up a targeted area for a discrete period of time, reportedly putting regional factories and Beijing's public vehicles on a compulsory holiday. The results were eerily impressive. But the greater significance of this fleeting transformation was that it exposed the limits of the party's power. The central government can clamp down abruptly and indomitably, but it can't do so everywhere, all the time.

In recent years, China's political leaders have embraced the environmental cause, not out of sentiment or idealism, but as a matter of survival. China's environment is becoming so degraded that it risks choking off the country's booming economy: the West balks at buying mercury-contaminated grain, while water shortages threaten Chinese paper mills and petrochemical plants. Also at risk is the country's political stability: peasant riots over land seizures and polluted rivers are becoming increasingly common, with some 51,000 pollution-triggered "public disturbances" annually—even by the government's estimates. But while the central government has issued stern directives aimed at reducing air and water pollution, it lacks the means to enforce them consistently, because over the past three decades, it has gradually relinquished certain types of authority to provincial governments in order to promote economic growth. The result has been dramatic gains in the country's gross domestic product, with new factories multiplying across the countryside. However, provincial autonomy has also enabled local officials to ignore cumbersome central directives, including regulations on matters ranging from food safety to environmental standards.

Understanding their diminished ability to enforce green statutes locally, China's leaders have turned cautiously to civil society for assistance. Since 1994, Beijing has empowered nongovernmental groups to expose polluting factories. Today there are more than 3,000 citizen green groups in China. In 2003 and 2004, the government enacted laws requiring environmental impact assessments and citizen input on major public works projects. (These measures took effect shortly after construction commenced on the first two phases of the water transfer project.) In 2005, China's first national public hearing—over the fate of the Old Summer Palace—was broadcast on national television. Progressive environmental officials are introducing the concepts of "public participation," "hearings," and "rights" to the public. Environmental lawyers are litigating China's first successful class-action lawsuits. Compared to a decade ago, the situation is remarkable.

Still, there are limits to the government's spirit of reform, and perhaps some in the Communist Party feel they've been moving too fast. Around the time of high-profile events like the Party Congress, the flashpoints become more apparent. For instance, the first promotion resulting from the 2007 congress was Li Yuanchao, former Party secretary of Jiangsu Province who was elevated to a seat on the Politburo, the inner circle of Chinese leadership. In announcing his ascent, newspapers extolled Li's "environmental" record. A few months earlier, however, his province had shut off water to four million people for a week because chemical pollution and algae blooms had turned the local water source, Lake Tai, a brilliant pea green. An environmental activist named Wu Lihong had tried to alert the authorities and the public to the problem. For his trouble, he was arrested on the orders of local officials and sentenced to three years in prison. To many observers, it seemed odd that Wu was silenced while more prominent environmentalists were allowed to operate freely. But Wen Bo, a veteran environmentalist in Beijing, decoded the message for me: Wu had been thrown in jail for questioning the real record of Li's Jiangsu government. "Li is a protégé of Hu Jintao," Wen said. "Jiangsu Province is the stronghold of Hu Jintao. If that area is quiet, their power-hold is strong."

The government does want citizen groups to help combat pollution, and it has created an opening for them to do so. But political power in China is still wielded behind closed doors, and that opening can constrict without warning when an activist crosses the agenda of an influential official. It is within this unpredictable sphere that Yong Yang is attempting to operate.

That October, I spoke with the 49-year-old Yong in Beijing. (We first met in 2007 in Sichuan.) He had thick black hair and hadn't shaved for a day or two. He was dressed in a black jacket, a gray sweater and black jeans. Despite his rugged appearance and the adventurous nature of his research, his eyes seemed more sad than rebellious. "I am not against the government," he explained, snuffing out what was likely his sixth or seventh cigarette of the evening. "What I want is to get the facts."

In Yong's hotel room, we hunched over his laptop to look at slides from his trip. There were photos of his SUV crashing through the ice; of someone pouring hot water from a teakettle to defrost the engine's water tank; of Tibetan herders who offered Yong and his colleagues' meat and milk along the way.

Then Yong opened a spreadsheet. On one side was a series of estimates, based on Yong's research, of the volume of water in the Yangtze. On the other side were the official estimates prepared by the government's Yellow River Conservancy Commission. The government data were supposed to be secret, but Yong had obtained them from a network of friends and former colleagues inside the government.

Yong found that the official figures were often "way off." In one section of the river, the government's plans call for diverting from eight to nine billion cubic meters of water north each year. However, Yong's research—supported by thirty years' worth of reports from hydrology monitoring stations—indicates that the average annual water flow for that section includes a low estimate of seven billion cubic meters. This means that when the river's flow is low, the government would be hoping to divert an amount of water greater than its total volume. Moreover, no sound engineering plan should call for redirecting all of the water, since downstream communities, including Shanghai, will still depend upon the Yangtze for agriculture, industry, and hydropower.

Yong is not alone in doubting the feasibility of the final section of the South-to-North Water Transfer Project. More than fifty scientists in Sichuan contributed to a 2006 collection of scientific articles and reports titled "South-to-North Water Transfer Project Western Route Memorandums" that raises serious concerns about the plan. At issue are the questions of construction at high altitudes, seismic stability, pollution in the Yangtze, climate change (the river's volume is expected to diminish as Tibet's glaciers melt), and the potential for reduced river flow to shut down hundreds of downstream hydropower stations, perhaps inflicting blackouts on millions. According to one former government researcher, there are even critics within the Ministry of Water Resources.

Why are the official projections so fantastically optimistic? Yong, who once worked as a government scientist in the Ministry of Coal Industry, thinks he has some idea of how the numbers were produced. "The government, they will make a goal," he explained. "Then their researchers think their job is just to say it works. Everybody will just say the good word, and try to find data to support it," he said, shrugging. "It's not a very scientific way of doing research."

Yong says he has asked the Yellow River Conservancy Commission how they arrived at their figures, but their staffers have refused to respond. "They just emphasize that there won't be much problem," he said. (My request for an interview with the commission was referred to the Water Ministry's Propaganda Department, where an official said that no one would be available for comment.) No matter whose figures are correct, what worries Yong most is that there is no independent system in place to determine whether such a colossal and disruptive undertaking will work.

Yet informed sources say that the project has a champion in retired President Jiang Zemin—still a powerful force in Chinese politics—and a handful of influential retired army officers. And many entrenched interests have reason to hope that construction proceeds. The steering committee that manages the water transfer project is led by Premier Wen Jiabao, and its members include high-ranking national government officials. A similar bureaucracy has been replicated in the affected provinces, creating hundreds of titles and salaries dedicated to moving the project forward. Five state banks have major investments in the plan, and expect loans to be repaid when water user fees are assessed. The two companies with multibillion-dollar contracts to build the early phases of the project are hungry for more. Yet the environmental impact assessment required by the 2003 law has still not been released, and the real deliberative battle over the project remains invisible.

The perennial unreliability of the available information pervades all aspects of China's environmental protection system, from water management to pollution control. Dr. Zhao Jianping, then the sector coordinator for energy in the World Bank's China Office told me, for example, that he was dubious of the government's ability to achieve its goal of obtaining 15 percent of China's energy from renewable sources by 2020. Beijing's characterization of the potential of wind energy was somewhat realistic, he said, but the official assessment of biomass potential was wishful thinking in his judgment. "In most other countries, you do the analysis first, then set goals," he said. "In China, you set the goal first, then you do the research and set the policy to try to achieve it."

Yang Fuqiang, vice president of the Energy Foundation, a research center and partnership of major international donors, reported similarly on Beijing's efforts to stem rising coal consumption. The central government relies on local cadres to report the number of new mines, but these officials often give faulty estimates, either for lack of accurate information or out of a desire to please Beijing. "Collecting reliable data is a major challenge," Yang said. There are no independent watchdogs to verify official statistics, which, unsurprisingly, often turn out to be wrong. In 2003, Beijing reviewed prior estimates of annual coal consumption and discovered that its estimates for 2000 had failed to account for fifty million tons of coal burned—"a rather large oversight," Yang remarked.

Optimists say that what China needs most is more technical training for its officials: to ensure that regional administrators are better equipped to count coal mines and local lawyers and judges understand the nuances of new environmental laws. China does need those things. But others are beginning to think that further changes are needed, too.

One person who has helped fund Yong Yang's research is Dr. Yu Xiaogang, founder of the nonprofit organization Green Watershed. Yu is also the architect of arguably the greatest success story of Chinese environmentalism to date. In 2004, he coordinated opposition to a proposed series of dam projects on China's last wild river, the Nu, or Salween, which flows from the Tibetan Plateau into the Burma Sea. Activists and scientists presented convincing evidence that the dams would have a ruinous effect on local communities and ecosystems. After a sustained campaign, Premier Wen Jiabao personally suspended the project, pending a new environmental impact assessment. When I visited Green Watershed's offices in western Yunnan Province, Yu surprised me when he said that his success was only temporary. "There will always be another dam proposal, another financier," he explained. He said he wants a reliable process for gathering public and expert input while plans are being drafted, not when the bulldozers are ready to roll.

"What we have got to do," Yu said, "is change the system." The veteran environmentalist Wen Bo had a similar take on things: "For China's environment to improve, I think the political system needs to change. I don't know exactly what the future needs to look like, but it needs to be more democratic, more free society, more free media."

In America, the popular and political momentum for creating our modern environmental apparatus was inspired by the work of a scientist, Rachel Carson, who challenged conventional wisdom and official policies governing the use of pesticides. After the U.S. Congress passed a series of landmark environmental laws in the 1970s, independent environmental lawyers ensured that those statutes were upheld by suing the government when it failed to enforce legislation such as the Clean Water Act and the Endangered Species Act. When Washington has dragged its feet, independent scientists and reporters have uncovered White House obfuscations and pushed for government action. Every industrialized country that has cleaned up its environment—apart from Singapore, a green authoritarian city-state—has done so with the help of civil society and a free press.

In countries where the government hasn't been able to control pollution, environmental crises have sometimes helped spur momentum for broader political change. By the mid-1980s, many in eastern Europe had grown resigned to life under repressive governments. That changed on April 26, 1986, when a nuclear reactor exploded at the Chernobyl power plant in the former Soviet Union, sending vastly more radiation into the air than an atomic bomb. In downwind Poland and Slovenia, uproar over nuclear reactors and official secrecy (the state presses initially refused to report on the disaster) provoked the first mass demonstrations against the government. "Chernobyl [alone] did not topple Communism," Padraic Kenney writes in *A Carnival of Revolution: Central Europe, 1989* (2002), a history of democracy movements in the former Soviet bloc. "But it became a popular symbol of government breakdown, a rallying cry for dissenters, a wake-up call for the population at large . . . and helped galvanize dissent in the years leading up to 1989."

Another case—closer to home for the Chinese—is Taiwan. The country was under martial law until 1986; any kind of open political opposition to the ruling Guomindang was strictly forbidden. As long as the government was delivering security and economic growth, the middle class tolerated one-party rule. Then the effects of environmental problems began to affect people's daily lives. The dissident groups that later became the Democratic Progressive Party first coalesced around environmental issues, especially air pollution and opposition to nuclear power. "Pollution was the one issue Taiwan's middle class couldn't tolerate," a former U.S. embassy official told me.

China's leaders are aware of these historical parallels. David Lampton, the director of the China studies program at Johns Hopkins University's School of Advanced International Studies, explained Beijing's conundrum: "The Chinese are caught between the logic of what they know they need to effectively implement environmental policy and the fear of whether these groups could become the opening wedge to political liberalization."

During my time in China I have often found myself wondering whether Beijing's experiment can succeed. Can a limited form of public participation help avert environmental ruin? Or are independent oversight, the rule of law, and the ability to vote out bad officials essential components of effective environmental protection?

Perhaps China will, once again, elide the apparent contradictions of its environmental politics in the same way that it has somehow melded capitalism and Communism. Or perhaps smoggy cities, dwindling water supplies, and peasant protests over pollution will force the Party to accept greater political openness. Or perhaps the environmental activists themselves will call for it. Whatever happens, the consequences will be epic. If China continues on its current course, within twenty-five years, it will emit twice as much carbon dioxide as all the thirty-four Organisation for Economic Co-operation and Development (OECD) countries combined. The Middle Kingdom's dilemma is ours, too.

For now, China's environmental politics have a slightly schizophrenic quality. In the summer of 2007, for instance, Beijing police shut down a long-running national environmental web site, China Development Brief, which had pages in both Chinese and English and was closely monitored by experts inside and outside the country. Observers speculate that authorities were worried about the site's role as a hub for green groups to network nationally without any kind of state supervision. In October, however, the State Environmental Protection Administration sanctioned a national conference of green NGOs, which gave environmentalists the opportunity to conduct their national networking in person.

I attended the conference in Beijing, and saw representatives of over three hundred citizen groups from across China behaving anything but furtively, exchanging business cards and debating President Hu's environmental theories in nearby restaurants. A few government officials showed up on the first morning to commend the work of notable attendees and encourage greater "public participation" in environmental protection. The program of speakers had been approved by the government, but as one participant told me, "The most important thing is not the schedule, but the chance to meet other environmentalists from everywhere in China." Some of the activists I spoke to said they wanted to be a "bridge" between the government and the public, helping to disseminate information about green priorities, while others said they wanted a greater role in setting or overseeing policy. Nearly all of them mentioned "the line"—the boundary between safe and potentially punishable forms of advocacy—which is perceived differently by the government and the public and fluctuates with changing political tides.

Yong Yang was at the conference too. He debuted a new PowerPoint presentation of his research, shared information, and gathered feedback. Having failed to open a direct line of communication with the government, he is now trying to telegraph his concern about the South-to-North Water Transfer Project through informal networks. (Over the summer, he had spoken with a reporter for the Hong Kong daily *South China Morning Post,* but the article was never published, because, he thinks, it was scheduled to appear right before the national Communist Party Congress.)

Although Yong's activities appear to bring him into increasingly open conflict with the government, he insists that his aim is not political—he sees himself as a scientist first, an environmentalist second. ("Science," he told me, "is the most damning kind of criticism.") Still, he is aware that his work is, as he put it, "a direct challenge to the system—to the government's decision-making process, and to the interest groups that benefit from it."

Yong has walked the line before. In the past, while researching power stations along the Min River, local business interests attempted—unsuccessfully—to silence him with bribes and threats. I asked if he was ever nervous about his safety. "Once you make up your mind to do this," he told me, "you have to be prepared for everything that happens."

CHAPTER 12

The Court Jester

JEFFREY PRESCOTT

In the spring of 2009, China's most outspoken law professor, He Weifang, was ordered to report for duty at the edge of the Gobi desert. For the next two years, he would teach in Shihezi, a windswept military outpost in Xinjiang, three thousand miles from his home in Beijing. He (pronounced Huh) is on the faculty at Peking University, and the transfer meant trading one of China's best schools for one of its most remote. The relocation recalled the punishment that Chinese emperors once reserved for serious criminals and the most wayward scholars: exile to "an insalubrious region" *(yanzhang)*.

China, like other authoritarian states, has a long tradition of sending troublemakers to distant borderlands. But He Weifang is no ordinary troublemaker, and, like so much else in his life, his exile was less straightforward than it initially seemed. His students call him a legal *budaozhe* (preacher). His faith is built on heresies to China's Communist Party line. He is an unabashed supporter of Western-style legal and political reform, and he openly demands free speech, democracy, and human rights. Unusually for someone of his convictions, he is also a figure of unique national prominence. His essays run in China's most-read newspapers, his blog has millions of hits, and his lectures generate the kind of enthusiasm usually reserved for pop stars. At Peking University, he won the teaching award so many years in a row that the law school took him off the ballot.

He's celebrity gave him one layer of cover, but he also had friends in high places. He is a member of the first class of college graduates after the decade-long suspension of higher education during the Cultural Revolution. His classmates enjoy a distinctive mixture of clout and fraternity that is rare in China and in their largely lost generation. They have been a vanguard in opening China to the world and, now mostly in their fifties (He was born in 1960), they hold senior positions in the country's artistic, intellectual, and political hierarchies. He Weifang was their anointed gadfly. Despite his outspokenness—indeed, because of it—he lectured as often to government officials and judges in Party-run training programs as he did to students. He thrived in a narrow gray zone in China's politics—between accommodation and outright dissent. That he could conduct himself this way and still hold on to his post at the country's most prestigious university signaled to many that China's reform was moving ahead, if slowly.

But 2009 was a bad year for Chinese legal advocates; it was the beginning of what would become the most serious crackdown on dissent in years. Many lawyers found themselves barred from courtrooms for work on "sensitive" cases; others were beaten by thugs or jailed. On Christmas day, a Beijing court convicted Liu Xiaobo, an essayist who later won the Nobel Peace Prize, of "inciting subversion." Liu was sent to prison for eleven years for drafting Charter 08, a petition calling for political reform through constitutional law. He Weifang, one of the first to sign the Charter, received the order banishing him to Xinjiang not long after Liu's initial arrest. Many assume that the cases are related, but He was never told this directly. Technically, all Peking University did was ask He to provide "teaching support" to a sister university. But his transfer landed like a blow, a win for critics who have long called for the Communist Party to "deal with him."

Still, He arrived in Xinjiang to something more complicated than forced obscurity. Shihezi University's propaganda office invited him out for a boozy welcome banquet. For his first lecture, students and faculty filled an auditorium beyond capacity. The *Economic Observer,* one of China's most respected national newspapers, extolled that lecture's "boundless eloquence." After his first week of classes, He was permitted to make the two-hour ride to the airport that put him just a four-hour flight from anywhere in China. In the weeks that followed, he returned to his usual routine, speaking in cities across the country: Wuhan, Suzhou, and Beijing. He continued to publish and blog. Exile, at least in this form, would not be enough to deal with He Weifang.

. . .

A few months before his transfer, I heard He lecture to a summer school program in the lakeside city of Hangzhou. I had seen him speak before at academic conferences, including one that we organized together, but never in the classroom. We first met in 2002, soon after I moved to Beijing to start up Yale's China Law Center. He was in the middle of a typical itinerary: he had just come from a conference in Suzhou, had given a lecture to Hangzhou's judges the day before, and would leave the next day for a series of events in Guangzhou before returning home. Five days, three cities, six events.

The Hangzhou lecture was scheduled for a hot, humid morning at Zhejiang University Law School, which occupies a group of dilapidated red brick buildings up a steep riverbank on the rear side of the hills that hug the city's downtown. The dean of the law school escorted He into a large function room, where students sat waiting behind rows of long tables. As they entered, the students gasped and jumped up to applaud, revealing their identical, oversized white T-shirts emblazoned with the name of the summer program. It seemed as though everyone had a digital camera, and everyone used them at once. It took a long time for the room to settle down.

A student introduced He, nervously reading from a sheet of paper. "He has the conscience of a public intellectual," she said. "The gentleman's speeches make us feel this is the voice a public-minded scholar ought to have." He, dressed casually in khaki pants and a striped, peach-colored polo shirt, smiled broadly and, bypassing the lectern, stepped to the front of the room. "Your introduction was too beautiful," he began. "Of course, mostly you described someone I aspire to become." Then he added a dig at the "Three Represents," an ideological catchphrase of China's former president Jiang Zemin. "Is it supposed to be a reflection of what the Chinese Communist Party has already achieved, or is it also an aspiration?" He asked with arched eyebrows. "I have never been so clear about that." In his first five sentences, he had managed to lampoon a former leader and a key piece of Party orthodoxy. Students glanced at one another, shifting in their seats. How political would this talk get?

He paced back and forth in front of the students, microphone in hand, and spoke without notes for nearly two hours. His expressive face is unlined; only a starburst of wrinkles around each eye and salt-and-pepper hair suggest his age. His eyes widen and an impish smile appears an instant before he delivers a crack or critical remark. The sharper the point, the bigger the grin. He laughed at the best of his own jokes. He made the large room feel intimate.

He lamented the unmarked addresses and unlisted phone numbers of government offices in Beijing, and then joked about a recent event staged by *People's Daily* in which China's president, Hu Jintao, "chatted" online. He drew a portrait with his arms of the photos that were published: a smiling Hu typing on a keyboard before a mission-control style console. "All that, but they don't even tell us his email address or his Internet handle."

He provided an insider's look at Chinese politics and spoke frankly about what he saw as the country's problems. Along the way, he referenced Marx, Weber, Confucius, nineteenth-century German jurists, a Chinese poet popular in the 1980s, and a statue of the Goddess of Justice in Lucerne, Switzerland. He spoke about the need for professional ethics, the role of legal education and critical thinking skills, and his vision of what the rule of law might mean for Chinese society. It was part pep talk, part stump speech, and part stand-up routine. He connected the students' own education with what was happening around them.

Artful and direct, He Weifang's public presentations are a rarity in China. In television and print, China's senior leaders invariably speak from stilted ideological scripts about "unswervingly building and safeguarding socialism with Chinese characteristics" or "firmly upholding the centralized and unified leadership of the Party." There is plenty of humor and sarcasm in China—the gap between rhetoric and reality provides abundant raw material—but He's lectures were the stuff of private conversation, not public discourse.

He concluded by nodding in my direction in the back of the room. "When I go to the United States, I am struck that China's legal scholars are more important than their American counterparts. Of course, American scholars are active. But the big issues have already been decided—separation of powers, basic democracy, basic rule of law, judicial independence." He feigned exasperation and laughed. "*Ai-ya!* These have all been resolved! The problems that they work on every day, I'm afraid, seem like minor details.

"What about us? Every day, from when we first open our eyes, we face immense problems. The political system is incomplete. Our basic democratic system is incomplete. We are called the 'People's Republic,' but we don't possess even a scrap of 'republic.' We don't have the rule of law." Squarely facing the students, he ended with a challenge: "We may not necessarily be able to say that we live in a beautiful age. But we live in an age where we can do great things." When He finished, nearly all the students rushed to the front of the room seeking autographs.

. . .

The thirty-year boom Deng Xiaoping launched in 1978 has made China's people freer and wealthier—but only in comparison to the equally long Maoist period that came before it. The Party, responsible for decades of misery, has now managed to deliver decades of relative prosperity. But a political disconnect remains. Although China's rulers, who still call themselves Communists, have enjoyed a disproportionate share of the spoils, they claim to represent "the fundamental interests of the overwhelming majority of the Chinese people." Few people in China actually believe this to be true. But the pronouncements the Party feeds its subjects—backed by force—still bind dissenters' tongues with gluey tenacity. He Weifang plays the part of a tall glass of cold water. People who spend time around him find their own speech, and even their actions, degummed. Those already inclined to opposition—a small but determined group of lawyers, scholars, and journalists—rely on He to help them pen their petitions or to articulate their ideas, as He does in frequent, frank interviews in the press and online.

In 2004, He and a few colleagues wrote a petition demanding the abolition of a harsh system of police detention, and it was changed after a public uproar. When a hapless security guard was given a life sentence for stealing from a faulty ATM in 2006, He's commentary and the resulting public outcry helped force the government to reduce the man's sentence to five years. He's reach extends to the symbolic. He led a crusade for China's judges to switch from military uniforms to American-style black robes. It was a partial victory: the Supreme People's Court made the switch to robes in 2002, but added a red stripe and four brass buttons, signifying "loyalty to the Party" above the law.

He Weifang's national reputation was sparked by a 1998 essay he wrote for a new weekly newspaper, *Nanfang Zhoumo* (Southern Weekend; also called Southern Weekly), which had become popular because of its willingness to take chances with China's censors and printed He's account of a lecture he had given to a roomful of judges. "Why is it that every year we place so many demobilized soldiers in the courts?" he had asked his audience. China's use of soldiers to fill the judiciary reaches back to the 1950s, when the communist legal order, inspired by Lenin, relied on politically dependable People's Liberation Army veterans to staff the *gong jian fa*—the police, prosecutors, and courts. The Cultural Revolution all but destroyed the legal system and, as the reform era began, China had to start from scratch. Law schools, shuttered for a decade, produced the first set of new graduates—He Weifang among them—in 1982. In the meantime, China turned to its troops as a stopgap. By 1998, with the legal profession rejuvenated, He argued that judges, like physicians, ought to be trained professionals. "The medical profession deals in matters of life and death. Don't judges also deal in life and death?" He asked. "Of course, there are differences. The doctor takes the dying and brings them back to life. The judge takes the perfectly healthy and sends him off to meet his maker!" Criticism of the army was (and is) a taboo, and the paper was forced to print an apology the next week. But the controversy only kept the issue alive and, it seemed, sold papers. Despite the reprimand, *Nanfang Zhoumo* signed He on as a regular contributor. He penned almost an essay a week over the next year—at the time, an unheard-of contribution by a scholar to the national popular conversation. In the years since, despite periods when censors have deemed his work too controversial to print, He has published hundreds of op-eds and essays. When a popular news magazine named him one of China's most influential public figures, his first *Nanfang Zhoumo* essay was cited as "the peak of poetic perfection."

. . .

He Weifang was born in 1960 in a village in Muping County, a hitchhiker's thumb of land on China's eastern coast that juts out toward the Korean Peninsula. His parents were both locals, but his father escaped village life by joining Mao's revolutionary army. Trained as a doctor, he served in the civil war that brought the Communists to power and later in the "Resist America, Support Korea" campaign (known to Americans as the Korean War). "When I was young, at home we had all these medals," He told me. "My father was never wounded in battle; he was in the rear. But he saw a lot."

Stationed in more prosperous Jiangsu after the war, with a decorated veteran and army officer as breadwinner, the young family should have been in a comfortable position. But He's father was discharged in 1963 and drew a poor transfer assignment. The family was sent back to Shandong, where He's father started work as the medic at a county high school.

His father did not flourish. "He was extremely direct," He told me during an interview, his normally fluid speech slightly hitched. "He was too direct. He criticized his leaders too bluntly, and when the Cultural Revolution began, he was attacked." He fidgeted and lit a cigarette. "Actually, he was an extremely honest and sincere man. He read the newspapers carefully and spent time on the education of his children. When I was six, I already had a huge vocabulary, because he took particular care of me."

"But all of a sudden, in the Cultural Revolution, he sank into a difficult position. And then, in 1970, he killed himself. I was ten when he died."

Suicide in that era was not just a matter of family shame. It carried a dangerous political edge. He's family was branded "anti-Party," stripped of their right to urban residence and military benefits, and sent back to live in Muping. He thought he would be "stuck as a peasant for life."

The family returned to discover that their village, Jianggezhuang, was now led by a war-hero Party secretary. It was one of a handful of Potemkin sites on the itinerary of state-sponsored tours for foreign travelers. As a result, the village enjoyed cultural resources unheard of in other parts of rural China (relatively speaking: a lit basketball court provided the luxury of nighttime sports). He joined the local Mao Zedong Thought Propaganda Troupe. Though limited in repertoire to a few politically correct plays, the group had access to cellos and violins. They performed for visiting delegations of the Sino-French Friendship Society.

He credits his father and mother for his love of reading and education. But He's formal schooling—a rudimentary nine years of primary education—focused almost exclusively on Mao Zedong Thought. Everyone graduated regardless of performance. For one entire year, students spent part of each day constructing a new teaching building. All over China, the education system was in chaos. Periodic campaigns attacking "revisionism of the capitalist education line" swept through the system, echoing political battles in distant Beijing. But his spot in the classroom kept He from the fields. His older brother, sent down to a farm, missed the chance for an education altogether.

He was assigned the chore of walking to the post office each day to pick up the school's newspapers. Instead of returning immediately, he went home for lunch, where he read the papers cover to cover before delivering them. "Every day was like that," he told me. It is hard to imagine finding literary sensibility in the turgid pages of the Party's propaganda-only mouthpieces, *Renmin Ribao* (People's Daily), *Zhongguo Qingnian Bao* (China Youth Daily), *Guangming Ribao* (Guangming Daily), and *Cankao Xiaoxi* (Reference News). Not long ago, He was invited to speak to the editorial staff of *Renmin Ribao*. Referring to this period, He told them, "I don't read your paper today, but I do have to give thanks to all of you. You taught me to love the written word."

. . .

I visited Xinjiang in May 2009, two months after He arrived. Shihezi's tree-lined avenues, four to six lanes wide, are set in a grid. Most roads have two generous bike lanes next to medians on either side. The buildings are low, four to six stories, and widely spaced, set back so far from the streets that it can take a full five minutes to get from one building directly across the road to another. This gives the city a thin, forlorn feel, as if it were built in anticipation of far more people, who never came. Actually, its population is aging. Over half of Shihezi's three hundred thousand registered residents are retired. Even around the university, which sprawls out on both sides of the main boulevard through town, there are few pedestrians on the streets save children and elderly couples. A billboard near the gate warns "Stay Far Away from Drugs, Build a Harmonious Society."

He and I spoke in the spare apartment that Shihezi University had arranged for He's two-year stay in Xinjiang. On the sixth floor of a tall concrete building, the window in the main room had a clear view to the snowcapped Tianshan range, south of the city. He sat at a plain table, which he used as a desk, with his laptop and a few books. A bright blue, overstuffed pleather couch and a matching pair of club chairs sat opposite a large flat-screen TV. A small stereo stood on the edge of a coffee table, along with an open pack of Lanzhou-brand cigarettes and a Mussorgsky CD. He took his meals at scruffy local restaurants. His bathroom was grungy.

Down the street, at the *bingtuan* museum, we toured displays of artifacts from the 1950s, including old wooden plows and hand tools used by soldiers-turned-settlers. The campus, the city, and the fields that surround Shihezi all owe their existence to the Chinese military. The Xinjiang Production and Construction Corps, known in Chinese by the shorthand *bingtuan*, or Corps, is a vestige of the military campaign to secure the vast territories of Tibet and Xinjiang in the early 1950s. The Corps stayed behind to develop this "liberated" land. Few of those who arrived to work in that era were allowed to leave. One exhibit told the story of the nearly forty thousand young girls brought out to wed the men, helping create the ethnic Han baby boom that populated Shihezi. "Many of the girls had political problems in their background," He told me as we looked at photographs showing young, scared-looking Shanghainese girls marching down a street lined with Corps men, crowding in on both sides in ragged uniforms. "They were promised that joining the army would help clear their names and give them a new chance. Then they were shipped out here."

In He's apartment, I had noticed a photocopy of James Millward's *Eurasian Crossroads: A History of Xinjiang*, a book that is banned in China. "Two years is long enough to see a bit of Xinjiang," He told me with a grin. "So I'm reading up on history." In his office on campus, a pile of books and half-opened packages, gifts sent by friends worried he might not have enough to read, covered a desk.

He has a way of turning any story drawn from the history of ideas, domestic or foreign, into an argument for the reforms he believes that China needs today. In his Shihezi classroom, he used my presence as an excuse to talk about the role of lawyers in American politics. He started with *The Federalist*, No. 50, quoting long sections from memory. "Madison said that if men were angels, no government would be necessary. If everyone were a Lei Feng"—a mythologized young military hero of Chinese propaganda from the 1950s, still celebrated with a national holiday—"then what need is there for law?" He argued that law should constrain government. "We formulate a constitution precisely because we assume man's base nature," He continued. "When we set up a government, we know it can go wrong, so we want to have separation of powers and checks and balances, to stop government from acting badly."

A student asked: "How can we balance the conflict between the rule of law and Chinese culture?" The question echoed the rhetoric the Party uses to explain away the inconsistencies in a reform agenda that has left its political monopoly unchanged. He cocked his head in thought before responding with another big smile. "Some people say that the biggest conflict between the rule of law and Chinese culture is that

Chinese people don't obey rules and regulations," he said. "But when Chinese people play mah-jongg, they obey the rules. Disputes are rare. Everyone follows the rules without asking." The students laughed as He moved his hands in a pantomime of shuffling tiles on a playing table. "We're even stricter with the rules in drinking games," he added, theatrically dispatching the contents of an invisible shot glass. "Examine carefully," he counseled the students, any claim about "China's national conditions."

A student at Peking University once told me about attending her first He Weifang lecture as a freshman. "For the first time in my life," she said, "I saw there was a new way of viewing the world." But this knowledge can be dangerous. In a recent lecture in Chongqing, a student put the issue bluntly: "You have spoken the truth to us on the stage this evening," she began. "But you used your status as a Peking University professor. I suspect if someone in my position were to get on stage and speak the truth like you, perhaps I would get in big trouble. So I would like to ask: to speak the truth, do you need a certain position or authority as a shield?"

In Shihezi, sitting in his makeshift living room, I asked He about who can speak freely in China. "That's a question with no easy answer," he replied. "I feel I need to be careful about encouraging people—particularly young people—to resist the political system. It is a moral question. I think that young people easily get intense. They go to extremes. There are some words that, perhaps, an elder can say in a more tactful way, a safer way."

I pressed him on the question of influence. How much of what he could do and say depended on his connections among classmates, his connections inside? "Actually, even if you have influence, you still need to know in what circumstances to use it, how to speak up. In this system, the art of speaking is extremely important." He continued, "I think the Middle Ages in Europe and today's China actually are similar. They had the Church and the king to dodge. We don't have that. But from top to bottom, we can control your actions, we can control your thinking. With all of that control, it is not so easy to know how to go out and solve problems."

To his own students, he often counsels patience on politics and a focus on scholarship. "There are so many cases where rights are violated," He explained a few years ago in a lecture transcript that circulates online. "A lot of people think that those of us in the law have some kind of miraculous cure. But actually we are also helpless." In the most outrageous cases, He explained, referring to a magazine punished for printing a critical article, "we law professors boil with rage, we talk it over. Should a bunch of us fly down to Guangzhou, have a sit-in in the Guangzhou High Court?" The students chuckled and clapped. "But think about it—so many cases are more unjust than that. We'd never be able to sit that long."

. . .

Most people date the beginning of China's reform era to a Party conclave in 1978, the Third Plenum, when Deng Xiaoping was restored to power. But a better marker might be the resumption of the national college entrance examination. Closed during the Cultural Revolution, China's dilapidated universities reopened in 1977 and 1978 to a group selected from millions of young people—aged from thirteen to thirty-seven—who tested into fewer than three hundred thousand slots available in all fields. Less than 5 percent of a decade's worth of prospective students were admitted. For He and his contemporaries, securing one of the impossibly few spots in college was the most important moment of their youth.

He failed on his first try. "As soon as I saw the math section, I knew I was ruined." In nine years of schooling, he had never been given a math class. He scored four out of a possible hundred points. The exam results, broadcast over the village loudspeaker system, left He despondent and embarrassed. He's mother insisted he try again. "The Cultural Revolution brought such bitterness to our family," He recalls her saying. "We have no other chance."

A few months later, in the spring of 1978, He tested again. He benefited from the obscurity of a small school in the Yangtze River city of Chongqing in Sichuan. China's Justice Ministry, seeing the need for lawyers, designated Southwest College of Politics and Law a "top-level" school, the only one outside a major city like Beijing or Shanghai. Southwest was picked for practical reasons. The school was remote enough that its scholars had not been sent too far away during the Cultural Revolution; being in Sichuan was, apparently, punishment enough. They could get back quickly to start over. Southwest's library had avoided the worst of the Red Guards' book burning and still had half its collection.

The school had trouble recruiting in 1978. "In a small place like ours, no one had heard that they were looking for students," He recalled. "Of course, even if I had seen it, I would not have dared to choose it, since it was a top-level university." A Southwest professor visiting Shandong to recruit examined a list of local college applicants with high enough scores for a national university. He picked two. He Weifang was one of them.

Arriving at Southwest was a shock, even for young veterans of the Cultural Revolution. After a five-day ride from Shandong to Chongqing, He Weifang was picked up at Chongqing's main train station by a sputtering Liberation-brand flatbed truck. The hour-long drive to the school's gate took him into the foothills of the Gele Mountains, past a villa occupied by U.S. General Joseph "Vinegar Joe" Stilwell during World War II and a monument marking a spot where Nationalist troops had massacred three hundred Communists at the end of the civil war.

A dirt road led from the gate of the university up to its only structure: an old administration building constructed by students and faculty in the atmosphere of self-reliance that prevailed in the 1950s. It had been repurposed to serve as dorm, classroom, and canteen that first year. The truck's bald tires slipped on the steep, unpaved slope, so the arriving students had to unload at the gate and walk up the hill. It was a miserable end to a long journey. Thirty years later, when recalling their arrival, almost every graduate mentions the mud.

The curriculum in those first years depended on the varied background of the cobbled-together faculty. No one had taught in ten years, after all, and many had destroyed their notes and files for fear of the Red Guards. The best-trained were those who had been treated worst. Lin Xiangrong, for instance, was a stern grader and father figure, whose lectures He called "pure and distilled." Lin had studied in Japan and Taiwan in the 1930s, working for the Communist underground. Accused of being a spy in the 1950s, he spent years in jail before being exonerated. At Southwest, Lin lectured on foreign legal systems, and he later helped He and other young scholars publish translations of classic legal works.

He Weifang thrived in the isolation of Chongqing. "There were no distractions, so you could concentrate on reading books," he recalled. He preferred to read alone, on the top bunk, nose to the ceiling, book over nose. He read *Selected Original Readings in Western Philosophy*. He read William Manchester's *The Glory and the Dream: A Narrative History of America, 1932–1972*, Yang Zheng's *Survey of Christianity*, and Qian Zhongshu's *Fortress Besieged*. His first book in English was Sidney Painter's *A History of the Middle Ages, 284–1500*. He befriended a librarian, Mrs. Xiao, who helped him with Hegel. After devouring the first volume of *Lectures on the History of Philosophy,* he looked for the second, but someone else had borrowed it. As soon as it was returned, Mrs. Xiao grabbed a passing student. "Go to Class 9 and look for He Weifang," she said. "Tell him that volume two of Hegel has come back. Tell him to get down here quickly to check it out."

. . .

In the 1980s, He did not consider becoming an activist. "When my generation started, we did not look to be rights defenders," He told me in Shihezi. "We just wanted to be scholars." He earned an MA in Beijing in 1985 and stayed on as a professor, writing well-received books about foreign law. "I enjoyed history and even useless hobbies: stamp collecting, playing chess, buying first editions."

The 1989 democracy protests in Tiananmen Square changed his thinking. "Before 1989, I did not really want to pay attention to real problems," He said. "It made me think—why does this country suffer one calamity after another?" He had briefly left his academic position to join a business startup, frustrated by scholars' low pay and poor housing. But he got caught up in the protest movement instead. His presence at Tiananmen Square made him unemployable after June 4, like many others. He was dismissed from the company, and a plan to join the Chinese Academy of Social Sciences fell through.

In desperation, He turned to a mentor, Jiang Ping, president of the China University of Political Science and Law, who had warned him against leaving his teaching position for business. "I was right, wasn't I? You are absolutely not cut out for that kind of work," He recalls Jiang telling him in his office. "Now, let's take care of this." Jiang ordered the personnel office to assign him to teach comparative law and to process the paperwork "as quickly as possible." Jiang saved He a job as one of his last official acts; a month later, he was dismissed for having supported the student protesters. (Jiang's firing earned him a hero's status. In an only-in-China twist, he maintained a position with the national legislature, and in the 1990s, he helped draft China's new corporate and securities laws.)

He looked around for a new scholarly direction. Improving the courts as an institution was not a sensitive issue, he realized, but it allowed him to address sensitive issues.

Starting in the late 1990s, his campaign to improve the judiciary seemed to be working. China's court leaders embraced "professionalism," and new policies encouraged the recruitment of judges with college degrees and backgrounds in law. By 2002, new judges were required to pass the same qualifying examination required of lawyers. Courts quietly downgraded many ex-soldiers from judges to "clerks." He Weifang emerged as one of the most prominent advocates for these reforms, and many of his ideas were put into practice.

The changes mirrored a larger effort to reconstruct China's legal system. A series of new laws began to address key questions of governance, limiting the power of China's domineering administrative bureaucracies, at least on paper. He hoped that making the courts more independent and professional would help speed up this process. In 2004, the Supreme People's Court asked He and a colleague to propose further structural reforms. Their plans called for separating the financing of local courts from local government and the creation of cross-regional "circuit courts," efforts to bypass entrenched local Party interests.

He could not resist inserting a symbolic change into his proposal: that the "people's courts" should simply be called "courts." Like the judges' new robes, the name change would emphasize the judiciary's enhanced institutional role. But in the People's Republic, this was no small suggestion. China still has a National People's Congress (legislature) and People's Daily (the official newspaper *Renmin Ribao*). The People's Bank (central bank) issues *renminbi*, "people's currency." The People's Armed Police are called out to deal with riots. "China," He likes to quip, "has too many people."

A banner headline appeared in *Xin Jing Bao* (Beijing News): "The 'People's Court' Might Change Its Name to 'Court.'" Once again, He had triggered a national debate. But this time, he had overreached. Asking to remove "people's" from the court was akin to stripping "under God" from the American Pledge of Allegiance. It struck too close to self-definition. The official reaction was swift and dismissive. "China's courts are the state judicial organs under the leadership of the Chinese Communist Party," a spokesperson emphasized. The court relieved He of his duties as an advisor. The national attention allowed He to reach a wide audience, but an official channel had been shut. "The name change issue attracted too much attention," He told a reporter, "so the other important suggestions in our draft were overlooked."

After a decade of preaching, He and other scholars had managed to help improve the quality of the judges, but they could not much alter the political environment in which courts operate. In 2007, somewhat chastened, He described in the authoritative British journal *China Quarterly* how judges fit into the power structure: "The police make the food, the prosecutor serves it and the court eats it." The legal system is still shackled by Chinese characteristics.

. . .

In 2008, to mark the thirtieth anniversary of the beginning of China's reform era and the reopening of the universities, He Weifang's alma mater held a reunion. The event offered a rare opportunity for He's generation of students to reconnect publicly and reflect on the direction of China's reforms.

The event was held at the Southwest College of Politics and Law's new campus in Yubei, a "development zone" across the Yangtze from Chongqing's old downtown. The boom has transformed the city into another Chinese megalopolis, dotting former fields with massive construction projects. A six-lane access road to the university, lined with spindly young trees and low shrubs, passes new "communities" in various stages of completion. The morning of the reunion, the sun rose hot but hidden behind the city's perpetual haze, silhouetting a horizon of cranes and the concrete shells of half-finished apartment towers.

In the center of the university's vast new campus, a plaza the size of a football field stretches in front of a gigantic convex structure of glass: the library. A concrete book, twenty feet square, sits over an artificial lake, open to a page with an embossed globe. Newly planted trees, held up with wooden braces, form part of a "scholar's forest" that includes life-size statues of Aristotle, Marx, Confucius, and the American jurist Nathan Roscoe Pound (1870–1964). On the way to lunch, we passed a sunken outdoor amphitheater, complete with Greek columns, overlooking a steep valley of cultivated fields holding out against earthmovers engaged in tunnel construction for a new expressway.

The reunion activities filled a wood-paneled auditorium large enough for a thousand. Students occupied every seat and aisle, and stood along the walls in the back. The morning and afternoon had been ceremonial. The main event took place that evening: a lecture by the current president of the China University of Political Science and Law, Xu Xianming, followed by comments from He Weifang.

A line of young women, dressed in long silk *qipao* and beauty-queen sashes, lined the stage as ushers. When Xu and other dignitaries walked in, the crowd began to clap. He Weifang entered last, wearing a gray suit and a bright orange tie, and the applause grew louder. There were even a few cheers. Looking sheepish, He waved to acknowledge the reaction. In introducing the evening's program, the moderator pointedly noted that He Weifang would speak last. Otherwise, the moderator said, "all of the students would leave immediately after his talk."

Xu Xianming's background is strikingly similar to He's. He was also born and raised in Shandong, entered college in 1978, and became an academic. But early in his career, he took a path toward officialdom. Xu is a scholar whose many articles and speeches, almost invariably, conveniently justify current policy. His early research, on modern interpretations of Marxism and Leninism, helped remold old doctrine to meet the ideological needs of the reform era. China's universities, all state-run, have an administrative structure that mirrors that of government, and soon after Southwest's 2008 reunion, Xu was promoted to head Shandong University, with his rank bumped up a half-step to the level of minister.

Xu looked ministerial, with Chinese characteristics. He was short, with a face and physique rounded by a life of banqueting, the lubricant of government interaction in China. He spoke slowly and clearly, with the cadence of a Chinese radio storyteller: folksy and heavy on slogans. He held forth for two hours, double the time allotted, but seemed oblivious to the clock.

Xu spoke of corruption, democracy, human rights, and constitutionalism. These are sensitive topics for a lecture, and Xu looked around the auditorium, mischievously, as he used each term for the first time. But his arguments followed a curious logic. China's corruption problem was the result of a lack of ethics, Xu asserted, adding that ethics could be cultivated by proper training, in school. China's law schools, therefore, were to blame for bribery in its courts. "Legal education," Xu declared, "should take responsibility for over 50 percent of judicial corruption."

According to Xu, Mao Zedong had led one of China's first "human rights movements" in the 1930s. Where did that leave us today? An analogy to the human body might help, Xu suggested: "A person has a torso. The torso of constitutionalism is democratic politics. In the past ten years or so, our achievements in democracy have been recognized around the world. A person has a heart. The heart of constitutionalism is the legislature. Our legislature with Chinese characteristics is the People's Congress system."

Xu extended the argument to include the "blood" (freedom) and "soul" (human rights) of constitutional government. "Thus, we had not found the soul of our constitutional government until we added 'respecting and protecting human rights' to the constitution," Xu said, referring to a toothless 2004 amendment. "So now we have a soul for our constitutionalism." He concluded by looking forward: perhaps President Hu Jintao's promotion of "harmony" might spark a new category of universal rights—the "right to harmony."

On the dais, He Weifang listened intently, occasionally writing a few notes. The other dignitaries on the stage stared straight ahead at the audience, with barely a reaction. Given the ubiquity in China of long boilerplate speeches, many of Xu's observations were familiar enough.

Though nearly three hours had passed by the time it was He Weifang's turn to speak not a single student had left. He got up with a huge grin, to loud applause, and stood behind the lectern, which was covered by an enormous bouquet of lilies and orchids. "Kelian de hua," he began. "Those long-suffering flowers."

He warmed up the crowd with a story about "his old friend" Xu. "I always speak very directly to him," he began. "For instance, Xu once predicted something with the strongest conviction: namely, that human rights would never be added to our constitution. He would die before that happened." He turned from looking at Xu and back to the audience as his hands gripped the podium. "So when it was added to the constitution in 2004, I wanted to call him up to say 'Are you preparing for death?'" The crowd roared. The table of dignitaries doubled over. Xu laughed too.

"I disagree with Professor Xu's view that legal education is responsible for more than half the corruption in the judicial system," He continued, looking directly at Xu. "I am a legal educator. Professor Xu, you are a legal educator's *boss*. Is that really your judgment?" Corruption comes from the lack of judicial independence, restrictions on the press, institutional weaknesses, perhaps, or even a lack of shame on the part of officials, He argued. Blaming the education system was an evasion. The audience erupted in applause.

He ridiculed Xu's metaphor of body and blood, suggesting it equated the truth "with something it is not." Where does human rights protection really come from? "Human rights comes from constitutional government," He told the students. "Constitutional government restricts autocracy and the reckless use of power." Political reform, He argued, would bring the conditions that would give protection of rights true meaning. "If we can restrict dictatorship, then we will naturally have human rights."

"Where is the path forward?" He continued, holding the podium and rocking slightly back and forth as he spoke, facing the crowd. His voice was excited, almost angry. "Where do you look for that kind of country?" he continued. "Sometimes we have impassioned scholarship, but we never seem to find the way forward. Where is the path?"

I have never before seen an audience in China respond so warmly and eagerly. Everyone seemed to know that they were witnessing something special: truth spoken bluntly to power, or at least to its academic proxy. When the speech was over, the students applauded loudly and enthusiastically. They filed out in excited conversation, energized despite the late hour. As always, a large group of students seeking autographs massed around He at the stage. He chatted and signed, laughing from time to time. A smaller group surrounded Xu, who was soon escorted away by Southwest's president. A jerky video of He's performance soon joined others like it online, along with transcripts, essays, and blog posts forming a living archive, bouncing around China, amassing an audience of millions.

. . .

Soon after arriving in Shihezi, He told a reporter that "before coming here, I joked that I wanted to be a frontier poet," invoking China's long history of a literature of exile. "But with modern communications that is impossible. A poet needs to face oppression, heaviness, anger, gloom. Only then can he distill these feelings into verse and song. Today, how can one distill? E-mail messages, phone calls, even text messaging—talk, talk, talk, talk—you have ranted yourself out."

But, after five months, events beyond He's control made his time in Shihezi far more isolated than anyone expected. Ethnic violence in Urumchi, Xinjiang's capital, burst out in July 2009, shutting down the city and highlighting the fragile nature of "harmony" in China's far West. The army occupied the city for weeks to help quell the massive riots, the worst unrest there in years. In the wake of the violence, the government shut off the entire province to outside communication. Shihezi, along with the rest of Xinjiang, had no Internet and only sporadic phone service for ten months. During a brief trip to Shanghai during this period, He posted an essay to his blog; after a long hiatus, he mentioned "coming up for air."

Back in March 2009, the night before He Weifang was due to leave for Xinjiang, one of his former students, the young activist scholar Xu Zhiyong, joined an impromptu farewell dinner for He in Beijing. In an essay written late that night, Xu invoked the eighth-century Tang poet Wang Wei's "Weicheng Melody":

> Morning rain in Weicheng dampens the dusty ground.
> Willow trees give the inn courtyard a fresh greenness.
> Why not drink one more bowl of wine?
> Beyond Yang Pass there are only strangers.

"The times have changed." Xu wrote. "Xinjiang is only four hours away. Perhaps a year or two is good. The Great Northwest is a beautiful place."

Later that night, a bit more sober, Xu reconsidered. "My heart was suddenly distressed. In my mind, the Great Northwest is most beautiful, but I don't know if Professor He will like it," he wrote. "In the past year, he has experienced so many twists and turns. It seems as if the fate of an intellectual who dares to speak the truth is entirely in the hands of unseen men."

"But, in fact, all of us—even those busy holding on to power—all of us await our nation's fate."

PART FIVE

Teachers and Pupils

It is an age-old Chinese story that young people are pressed to study hard and do well. This trope can be found in memoirs and works of fiction that long predate the 1911 Revolution; educational success has been a strategy for upward mobility in China for centuries. But many things have changed over the past few decades, from the nationalities of the children attending Chinese schools to the gender makeup of classrooms, as the chapters in this section show. In the first of these, we meet an expat couple (Canadian mother, British father) who have made the unusual decision to send their children to a neighborhood school in Shanghai, rather than an international one. In the second, we meet a young woman who struggles in a materialistic metropolis not just to learn traditional core subjects but to excel in novel ones ranging from piano to swimming. And in the third chapter, we learn about the curious history of the guitar in China, and meet a pair of quite different Chinese virtuosos of the instrument who respectively believe that teaching students to rock and master Bach is good for the nation.

CHAPTER 13

The Great Wall of Education

ANNA GREENSPAN

We gather for national day at a local kindergarten in downtown Shanghai. Outside, in the yard, tiny chairs are set up in a semicircle facing the country's red flag. The teacher stands in the center. Microphone in hand, she tells her young pupils of the great gifts *zuguo mama* (the motherland) has given them. We all stand at attention as the flag is raised and China's national anthem, "The March of the Volunteers," is played—too loudly—over a scratchy PA system.

"Arise! Arise! Arise! A million hearts beat as one. Brave the enemy's fire, March on!" I know the song well. My kids enjoy belting it out while riding on the back of my bicycle through the streets of the old French Concession. When I found a version online, they begged me to play it over and over again, while they stood in the middle of the living room, straight as soldiers, saluting. Now, every time we pass a red flag, they ask to stop and sing.

When the anthem ends, the atmosphere of the assembly lightens. A popular tune comes over the loudspeaker. The children start to twirl. "I have black hair, I have black eyes, I am a Chinese baby." The words are lost on my 4-year-old daughter Zoe. Despite her blond hair and white skin she spins, dances, and sings along.

We are a new breed of foreigner living in China, a symptom of the country's increasing growth and globalization. We didn't come as sinologists, missionaries, diplomats, or to further our business or engage in trade. No one offered us an expat package, with special "hardship" pay, that would allow us to recreate the comforts of home in a far-away land. Rather, we have come to live in Shanghai for the same reasons foreigners have always flocked to cities like London or New York. We were drawn by the opportunities it made available—editing and university teaching jobs that we struggled to find in Canada were ours in Shanghai just for the asking—but also by the excitement of the giant metropolis. We had the sense that Shanghai today is positioned at the edge of tomorrow. Our children go to the local neighborhood school because this, for now, is our home.

Picking a local school was a natural choice, but also a strange one. Our kids are among the first foreigners ever to go to Chinese public schools. To get them in required dogged persistence. There are many teachers and parents who feel that the neighborhood school is simply not where an outsider belongs. My own search involved wandering the neighborhood, banging on gates, and being turned down at the door. School guards were the first line of defense. The main guard at our school is a gruff middle-aged man with a thuggish demeanor. He wields his power with sadistic delight, and brusquely declines entrance with a backhanded wave to anyone who has forgotten to bring the proper ID. When not policing the door, he is most often found lounging outside, chain-smoking.

When my son Max was just a toddler, I eyed the school on our walks and was keen to explore. One spring afternoon, I waited among the other parents at pick-up time and, unnoticed in the crowd, snuck in. Once inside, I was surprised and delighted to spot another foreign parent and eagerly approached him.

Brent's kids had been going to the school for some time, and he told me that in most respects they were satisfied. In truth, our family had stumbled upon one of the best preschools in town. Jianguo Kindergarten, two blocks from our home, is in an old colonial villa set on large, leafy grounds. The garden is dotted with magnolia trees, and flower-beds. At the front is a small fountain, with a scholar's rock, a pet turtle, and a waterwheel that the children like to spin. The classrooms, filled with crafts and toys, have high ceilings, large windows, and wood floors.

Bolstered, I poked my head into an office and introduced myself to a school administrator, a no-nonsense woman with a round face and red glasses. I had not planned to apply that day. I was just on a recon mission, but the administrator began helping me fill out forms I could barely comprehend (despite all my efforts, I am still pretty much illiterate in Mandarin), and I happily complied. I wrote Max's name, date of birth, and contact details and left all the other spaces blank. Local Shanghainese, well versed in the city's ways, know how to navigate in through both the front and back doors of local schools. Outsiders bumble through these intricacies. I left with no idea whether Max would be accepted by Jianguo Kindergarten. When I got a phone call a few days later saying that he could start in the fall, I felt triumphant. Somehow we had passed our first test.

Shanghai is a migrant city. Throughout modern times, it has attracted people from both inside and outside China. Shanghai's schools, however, have until very recently been almost entirely closed off. In the early twentieth century, thousands of foreigners made Shanghai their home and built their own schools. These enclaves—the French, British, and American schools—exist again today to serve an ever-growing number of expats, who pass through the flourishing city on three-, four- or five-year stints. For locals, education is firmly tied to the *hukou,* or household registration, system, which binds people to their towns or villages of birth. Under this system, it is basically impossible for a Chinese child without a Shanghai *hukou* to get into a Shanghai school. Today, there is growing pressure to reform. Millions of internal migrants who want to make Shanghai their home are pushing against the door. Laws are changing fast and are difficult to decipher, and individual schools seem free to set their own policies. Yet most of the best schools in Shanghai remain closed to migrants from the Chinese countryside. Two years ago an Australian friend tried to get her godson admitted into our school. The boy was born in Shanghai but lacked proper papers. We approached Principal Zhang, a stylish woman with perfectly plucked eyebrows, immaculate makeup and a wide, friendly smile. I have always found her flexible and accommodating, but in this case, after leafing through the papers, she shook her head with a frown. There was no way a Chinese child without a Shanghai *hukou* could be admitted. Outsiders like us, however, who hold a foreign passport and are willing to pay the extra fee, can now usually get in.

Foreign children who enter this once-gated zone get an insider's view of China available to few others—including their parents. When Zoe had a school trip to visit the People's Liberation Army, we were told that she had to go alone. The other children were to be accompanied by their parents, but as foreigners we would not be able to do so. At a recent assembly held to celebrate the upcoming lantern festival, we gathered in a hall to hear stories about the Yellow Emperor. Parents were then asked to join in the holiday ritual of solving cryptic riddles. While I hid in the back, with only the vaguest notion of what was going on, the other parents enthusiastically participated in this revival of a tradition, proudly raising their hands when they knew the right answer and cheering loudly when their team won a point. Like a first-generation immigrant in the West, I follow my children—who act as my probes and translators—trying as best I can to keep up with a deep cultural integration that I know I shall never achieve

For foreigners, the biggest advantage of local schools is the opportunity for linguistic immersion. Our kids are gaining a natural sense of Mandarin's rhythms and tones. They have full-time exposure to a language that is gaining increasing importance on the global stage. The Confucius Institutes, centers set up by the Chinese government to promote Chinese language and culture abroad, claim that there are forty million foreigners around the world studying Chinese. American elementary schools are beginning to add it to their routine curriculum. In Shanghai, Mandarin is the lingua franca. Zoe's best friend Upe, a tiny, delicate girl with white blond hair, is the only other foreigner in her class. Upe is Italian and Lithuanian. When she and Zoe get together, they play in Chinese. Though Mandarin is on the rise, it is still pretty rare for non-native speakers to achieve any kind of fluency. Even in Shanghai, China's most cosmopolitan city, anyone who doesn't look Chinese and manages even a few mangled sentences is met with shock and congratulations. With kids, the oddity is even more acute. My children's fluency is a novelty. Passers-by always say the same thing about Zoe. "She looks like a Barbie doll." When she opens her mouth and responds, they are astonished. "She speaks!"

There is much to admire in Shanghai's local schools. Chinese compare their educational method, with all its rote learning and relentless memorization, to force-feeding a duck (the technique used to create Beijing's famous roast duck). The grotesqueness of the image is mitigated by the deliciousness of the dish. In the "duck-feeding education style," rigorous techniques ensure that the teaching of foundational skills in math and literacy is superb. In 2009, when Chinese students were included in the Programme for International Student Assessment (PISA), international tests in math, reading, and science, educators were stunned to discover that in every subject, students from Shanghai came out on top. Even more important, schooling in China is embedded in a culture that cares deeply about education, celebrates smart kids, rewards hard work, and instills the values of patience, concentration, and respect.

Locals who move abroad are acutely aware of the advantages. Zoe's classmate Long Long, a sweet boy with dimpled cheeks, has only recently returned to the city after spending the first years of his life abroad. The only reason his family came back, his mother confessed, was so that their son could go to a Chinese school. Another friend lives in Australia but won't take citizenship there because she doesn't want to renounce her Shanghai *hukou* and thus give up her easy access to the city's schools. When she comes to Shanghai on holiday or for work, her 5-year-old daughter attends a local kindergarten. An open-minded scholar who is researching Shanghai's burgeoning creativity, my friend is stunned at what her daughter can learn in only a few weeks. "I don't know what they are doing over there," she says of the expensive preschool in Australia. "It just seems so lazy."

Jianguo Kindergarten is at the forefront of Shanghai's experiments with "quality education" that tries to temper the rigidity and pressures normally associated with Chinese schools. Homework is basically nonexistent and, until the final year, when they start learning math (numeracy is taught before literacy here), students do little more than read books, play games, and sing songs. Zoe, who has been placed in the ballet class, has "open days" when we are invited to watch as the children dress up in fancy clothes and show off various forms of interpretive dance. The educational emphasis is on teaching morality and life skills. My kids now know how to use chopsticks and sit nicely in their chairs. In conjunction with various citywide campaigns, they have been taught that it is wrong to indulge in meals of ibex and shark fin soup. No one seems to care how well my kids count or read. We haven't been given any development charts of personal growth. I stopped attending parent-teacher meetings when I realized that personal communication was impossible. Instead, adults sit together in rows listening to PowerPoint presentations on how best to raise their kids—the proper way to brush their teeth, when to put them to bed, and how to check their eyes. The written student evaluations we do occasionally receive say things like: "Zoe has a big tummy. She can eat two bowls of rice—wow!"

After four years, however, we are nearing the end of preschool. Our son, Max is now in *da ban,* the highest grade. For the past months I have been compulsively, obsessively, speaking to those who have gone before me—foreign families in local schools with children older than mine. What I have found is that it is rare for non-native students to make it past grade two or three. In my research so far, I have only discovered a few families with children who have stayed in local schools through middle school. Initially, I had assumed that my kids would continue in the local public system. Now, as the decision nears, I find that despite everything I admire about China's education system, I am reluctant to send Max to the same elementary schools his Chinese classmates will attend. The majority of outsiders—both children and their parents—simply can't endure a regular public education, and the few who can most often choose not to. Chinese education, even in the best local schools in the most open city, forms a nearly impregnable wall.

Language is the first and most obvious stumbling block. For young kids, who have malleable brains, learning to speak Mandarin is not particularly hard. The tones, which older people (like me) find difficult to hear, never mind repeat, come with ease. In fact, the monosyllabic, sing-songy nature of the language seem to make it easier for children to learn than English. Max's and Zoe's baby babble was bilingual, and many of their first words were in Chinese. By age four, their proficiency in the pronunciation of Mandarin far exceeded my own. Max now frequently—and somewhat annoyingly—insists on correcting my accent. The benefits of his fluency extend beyond China. A fishmonger gave us a discount in Canada last summer because Max could speak to her in her native tongue.

While the spoken language is relatively easy, learning to read and write is not, even for native speakers. Becoming literate in Mandarin is very, very hard. Highly educated Chinese regularly forget how to write the commonest words. In his essay "Why Chinese Is So Damn Hard," the sinologist David Moser admits to taking some joy in detailing this incompetence. He writes of a lunch with three Ph.D. students in the Chinese Department at Peking University (Beijing Daxue), the most prestigious university in China, where though all three were native speakers, not one could remember the characters that make up *da penti,* "to sneeze." "Can you imagine," writes Moser, "three Ph.D. students in English at Harvard forgetting how to write the English word 'sneeze'?" Without an alphabet, Mandarin offers few phonetic cues. Radicals, components of characters, sometimes provide clues, but these are vague and unreliable. In the end, the only way to learn a character is to memorize it. In English, it is worth noting, precisely the opposite holds true. When Max has memorized an English story, I know it is no longer useful as a reading tool. I only feel he is truly reading when he sounds out the letters. In Mandarin, on the other hand, reading and remembering are one. To become literate in Mandarin, then, takes enormous patience and discipline. The entire education system extends from this basic, fundamental fact, and the inherent difficulty of the written language infuses the whole of culture in profound ways. In China, the act of writing itself has deep—even cosmic—implications. Calligraphy is one of the highest forms of art. Mastering a beautiful script is traditionally the surest sign of having attained culture's most esteemed goal: self-cultivation.

This year, we hired a tutor for Max to boost his writing skills. She started with the strokes, paying minute attention to the horizontal and vertical line and the short curving diagonal dash. Each has a name and an order. It is crucial to get these exactly right from the start. Young students are given little writing notebooks, in which they copy out the characters line after line after line. We do this with the English letters too, of course, but it is not the same at all. In a pictographic language, each character has the meticulous precision of a painting. Even numbers are subject to this exactitude of inscription. For Chinese kids, it is not enough to know the number 5. The straight lines and round curves must be written exactly right. And so, week after week, Max's tutor leaves him with the same exercise: to write out the most basic strokes over and over again as neatly as he can.

A related obstacle is the burden of homework, which starts early and hits hard. By first grade, kids get at least an hour of homework a night. The next year, it doubles, and by age ten, kids regularly miss sleep so that they can complete their assignments. Parents, of course, suffer as well, since someone has to stay home to coax and cajole. I have at least one colleague at the university where I teach who insists on holding his class in the evening so that he can avoid homework time for one night a week. From the start, family life is restructured around the onerous task of education. The little time left over is taken up with extra classes. Teachers supplement their salaries through after-school tutoring. The Ministry of Education has prohibited the practice, but the ban is routinely ignored, like everything else aimed at curbing the intense pressure on children. Weekends are spent at Children's Palace community centers, which offer classes in English, painting, and training for "Olympic Math." Piano is especially popular. Amy Chua's notorious 2011 memoir *Battle Hymn of the Tiger Mother* was typically Chinese in its almost delirious insistence that her children excel at a musical instrument. I am considered strict among my expat friends for having started Max at piano at six and demanding that he practice five to ten minutes a day. The local Chinese parents I know with children Max's age, however, are already making their little musicians practice between forty minutes and two hours a night.

This extreme pressure is at least in part a product of history. China's contemporary educational culture is only a few decades old—people as young as thirty remember street games and lots of free time. The harshness of the system, many argue, is a result of its emergence from the shattered dreams of the "lost generation" whose opportunities were wasted by the Cultural Revolution. This generation was also the first to be restricted by the one-child policy. The result is a generation of single children, the famed "little emperors," who bear the brunt of their parents' unfulfilled ambitions.

The strain of expectation has drastic effects on the nature of friendships. Kids spend time together at school and now—with an increasing intensity—online. But the type of friendships common among kids in the West, which are based on spending lots of time together, are remarkably rare. Foreign parents who send their kids to local schools often comment on this fundamental difference in socialization. Dropoffs and pickups are generally done by grandparents and *ayis* (housekeeper-maids), which makes communication with other children's parents difficult. I've managed to invite a few of Max's classmates to birthday parties, and Zoe sometimes plays outside with hers, but my children's relationships with their Chinese classmates are nothing like the deep, intimate friendships of playdates and sleepovers that are common amongst the children who attend international schools. "Playdates are hard," said one British mom I talked to, who sent her kids to local schools until the fourth grade. "Kids often come over with a personal video game that they never put down. They don't really know what to do with boxes of costumes and toys."

Much of what I know about local teenage life comes from Ruru, whom I met years ago when she was sixteen. Her mother, who works as a senior manager in a pharmaceutical company, asked if Ruru could come over on the weekends to practice English. We agreed apprehensively. The first few times we saw her, Ruru seemed sullen and shy, her gaze fixed downward as she fiddled with whatever gadget she happened to be carrying. It turned out, however, that once unleashed Ruru could talk passionately, fluently for hours. She has defiant opinions, likes history, manga cartoons, and video games, and she complains bitterly about her mother—often while her mother is still in the room. She seems, in short, a typical teenager. Yet when I asked Ruru how often she went out with her friends, her answer astounded me: once or twice a year.

One of the most surprising things about Shanghai is that aside from the hour when school is let out, teenagers are barely visible. Expressions like "hanging out" or "just chilling" have little meaning here. In Shanghai, public places belong to the old, not the young. Ruru, now a student at Tsinghua University (Qinghua Daxue) in Beijing, one of China's top universities, complains about her classmates' lack of "EQ," a term for Emotional Intelligence that has become quite popular here. "They don't know anything about movies or music," she complains. "I feel totally out of the loop." Only students from the big cities, Shanghai and Beijing, do anything other than study, she said. Last time I saw her, Ruru told me her roommate was a mean, selfish girl who wouldn't do anything not sanctioned as study. "She only started to talk to me after the dean made a speech about the importance of social relations," Ruru said.

Underlying this rigidity is the fact that the Chinese education system is based almost entirely on standardized tests. Students are tested early and often. I've been told to expect exams in math, English, and Chinese almost every week by grade one. In the senior year of high school, students undergo at least eighty exams. All this testing is designed as preparation for the dreaded the three-day college entrance exam, or *gao kao* (high test), reportedly far more difficult than anything equivalent in the West. The *gao kao* is a collective rite of passage in China. For many, it is the single most important factor in determining the course of their lives. In June, when the *gao kao* is written, the whole country is drawn into the ritual. The media are filled with stories of the extreme measures resorted to by students and their families. Girls go on the pill to control their periods. Parents take time off work to prepare special meals. In Shanghai, construction anywhere near the testing zones is stopped. Traffic is rerouted. Students who wake up late can call for a police escort to get to the test on time. Many lament the all-consuming influence of the test. China is a country where backdoor *guanxi* (personal connections) and corruption are commonplace, however, and there is extreme hesitation to move away from the objective testing of the *gao kao* system, whatever its flaws. Educational experiments aimed at producing more well-rounded individuals are invariably abandoned when it is discovered that they lead to lower tests scores. China is still a poor country, and millions who feel trapped see a good *gao kao* score as the only way out.

The educational methods—the stress of excessive homework and the routine drudgery of test-based learning—are off-putting, but it is the culture in which education is embedded that, for me, forms the ultimate barrier to a full immersion in Chinese public schools. One of the most widely held clichés about China is that it counters American individualism with a deep-rooted collectivism. If this is true, it is only in a very particular sense. There are no team sports or group projects at Chinese local schools. The Chinese university students I teach have told me that they have trouble translating the terms "school project" or "class presentation" into Mandarin. Collectivity is not about finding ways to work together. In fact, the Chinese incapacity for teamwork is one of the most frequent complaints made by people trying to do business on the mainland. What the Chinese education system instills into children instead is a sense of group belonging coupled with a rigorous reinforcement of the norm. There is an intense—sometimes almost zombie-like—groupthink mentality, which presumes that everyone should follow exactly the same path. In Shanghai, people will stop and get in a line simply because the line exists. Crazes are commonplace. After the 2011 Japanese earthquake, for example, rumors on the Internet sparked a nationwide run on salt. The mass collective behavior extends to all facets of life. Get a top score in the *gaokao* and everyone knows in advance, not only what university you will attend, but also what your major and future job will be. Personal desire plays almost no role at all.

The mechanism through which this is instilled into students is a continual reinforcement of collective triumph or shame. To do well or poorly is a reflection on your family, your class, your school, your village or town, and, in the end, on China itself. The method is clearly effective. When Max forgets to bring his handkerchief or cut his fingernails, he panics. He is not worried for himself. Rather what he fears is that his own failure at morning inspection will reflect badly on the class. Students are appointed as monitors and told to rat out their classmates. Max always makes sure his shirt is tucked in, lest the bathroom monitor berate him. This shame-based collectivism produces group identity, but it has a fiercely competitive edge as its flip side. Max, like most children, is deeply upset when he doesn't come in first, and I fear that the principle "it doesn't matter if you win or lose, it's how you play the game" is not one that is being reinforced at school. Perhaps this is the inevitable result when unemployment is growing and a vast population fights fiercely for the few spots in the country's top

universities. But from an outsider's perspective, the brutal competitiveness seems to run deep in Chinese culture. Overt expressions of favorit-
ism from teachers and even parents and grandparents are commonplace.
"Whom do you like better, your mom or your dad?" adults routinely
ask children. At school, students are publicly ranked. Every question
has only one right answer, precisely because this is the only clear and
fair way to determine who is best. Count the number of stripes on a
child's school uniform and the well-initiated instantly knows how well
he or she has performed.

Chinese parents are severe when it comes to education. It is not
uncommon to hear stories of children being beaten for getting bad
grades. The more subtle and profound strategy of shame is a frequent
tool of reproach used by many of the local teachers and parents I know.
Children are taught to fear a poor performance, lest they make their
elders lose face. In China, to do badly at school is a disgrace. Strictness
in teaching is regarded as essential. Max learned the words *piping* (to
criticize) and *ma* (to scold) in his first months of school.

In North America—with its special "gifted" classes—one of the signs
of being good at something is that you don't have to work too hard to
excel. Chinese culture tends to precisely the opposite view. People don't
give much credence to the idea of natural skills. They assume instead,
that the kids who do best are the ones who work the hardest. The
students Ruru always praised most were the ones who stayed up latest
studying. She argued fiercely that among her peers little weight was put
on the sense of individual talent and parents felt little obligation to
foster natural strengths. That there can be no learning without suffering
is a commonly held belief. Max is a little frightened of his kung fu
teacher, Zhang Yi, a lovely man, who occasionally shouts to control
the unruly rabble of foreign kids who take his class. His strictness is
only a shadow of how *wushu* (Chinese kung fu) is traditionally taught,
however. "My *wushu* master used to beat us black and blue," Zhang
told me. "If I came home without bruises, my mother accused me of
not going to class." In Shanghai, even yoga teachers adopt this stern,
hard-work attitude. Go to a yoga class taught by a local teacher and
there is no soothing suggestion that you "relax and listen to your
body." Instead, the teacher watches the class like a hawk, yelling at
anyone who releases a pose too soon. In order to instill the supreme
value of hard work into them, parents teach their children what is called
"eating bitterness," *chi ku*. This is taken literally at birth, when parents
follow the old Chinese custom of giving their newborns something

bitter to taste. "After that," my friend Xiong Wei explained, "life is guaranteed to seem sweet."

My intuition is the opposite. I tend to encourage rather than berate. When Max and Zoe show me their creations, my instinct is to shower them with praise. Every random scribbling is taken as a sign of creativity and individual expression. In China, however, what is valued is technique. When you send your kids to a local preschool, you notice a change in their drawing almost straight away. Within a few weeks, the incoherent scrawls of a toddler are transformed into recognizable shapes and lines. In art education, teachers lead by example and guide by holding the hand: this is how you draw a house, a bird, a face. Max, who is now capable of sophisticated, well-disciplined drawings, shares the Chinese tendency for harsh judgment. He dismisses Zoe's doodles with disdain. "Bu hao kan" (It looks ugly), he says, staring at her scrawls. I try to temper the criticism, explaining that there are all sorts of ways to draw. But I have begun to doubt my sincerity. Some kids' drawings are better than others. Not everyone's skill or talent is the same.

Recently, a wave of research has also begun to question the value of overabundant applause. The trailer for *Waiting for Superman*, a documentary film about America's failing schools, mocks the culture of overconfidence. International PISA rankings, says the voice-over, show that American students are falling behind in all categories but one: self-esteem. In their 2009 book *NurtureShock: New Thinking about Children*, Po Bronson and Ashley Merryman describe an experiment by the psychologist Carol Dweck. Two groups of students were given the same test. Midway through, the students were interrupted and given feedback. One group, in true American fashion, were told that they were doing great; the other group was asked to try harder. Those who were berated ultimately did better on the test. Children who are constantly commended, say Bronson and Merryman, tend to give up too quickly when things don't come easily. American kids "think they can do everything, but they can't do anything," laments a Californian parent who now sends hers to a Shanghai school.

Chinese schools are undoubtedly superior to their Western counterparts in teaching respect, patience, concentration, and the value of hard work. Yet self-confidence is vital in itself, irrespective of achievement. Graduates of the Chinese system may be able to whiz through tests, but according to every manager I've talked to—whether local or foreign—they are incapable of taking risks and terrified of failure. Few dare go against the grain. Most important (and it seems to me, at the heart of the cultural clash) is a sense that there is embedded in Chinese education a certain denial of childhood itself. Perhaps this is not surprising. In the West, the notion of childhood, the idea that there is a special time of life that should be treasured as productive of imagination and play is a recent invention. Childhood is one of the products of modernity. In China, it is a conceptual category that has not yet fully arrived. Chinese society is wonderfully kid-friendly. Max and Zoe regularly accompany us to gallery openings, fancy restaurants, and bars. Walk down the street in Shanghai with a baby and everyone—from elderly couples to hip-looking teenage boys—stops to coo. At the same time, however, there is an obliviousness to how children think and feel. A favorite adult game, for example, is to pretend to steal a toddler's toy, despite the fact that the "fun" almost always leads to tears. Chinese children's stories are overly schmaltzy and highly moralistic. Indigenous cartoons, which are enormously supported by the state, all seem weirdly off-key, not quite appropriate for either children or adults. "Chinese people," my Mandarin teacher once told me, "see kids a lot like animals at the zoo. They view them as cute and cuddly, fun to prod and pat. Little attention, however, is paid to their internal states."

Many fear in China that the education system is unkind. Everyone agrees at least in principle that children should be given more free time. Yet the idea that there is something truly, inherently valuable in just leaving children alone and letting them play is extremely unusual. Attempts to encourage playfulness further serve to highlight the problem. Right before Chinese New Year, for example, the *New York Times* reported on an official in Hebei Province who released a 32-point "play plan" to get young students to stop studying and have some fun during the holiday. Closer to home, but in a similar vein, Long Long's mother recently asked me if I knew any psychologists. Apparently, the kindergarten was looking for one who would consult on the proper methods of play. Yet play, directionless and without purpose, but full of creative potential, is precisely what is required to develop the creative economy China is so desperate to produce. As the urban activist Jane Jacobs taught, play, rather than strategic goals and targeted growth, is almost always at the heart of invention and economic expansion. This is why Google allows its employees to spend 20 percent of their time pursuing their own interests, no matter where they lead. It's also why so many leaders advise young people to do what they love, rather than try to live life according to a prescribed plan. The pursuit of childhood passions—even when unpredictable and seemingly frivolous—is a key to the creation of wealth, as well as a privilege that follows from economic achievement.

I struggled—obsessively—over the question of primary school for many months. The two feeder schools in my area are both fiercely competitive "key schools," meaning that they rank at the top of the local system and are geared toward an intensely pressured elite. I ruled these out early. Xiangyang Primary School, also located nearby, seemed more promising. Local parents told me it had a reputation as a "happy school," with an emphasis on rounded personalities and having fun. I went to check it out, but I didn't see a single other foreigner there, and my minimal encounters with teachers and guards gave me the impression that I would have to push my way in. That prospect alone exhausted me. I started looking elsewhere.

We live at the bottom of Ulumuqi Road, one of the main arteries of the former French Concession. The tree-lined street is filled with a jumble of fruit and vegetable sellers, diplomatic headquarters, regional restaurants, and random tiny stores. About half way up, near the corner of Anfu Lu, is a cluster of high-rise housing that is popular among Shanghai's ever-growing foreign population. Outside the apartments, street peddlers gather on the corner, selling flowers, household goods, and pirated DVDs. On Anfu Lu itself, much of the old art deco architecture has been converted and now houses coffee shops, designer boutiques, wine bars, and the best bakery in town. Aiju Primary School, a private school that specializes in the arts, is located at the end of this intensely cosmopolitan street in new airy structures built with lots of glass. For the past few years, it has operated an international class open to children with foreign passports. It thus hovers at the edge of the local system, geared toward parents who want Chinese linguistic immersion and some of the discipline, but with less of the pressure and more time for play.

Max and I toured the school in the fall. We saw the art classes, one specializing in Western techniques, the other in Chinese ones. There were rooms dedicated to piano, *erhu* (the Chinese two-stringed fiddle), and the study of Go. On the top floor, there was even a place for robot races. Max and I agreed that it seemed pretty great. In the week after Chinese New Year, we went for an interview. Waiting in the conference room, I bribed Max with a chocolate bar to promise not to be shy. The principal called him in and I waited nervously. About ten minutes later, they returned smiling, and the principal detailed all the things Max had gotten wrong. Answering a math question, he had mistaken *ba shi* (80) for *shi ba* (18). He couldn't recognize most of the characters she had pointed to and didn't know the number to call the police or fire department (information that no one had taught him, but that the school apparently felt he should know). Still, he had apparently been chatty and charming enough to get in. The principal told us that if we wanted a space, we could have it.

"Are you sure?" I asked. "Can I stop my search?"

"I promise," she said. "Call in May to pick up his uniform and books. He starts in the fall."

CHAPTER 14

Gilded Age, Gilded Cage

LESLIE T. CHANG

At the age of four, Zhou Jiaying was enrolled in two classes—Spoken American English and English Conversation—and given the English name Bella. Her parents hoped she might go abroad for college. The next year they signed her up for acting class. When she turned eight, she started on the piano, which taught discipline and developed the cerebrum. In the summers she went to the pool for lessons; swimming, her parents said, would make her taller. Bella wanted to be a lawyer, and to be a lawyer you had to be tall. By the time she was ten, Bella lived a life that was rich with possibility and as regimented as a drill sergeant's. After school she did homework unsupervised until her parents got home. Then came dinner, bath, piano practice. Sometimes she was permitted television, but only the news. On Saturdays she took a private essay class followed by Math Olympics, and on Sundays a piano lesson and a prep class for her entrance exam to a Shanghai middle school. The best moment of the week was Friday afternoon, when school let out early. Bella might take a deep breath and look around, like a man who discovers a glimpse of blue sky from the confines of the prison yard.

For China's emerging middle class, this is an age of aspiration—but also a time of anxiety. Opportunities have multiplied, but each one brings pressure to take part and not lose out, and every acquisition seems to come ready-wrapped in disappointment that it isn't something newer and better. An apartment that was renovated a few years ago looks dated; a mobile phone without a video camera and color screen is an embarrassment. Classes in colloquial English are fashionable among Shanghai schoolchildren, but everything costs money.

Freedom is not always liberating for people who grew up in a stable socialist society; sometimes it feels more like a never-ending struggle not to fall behind. A study has shown that 45 percent of Chinese urban residents are at health risk due to stress, with the highest rates among high school students.

Fifth grade was Bella's toughest year yet. At its end she would take entrance exams for middle school. Every student knew where he or she ranked: when teachers handed back tests, they had the students stand in groups according to their scores. Bella ranked in the middle—twelfth or thirteenth in a class of twenty-five, lower if she lost focus. She hated Japan, as her textbooks had taught her to: the Japanese army had killed 300,000 Chinese in the 1937 Nanjing massacre. She hated America, too, because it always meddled in the affairs of other countries. She spoke a fair amount of English: "Men like to smoke and drink beer, wine, and whiskey." Her favorite restaurant was Pizza Hut, and she liked the spicy wings at KFC. Her record on the hula hoop was two thousand spins.

The best place in the world was the Baodaxiang Children's Department Store on Nanjing Road. In its vast stationery department, Bella would carefully select additions to her eraser collection. She owned thirty erasers—stored in a cookie tin at home—that were shaped like flip flops and hamburgers and cartoon characters; each was not much bigger than a thumbnail, and all remained in their original plastic packaging. When her grandparents took her to the store, Bella headed for the toy section, but not when she was with her parents. They said she was too old for toys.

If Bella scored well on a test, her parents bought her presents; a bad grade brought a clampdown at home. Her best subject was Chinese, where she had mastered the art of the composition: she could describe a household object in a morally uplifting way.

> Last winter Grandmother left her spider plant outdoors and forgot about it. . . . This spring it actually lived. Some people say this plant is lowly, but the spider plant does not listen to arbitrary orders, it does not fear hardship, and in the face of adversity it continues to struggle. This spirit is worthy of praise.

She did poorly in math. Extra math tutoring was a constant and would remain so until the college entrance examination, which was seven years away. You were only as good as your worst subject. If you didn't get into one of Shanghai's top middle schools, your fate would be mediocre classmates and teachers who taught only what was in the textbook. Your chances of getting into a good high school, not to mention a good college, would diminish.

You had to keep moving, because staying in place meant falling behind. That was how the world worked even if you were only ten years old.

The past decade has seen the rise of something Mao sought to stamp out forever: a Chinese middle class, now estimated to number between one hundred and one hundred and fifty million people. Though definitions vary—household income of at least $10,000 a year is one standard—middle-class families tend to own an apartment and a car, to eat out and take vacations, and to be familiar with foreign brands and ideas. They owe their well-being to the government's economic policies, but in private they can be very critical of the society they live in.

The state's retreat from private life has left people free to choose where to live, work, and travel, and material opportunities expand year by year. A decade ago, most cars belonged to state enterprises; now many families own one. In 1998, when the government launched reforms to commercialize the housing market, it was the rare person who owned an apartment. Today home ownership is common, and prices have risen beyond what many young couples can afford—as if everything that happened in America over fifty years were collapsed into a single decade.

But pick up a Chinese newspaper, and what comes through is a sense of unease at the pace of social change. Over several months in 2006, these were some of the trends covered in the *Xinmin Evening News,* a popular Shanghai daily: high school girls were suffering from eating disorders. Parents were struggling to choose a suitable English name for their child. Teenage boys were reading novels with homosexual themes. Job seekers were besieging Buddhist temples because the word for "reclining Buddha," *wofo,* sounds like the English word "offer." Unwed college students were living together.

Parents struggle to teach their children but feel their own knowledge is obsolete; children, more attuned to social trends, guide their parents through the maze of modern life. "Society has completely turned around," says Zhou Xiaohong, a sociologist at Nanjing University, who first noticed this phenomenon when his own father, a retired military officer, asked him how to knot a Western tie. "Fathers used to give orders, but now fathers listen to their sons."

Because their parents have such high hopes for them, children are among the most pressured, inhabiting a world that combines old and new, and features the most punishing elements of both. The traditional examination system that selects a favored few for higher education remains intact: The number of students entering college in a given year is equal to 11 percent of the college-freshman-age population, compared with 64 percent in the United States. Yet the desire to foster well-rounded students has fed an explosion of activities—music lessons, English, drawing, and martial arts classes—and turned each into an arena of competition.

Such pursuits bring little pleasure. English ability is graded on five levels, stretching through college, and parents push children to pass tests years ahead of schedule. Cities assess children's piano playing on a ten-level scale. More than half of preteens take outside classes, a survey found, with the top reason being "to raise the child's future competitiveness."

Parents tend to follow trends blindly and to believe most of what they hear. The past is a foreign country, and the present too. "We are a traditional family" was how Bella's mother, Qi Xiayun, introduced herself when I first met her in 2003. She was thirty-three years old, with the small, pale face of a girl, and she spoke in a nonstop torrent about the difficulty of raising a child. She teaches computer classes at a vocational college; her husband works in quality control at Baosteel, a state-owned company. They were appointed to those jobs after college as part of the last generation to join the socialist workforce before it started to break apart.

Bella's parents met the old-fashioned way, introduced by their parents. But after they had Bella in 1993, they turned their backs on tradition. They chose not to eat dinner with their in-laws every night and rejected old-fashioned child-rearing methods that tend to coddle children.

When Bella was not yet two, her grandmother offered to care for the baby, but her mother worried that the grandparents would spoil her. Bella went to day care instead. When she entered third grade, her mother stopped picking her up after school, forcing her to change buses and cross streets alone. "Sooner or later she must learn independence," her mother said.

So Bella grew up, a chatty girl with Pippi Longstocking pigtails and many opinions—too many for the Chinese schoolroom. In second grade, she and several classmates marched to the principal's office to demand more time to play; the protest failed. Her teachers criticized her temper and her tendency to bully other children. "Your ability is strong," read a first-grade report card, "but a person must learn from the strengths of others in order to improve." In second grade: "Hope you can listen to other people's opinions more."

The effort to shape Bella is full of contradictions. Her parents encourage her independence but worry that school and the workplace will punish her for it. They fret over her homework load, then pile more assignments on top of her regular schoolwork. "We don't want to be brutal to her," says Bella's father, Zhou Jiliang. "But in China, the environment doesn't let you do anything else."

Bella teaches her parents the latest slang and shows them cool Internet sites. When they bought a new TV, Bella chose the brand. When they go out to eat, Bella picks Pizza Hut. One day soon, her parents worry, her schoolwork will move beyond their ability to help her. When Bella was younger, her parents began unplugging the computer keyboard and mouse so she wouldn't go online when she was home alone, but they knew this wouldn't last.

Recently, Bella's father and his sister and cousins put their grandfather in a nursing home. It was a painful decision; in traditional China, caring for aged parents was an ironclad responsibility, and Bella's parents have extra room in their apartment for their parents to move in some day. But Bella announced that she would one day put her parents in the best nursing home.

"The minute she said that, I thought: It's true, we don't want to be a burden on her," Bella's father says. "When we are old, we'll sell the house, take a trip and see the world, and enter the nursing home and live a quiet life there. This is the education my daughter gives me."

I went to school with Bella one Friday in her fifth-grade year. She sat up in bed at 6:25, pulled on pants and an orange sweatshirt, and tied a Young Pioneers kerchief around her neck. Her parents rushed through the cramped apartment getting ready for work, and breakfast was lost in the shuffle. Bella's mother walked her to the corner, then Bella sighed and headed to the bus stop alone. "This is the most free I am the whole day."

Today there would be elections for class cadres, positions that mirror those in the Communist Party. "My mother says to be a cadre in fifth grade is very important," Bella said.

The bus dropped us off at the elite Yangpu Primary School, which cost $1,200 a year in tuition and fees and rejected 80 percent of its applicants. Her classroom was sunny and loud with the roar of children kept indoors. It had several computers and a bulletin board with student-written movie reviews: *The Birth of New China*, *Finding Nemo*.

By 8:30 the students were seated at their desks for elections. Their pretty young teacher asked for candidates. Everyone wanted to run.

"This semester I want to change my bad nail-biting habits, so people don't call me the Nail-Biting King," said a boy running for propaganda officer.

"I will not interrupt in class," said a girl in a striped sweater running for children's officer. "Please everyone vote for me."

The speeches followed a set pattern: name a personal flaw, pledge to fix it, and ask for votes. It was self-criticism as campaign strategy.

Those who strayed from the script were singled out. "My grades are not very good because I write a lot of words wrong," said one girl running for academic officer. "Please everyone vote for me."

"You write words wrong, please vote for me?" the teacher mimicked. "What have you left out?"

The girl tried again. "I want to work to fix this bad habit. Please everyone vote for me."

Bella delivered her pitch for sports officer. "I am very responsible, and my management abilities are pretty good," she said breathlessly. "Sometimes I have conflicts with other students. If you vote for me, it will help me change my bad habits. Please everyone give me your vote."

In a three-way race, Bella squeaked to victory by a single ballot. Election day, like everything in school, ended with a moral. "Don't feel bad if you lost this time," the teacher said. "It just means you must work even harder. You shouldn't let yourself relax just because you lost."

The language of child education is Darwinian. "The elections teach students to toughen themselves," Bella's teacher, Lu Yan, said over lunch in the teachers' cafeteria. "In the future they will face pressure and competition. They need to know how to face defeat."

Some schools link teacher pay to student test performance, and the pressure on teachers is intense. Bella's class had recently seen a drop in grades, and the teacher begged parents to help identify the cause. Lu Yan had just gotten her four-year college degree at night school and planned to study English next. All her colleagues were enrolled in outside classes; even the vice-principal took a weekend class on educational technology. A math teacher was fired three weeks into the school year because parents complained she covered too little material in class.

Life will not always feel like this. The next generation of parents, having grown up with choice and competition, may feel less driven to place all their hopes on their children. "Right now is the hardest time," says Wang Jie, a sociologist, who is herself the mother of an only child. "In my generation we have both traditional and new ideas. Inside us the two worlds are at war."

In math class later that day, the fifth graders whipped through dividing decimals using Math Olympics methods, which train kids to use mental shortcuts. They raced across a field in gym class, with the slowest person in each group punished with an extra lap around the track. School ended at 1:30 on Fridays. The bus let Bella off outside her building, where she bought a popsicle and headed inside. Her weekend was packed with private tutoring, so Friday was the best time to finish her homework.

I told her that no American ten-year-old did homework on a Friday afternoon.

"They must be very happy," Bella said.

In the five years since I met Bella and her family, their lives have transformed. They moved into a new three-bedroom apartment—it is almost twice the size of their old one, which they now rent out—and furnished it with foreign brand-name appliances. They bought their first car, a Volkswagen Bora, and from taking the bus, they went straight to driving everywhere. They eat out a couple of times a week now, and the air-conditioner stays on all summer. At twelve, Bella got her first mobile phone—a $250 Panasonic clamshell in Barbie pink. Her parents' annual income reached $18,000, up 40 percent from when we first met.

As the material circumstances of Bella's family improved, the world became to them a more perilous place. Their cleaning lady stole from them and disappeared. Several friends were in near-fatal car accidents. One day Bella's father saw her holding a letter from a man she'd met online. Bella's parents changed the locks and the phone number of the apartment. Her father drove her to and from school now, because he thought the neighborhood around it was unsafe.

Bella's mother took on more administrative responsibilities at work and enrolled in a weekend class to qualify to study for a master's degree. Bella's father talked about trading in their car for a newer model with better acceleration and more legroom. They frequently spoke of themselves as if they were mobile phones on the verge of obsolescence. "If you don't continue to upgrade and recharge," Bella's father said, "you'll be eliminated."

Social mobility ran in both directions. A friend of Bella's mother stopped attending class reunions because he was embarrassed to be a security guard. A company run by a family friend went bankrupt, and his daughter, who was Bella's age, started buying clothes at discount stalls. Society was splintering based on small differences. Family members only a decade younger than Bella's parents inhabited another world. One cousin ate out every night and left her baby in the care of her grandparents so she could focus on her career. Bella's father's younger sister, who was childless, thought nothing of buying a full-fare plane ticket to go somewhere for a weekend. Friends who were private entrepreneurs were having a second child and paying a fine; Bella's parents would probably be fired by their state-owned employers if they did that.

Bella tested into one of Shanghai's top middle schools, where teachers often keep students past five in the evening, while their parents wait in cars outside. She is in level three in English and level eight in piano. She still ranks in the middle of her class, but she no longer has faith in the world of adults.

She disdains class elections now. "It's a lot of work," she says, "and the teacher is always pointing to you as a role model. If you get in trouble and get demoted, it's a big embarrassment." She loves Hollywood films—especially *Star Wars* and disaster movies—and spends hours online with friends discussing Detective Conan, a character from Japanese comic books. She intends to marry a foreigner because they are richer and more reliable.

Her parents no longer help with her homework; in spoken English, she has surpassed them. They lecture her to be less wasteful. "When she was little, she agreed with all my opinions. Now she sits there without saying anything, but I know she doesn't agree with me," her mother said one afternoon in the living room of their new apartment, as Bella glared without speaking. "Our child-raising has been a failure." In China, there is no concept of the rebellious teenager.

Across Chinese society, parents appear completely at sea when it comes to raising their children. Newspapers run advice columns, their often rudimentary counsel—"Don't Forcibly Plan Your Child's Life" is a typical headline—suggesting what many parents are up against. Some schools have set up parent schools where mothers, and the occasional father, can share frustrations and child-raising tips.

At times educators go to extremes: At the Zhongguancun No. 2 Primary School in Beijing, vice-principal Lu Suqin recently took two fifth-grade boys into her home. "Their parents couldn't get them to behave, so they asked me to take them," she explains. "After they learn disciplined living, I will send them back."

Bella had one free day during the 2006 weeklong National Day holiday. Some of her extended family—seven adults and two children—took a trip to Tongli, a town of imperial mansions an hour's drive from Shanghai. Bella's father hired a minibus and driver for the trip; a friend had just been in a car accident and broken all the bones on one side of his body. Bella sat alone reading a book.

Developing China zipped past the window, city sprawl giving way to a booming countryside of fishponds and factories, and the three-story houses of prosperous farmers. Bella's mother indulged in the quintessential urban dream of a house in the country. "You have your own little yard in front," she said. "I'd love to live in a place like that when we retire."

She was thinking seriously about Bella's future. If she tested into a good college, she should stay in China; otherwise, she would go abroad, and they would sell the old apartment to pay for it. She had decided that Bella could date in college. "If she finds someone suitable in the third or fourth year of college, that's fine. But not in the first or second year."

"And not in high school?" I asked.

"No. Study should be most important."

Tongli was mobbed with holiday visitors. Bella's family walked through its courtyards and gardens like sleepwalkers, admiring whatever the tour guides pointed out. They touched the trunk of the Health and Long Life Tree. They circled a stone mosaic said to bring career success. They could not stop walking for an instant, because crowds pressed in from behind. It was the biggest tourist day of the year.

Bella politely translated for a great-aunt visiting from Australia who didn't speak Chinese, but it was just an act. "This is boring," she told me. "Once you've seen one old building, you've seen them all."

I sat with her on the ride home. She was deep into a Korean romance novel.

"It's about high school students," she said. "Three boys chasing a girl."

"Do people have boyfriends and girlfriends in high school?" I asked.

"Yes."

"What about middle school?"

"Yes. Some."

"Do you have a boyfriend?"

She wrinkled her nose. "There's a boy who likes me. But all the boys in my grade are very low-class."

She wanted to go to Australia for graduate school and to work there afterward. She could make more money there and bring her parents to live with her. "On the surface China looks luxurious, but underneath it is chaos," Bella said. "Everything is so corrupt."

Some observers of Chinese society look at children like Bella and see political change: her generation of individualists, they predict, will one day demand a say in how they are governed. But the reality is complicated. Raised and educated within the system, they are just as likely to find ways to accommodate themselves to it, as they have done all along.

"Just because they're curious to see something doesn't mean they want it for themselves," says Zhang Kai, Bella's middle-school teacher. "Maybe they will try something—dye their hair, or pierce an ear—but in their bones, they are very traditional. In her heart, Zhou Jiaying is very traditional," he says, and he uses Bella's Chinese name.

Bella is fifteen now, in the ninth grade. She has good friends among her classmates, and she has learned how to get along with others. School is a complicated place. One classmate bullied another boy, and the victim's parents came to school to complain. Because they were politically influential, they forced the teacher to transfer the bully out of the class.

The incident divided Bella's class, and now her friends in the Tire Clique won't speak to her friends in the Pirate Clique. A friend got into school without taking the entrance exam because her mother's colleague had a cousin in the education bureau.

Bella's teacher nominated some students for membership in the Communist Youth League. Bella thought it meaningless, but she fell into line and pulled an application essay off the Internet. She couldn't afford to get on her teacher's bad side, she told me, citing a proverb: "A person who stands under someone else's roof must bow his head."

The high school entrance exam is a month away. In the evenings, Bella's father watches television on mute so he won't disturb her studies. A good friend is also an enemy, because they vie for the same class rank. Her compositions describe what the pressure feels like:

> I sit in my middle-school classroom, and the teacher wants us to say goodbye to childhood. I feel at a loss. Happiness is like the twinkling stars suffusing the night sky of childhood. I want only more and more stars. I don't want to see the dawn.

CHAPTER 15

Shredding for the Motherland

JAMES MILLWARD

In the fall of 1990, less than a year after the crushing of student-led protests in China, the U.S. government dispatched Vic Trigger to Beijing. Trigger's mission? To teach China's youth to shred.

"He had the hair, he had the clothes," recalls R. Bin Wong, a professor of Chinese history at the University of California, Los Angeles, who happened to be seated next to Trigger on the plane. "His only carry-on was the guitar."

Tall and lanky, with dark wavy hair tumbling around a mousy face, Vic Trigger had been tasked, at that delicate moment in Sino-U.S. relations, with showing aspiring Chinese guitarists how to play hard and fast rock guitar. Trigger was teaching guitar and music theory at the Guitar Institute of Technology (GIT) in Hollywood, California, when the U.S. Information Agency invited him on a three-week teaching tour of China. Before that, Trigger had his own band and taught guitar out of a house that he shared with band mates and various hangers-on in the San Jose area. Greg Kim, who was Trigger's student in the late 1970s, recalls Trigger jotting notes in a journal or fiddling with guitar effects during their lessons. (The lessons grew longer once Kim's sister, forced by their parents to drive her little brother to guitar lessons, started passing the time by smoking pot and fooling around with the bass player in a locked bedroom.) The Vic Trigger Band played the local Veterans of Foreign Wars hall and released one album. Song titles such as "Get High and Space Out" and "Roll and Smoke and Deal" "pretty much summed up the philosophy of the band," Kim recalls in his blog.

Thus ideally suited as a U.S. cultural ambassador, Trigger found himself a few years later standing in front of a hundred students in Beijing, one of four cities on his China tour. Most of the Beijing kids had backgrounds only in classical music or Chinese traditional instruments. A third of them were members of the classically focused Beijing Guitar Association, then just a few years old. They nonetheless formed an eager audience for his progressive rock style and—despite translation problems, a large dose of theory, and classes that began too early in the morning for budding rock stars—U.S. embassy officials pronounced the tour a resounding success.

But Vic Trigger had hardly parachuted into a rock music vacuum. The Chinese folk-rocker Cui Jian's music was ubiquitous in Beijing that year, and his songs—steeped in alienation, if not shredding—had served as anthems on Tiananmen Square in 1989. The pointed love-and-politics allegory "A Piece of Red Cloth" was quickly banned, but Cui's "Nothing to My Name," a youth lament set to a northwestern Chinese folk melody, resonated through the grim months that followed the crackdown. Moreover, Trigger encountered many good guitarists who were living long-haired, high-volume, hash-smoking lives in the Beijing rock demimonde. Kaiser Kuo, the Chinese-American co-founder of the Chinese metal band Tang Dynasty (Tang Chao) and a heavy metal missionary himself (he is now head of international public relations for Baidu, China's Google), recalls Vic Trigger's USIA-sponsored visit as a "transparent and comical attempt at subversion of state power through rock—a kind of hard rock soft power."

He has a point: Tang Dynasty, like Cui Jian and other formative rock bands, were still marginal compared to syrupy Hong Kong pop stars, but they enjoyed popularity and influence orders of magnitude beyond that of the Vic Trigger Band's brief heyday. Still, the eager intermediate guitarists who made up Trigger's audience got much from the encounter: one admitted to having been "converted" from classical to rock music by exposure to a foreign musician. And whatever State Department official dreamed up the idea of sending a guitar missionary to China in 1990 was on the right track; the guitar was huge in China then.

I never met Vic Trigger, though I was in Beijing at the same time and was in a modest way caught up in rising guitar fever. In my spare time away from dissertation research at People's (Renmin) University,

I made friends with Zhang Zhining, an international business student whose intense interest in the guitar was nearly overwhelming. As an English-speaking guitarist, I was irresistible to him, and he dropped by my dorm room almost daily. My finger-style playing or the idea of just jamming for fun intrigued but failed to impress Zhang. Instead, he brought photocopies of pirated Japanese transcriptions of Mozart and Beethoven: he wanted us to practice these awkward duets outdoors in the campus park, where we could better meet girls. (Some things are universal.) Though dubious of the musical and amatory prospects of this approach, I couldn't resist Zhang's energy and duly dusted off my classical chops.

One day Zhang casually mentioned an upcoming meeting of the People's University Guitar Club. He asked me to play for the group. "No big deal," he said. "Just drop by Friday night and play some of those American things you play."

What Zhang failed to tell me was that the Guitar Club was one of the few college clubs allowed to convene following the suppression of the Tiananmen Square protests of 1989, and its meetings were the most popular events on the People's University campus in those days. I only learned how popular the meetings were when I was thrust onto a large stage in front of several hundred students. I was the main act and apparently billed as a noted American guitar *gaoshou* (master). Alas, many in the audience were disappointed.

Despite its name, People's University was known as a school for the well-connected, politically reliable children of Party and government officials. Peking University, aka Beida (short for Beijing Daxue), where much of the momentum for the 1989 student movement was built, was a different story. Its campus activities remained restricted far longer than those of People's University. In the early spring of 1990, however, Zhang told me that the Beida Guitar Club had been given the green light to reconvene. He had Beida connections and took me along to one of the Beida Guitar Club's first meetings.

The Beida Guitar Club meeting was a much more intimate affair than the big show at People's University. Because university authorities would have been alarmed to see a foreigner at the club session, Zhang walked me into Beida without fanfare or officially registering me at the gate. The meeting was in an older building on campus, where thirty or forty students were gathered in a classroom lit with dozens of candles, clutching their guitars. True to the coffee-house atmosphere, the music was folksy and a bit political; the climax of the evening came when the

Beida students collectively strummed and sang Cui Jian's "A Piece of Red Cloth," in which a narrator ironically relates his happiness at being blindfolded in red cloth and led down the road by a master with hands as warm as fresh blood. Today, the image of these students at Beida—roughly, China's Harvard—reviving a banned Tiananmen anthem in a candle-lit classroom seems like a final frisson of student political engagement that has given way to the present's frenzied consumerism. But what struck me at the time was the bizarreness of forty guitars strumming at the same time. The candles, the tweaking of authority, and the bohemian ethos were all familiar to someone whose college years began before the Reagan presidency. But you'd never have heard forty guitars together like that on an American campus. The guitar in China struck many familiar notes, but something about the whole chord rang differently.

Although not a recent arrival, the guitar was still new enough in China in the early 1990s to cause excitement. In fact, in our own ways, Vic Trigger and I had stumbled onto the second guitar boom in China's modern history. Western missionaries may have brought lutes, vihuelas, and other guitar-like instruments to parts of China by the sixteenth-century, but their memoirs mention only keyboard instruments and bowed string ensembles. It was probably in the late nineteenth or early twentieth centuries that the guitar became known in China's coastal cities. By the 1920s and 1930s, the instrument was all the rage in Shanghai and Hong Kong, cosmopolitan cities with broad Western and Asian connections. Famous stars appeared with guitars in movies made in Shanghai's film studios. Models posed with Western stringed instruments. *Ling Long,* a magazine for sophisticated "modern girls," ran several portraits in the mid-1930s of fashionably dressed young ladies playing or holding guitars, ukuleles, or mandolins. In one, a woman with bobbed hair and a *qipao* dress with modish diagonal stripes mimes playing guitar in a garden. The caption reads, "Miss Xu, in this tranquil place, play a song for us!" In another, a girl labeled "healthy and beautiful" lounges in a bathing suit, cradling a ukulele in her lap. In a third, a girl in revealing tank top and short shorts lies on her back, one knee raised, her loose hair provocatively splayed on the courtyard floor behind her. "Only *she,*" the caption sighs, "can fully express such a life of natural beauty." The head of a mandolin rests against her breast and her slender fingers toy with the tuning pegs.

These Western stringed instruments made it possible (in a way Chinese instruments do not) for young Chinese to accompany themselves singing popular songs of the day, and to do so in parks and other outdoor settings (as the piano does not). The guitar in China in this era was associated with youth and freedom—as it was in many other places. But in China it bore an added sense of sophistication and cosmopolitanism, because the guitar was—and would remain for decades—classed as a foreign instrument.

These associations got the guitar in trouble when China's political vicissitudes led to anti-Western isolationism during the Cultural Revolution in the 1960s and 1970s. Notwithstanding their revolutionary romanticism, the millions of young Red Guards then roaming the country and challenging authority were not playing guitars, which were condemned as Western and decadent, associated with "hooligans" (*liumang*). Young people might accompany anthems to Mao on the accordion, harmonica and autoharp. And it was permitted to play the "balalaika," a three-stringed banjo-like instrument. These were functionally similar to simple guitars, but round in shape—Russian balalaikas are in fact triangular—with backs decorated with such Maoisms as "Never forget class struggle!" Now these instruments are coveted pieces of Cultural Revolution memorabilia.

As the Cultural Revolution wound down in the late 1970s, the guitar returned, as much an icon as a musical instrument. One emblematic figure of that era was the "false foreign devil," the newest avatar of the *liumang* hooligan. He wore long hair, tight or bell-bottom pants, sunglasses (often with the tag still dangling), and carried a guitar. The philosopher Zhao Yuesheng describes his first encounter with the type in 1978 or 1979:

> I opened the gate and entered the yard [of a friend's old courtyard home in Beijing] and saw a guy standing under the big tree. He was tall—close to six feet—with broad shoulders, a narrow waist, and long legs. On close inspection he looked like a wild tartar [*huren*] with his fair complexion, prominent brows, deep-set eyes, broad forehead, square face, and high-bridged nose. His long hair swept his shoulders, and the tight trousers left the rounds of his buttocks clearly visible. Today, we'd call this "sexy." In the opinion of the time, it was "hooligan." His left hand leaned against the trunk of the walnut tree; from his right shoulder hung a big guitar, its coppery finish already worn off.

Used to seeing people dressed in standard loose-fitting workers' and soldiers' clothes, Zhao was startled by the man's getup, which reminded him of Hong Kong or Taiwanese styles. They went inside the house, which belonged to a young woman of their mutual acquaintance. Zhao was curious to hear this young man, whose name was Tang-ke, play the guitar and sing—something Zhao had only read about in novels, but had never heard before. Though Tang-ke was obviously courting the woman, Zhao was the one most affected when the guitarist softly strummed chords and sang a love song called "Blue Streetlight" in a rough but melodic voice. Compared to the strident martial anthems to Mao Zedong that Zhao had grown up with, this song was drenched in "consumptive sentimentality, and so—'capitalist'"! In the late 1970s, then, while no longer entirely banned in China, the guitar was not familiar to everyone. In America, the instrument often signified a bohemian or hippie lifestyle and conveyed a folksy authenticity. In China, the guitar was an accessory to jeans and long hair and suggested something foreign, new, transgressive, and even sophisticated. Some Chinese disdained the guitar for its associations with social rebels, long-haired lowlifes, and the blindly xenophiliac. But to others, for largely the same reasons, it exercised an irresistible allure.

Disdain for déclassé uses of the guitar was not unique to China, of course. The guitar maestro Andrés Segovia, who sought to "rescue" the instrument for classical music, hated both the flamenco music of his native Spain, which he thought coarse, and the abomination of rock. Nevertheless, Chen Zhi, who more than anyone else is credited with making the guitar respectable in China in the eyes of both the Party state and Chinese parents, knows a good deal about surmounting a bad reputation.

I went to see Chen in Beijing one November afternoon in 2007. A pretty young woman in red cashmere, with a neat short hairstyle and long fingers, met me outside the subway exit. She introduced herself as Li Jie, and she looked to be in her early twenties, so I took her for a student just starting a musical career. I somehow imagined her teaching small children, maybe in a kindergarten somewhere. She chatted with me nervously while we walked past an enormous new Wo-er-ma (Walmart) and rounded the corner to the clean, new buildings of a high school associated with the Central Conservatory of Music. In the elevator, with an apologetic air and some self-deprecatory words, she handed me her doctoral dissertation on Segovia. I later learned that besides holding a Ph.D., Dr. Li Jie is an internationally recognized virtuosa, winner of the second international guitar competition in Hong Kong and a frequent performer throughout China and East Asia with the "super trio" known as "God's Favored Girls" and with a quartet of Chen's former students called the "Four Angels."

Chen was teaching a roomful of students aged nine to their late teens, all eagerly attentive despite the fact that it was a Sunday, their one day off each week. Winter sunlight slanted through upper-story windows while Chen, trim in slacks and a turtleneck sweater, put them through their paces. As Li Jie led me in, one student, performing a study by the Paraguayan composer Agustín Barrios, was having some trouble with his tone on a guitar he'd borrowed for the day.

"If you ride your own steed, it doesn't matter if it's a donkey, it will run like a horse. If you ride someone else's, even if it's a stallion, it will run like a donkey," Chen told the boy.

For another student, Chen compared the structure of Johann Sebastian Bach's *Prelude, Fugue and Allegro for Lute* (BWV 998) to that of a four-story building. With a third, who was attempting to practice a challenging piece too fast, he discussed tempo using the metaphor of money. The students intently absorbed their teacher's epigrams and talked easily with him, notwithstanding the five or six decades dividing them.

Chen was born in 1936 in Shanghai on the eve of the Japanese occupation. His father, General Chen Cheng, was then leading the Nationalist (Guomindang) military campaign to eradicate the Communists. Chen Cheng later fought the Japanese invaders, then fought the Communists again. Following the defeat of the Guomindang, he went with Chiang Kai-shek to Taiwan, where he served in several top government posts. Chen Zhi, however, remained on the mainland with his mother. With such a famous father, Chen could not go to ordinary schools, so he was taught at home by tutors, including aristocratic White Russians, for whom Shanghai was a haven after the Bolshevik Revolution. The Russians taught him violin and piano formally, but some of them also played guitar for fun, leaving a deep impression on Chen. He fooled around with the instrument on his own, learning a bit from books, recordings, and concerts in Shanghai. At university in the 1950s, Chen majored in mathematics and was assigned to work as a math instructor at the Beijing Engineering Institute when he graduated. He began studying guitar more seriously, but still as a hobby.

The guitar was not at all popular outside of the cosmopolitan cities of Shanghai and Hong Kong. When a state film production company wished to use guitar in the soundtrack to a documentary entitled *Chairman Liu Shaoqi's State Visit to Indonesia*, they scoured the official music and arts groups in Beijing in vain for a guitarist. Finally, Chen was seconded from his math teaching to record the guitar parts. This footage of President Liu Shaoqi's 1963 tour of Southeast Asia would play an infamous role in later history. At official events, including a state dinner with Indonesia's President Sukarno, Liu's wife, Wang Guangmei, wore a tight-fitting *qipao* dress and a string of pearls. When Mao turned on Liu as a "capitalist roader" in the late 1960s, Red Guards dragged the former first lady to mass criticism rallies in *qipao*s accessorized with necklaces of ping-pong balls to mock her. Chen's foreign-sounding guitar soundtrack to the film cannot have helped.

The Cultural Revolution was also difficult for Chen Zhi personally. He doesn't like to discuss this period, but the Maoist chaos of the Cultural Revolution in the late 1960s and early 1970s was a bad time to be the guitar-playing White-Russian-educated biological son of the second-in-command of Communist China's arch-enemy. During the Cultural Revolution, Chen Zhi pedaled a tricycle cart at a vegetable farm for ten years. On the side, he taught a bit of harmonica, but he had no chance to practice guitar.

In 1980, Chen went abroad, reunited with relatives, and came into some property. Back in Beijing, he launched the first of many initiatives to promote the guitar in China. In 1982, he opened the Beijing Sincere Will [*chengzhi,* a word combining his father's and his own given names] Classical Guitar School, said to have been the first such institution in China. Two years later, he began broadcasting weekly guitar classes on Central People's Television. In 1986, he founded and became chairman of the Beijing Guitar Association, which, like all civic organizations in China, had to be officially approved, and whose members would make up a third of Vic Trigger's students in 1990. In subsequent years, under Chen Zhi, the Beijing Guitar Association organized China's first international guitar festival and a training class for teachers in 1987, a guitar competition in 1988, and an ongoing series of concerts and exchanges with international performers. Chen established the classical guitar major and became the first professor of guitar at the Central Conservatory of Music. As the Chinese publication *Zhonghua Yingcai* (China's Talents) put it, "He wants to make China, with her ten million guitar enthusiasts, into a 'guitar world power.'"

I talked with Chen Zhi after his class, while Li Jie hovered over us, poured tea and then ran off to photocopy materials Chen wanted to give to me. Chen had just returned from the Guitar Federation of America's convention in Los Angeles, where two of his students had placed first and third among children aged fourteen and under, and another had tied for second place among those aged from fifteen to eighteen. Chen's students (including one from Korea) thus took three of the eight youth prizes in this truly international competition. Chen has made a specialty of turning out guitar wunderkinder in short order. His first student to claim international attention was Wang Yameng, who took first prize in the thirty-sixth Tokyo International Guitar Competition in 1993. Though she was participating in an adult competition, Wang won at age twelve, after only five years of study. Wang's victory in Tokyo was especially sweet, because just six years earlier, the Japanese classical guitarist Fukuda Shinichi had predicted, while visiting China for one of Chen's festivals, that Chinese guitar music would need three decades to catch up to "world levels." Other young students of Chen's have taken prizes in Hong Kong, Paris, and Vienna. Several of his former students—so far all young women—now perform around the world as soloists, or with one another in various duo, trio, and quartet ensembles. Like so many other things in China, classical guitar has developed fast.

"I'll speak frankly with you," Chen said, sitting back in an armchair in an office adjacent to his classroom. "The piano has been in China for a century, with several generations studying it, so we can have someone famous like Lang Lang on the international stage. The violin likewise—there are many international-class Chinese violinists. But the guitar only started with me, with my school in 1982 and at the Conservatory from 1990. Now my students are winning these competitions—in terms of speed, this is much faster than violin or piano."

With his students' sudden emergence to global prominence, Chen himself has become an international figure, sought after to give master classes and speak about his methods that raise students to technical mastery in just a few years. In conversing with Chen Zhi, it was clear how much the growth of the guitar in China is measured in terms of international recognition and acclaim, and what a nationalistic project it is. "Without Deng Xiaoping's reform and opening up," Chen told me, "I would not have been able to learn on my own how to teach guitar." But, he hastens to add, he developed his own method and does not subscribe to any of the known established "schools" of guitar training.

"Now, I could be abroad all the time," he told me. "When I teach in Korea, or Paris, I get 1,000 euros for a day's work—much more than I could earn here. But I choose to stay in China. Chinese children are like the fine woods used for making instruments: without good wood, you can't make a good guitar." Chen's hands, the right-hand nails carefully filed and buffed, shaped a guitar in the air. "So I want to live in China, with all this good wood, where I can chose among them. There are good children in the West as well, but because those countries are so developed, there are too many things to play with. To learn an instrument, you have to study really hard. And compared to my kids—the Western kids are just playing around."

Chen's goals go beyond elevating Chinese concert guitarists to the world stage. He hopes to bring the guitar to the Chinese masses, to use the guitar to "raise their level of spiritual civilization," as a "bridge from cultural illiteracy to literacy." Pianos, he goes on, are too expensive and delicate for the countryside, and the violin is simply too hard to get started on. "But anyone can learn to play simple guitar and sing songs. Even in the army now, every unit has a few guitars. You have to start simple with guitar, especially with young people. Therefore, I say, Chen Zhi is not only a teacher of a musical instrument, but an education worker constructing spiritual civilization. I see myself as having quite a significant job, to raise the level of spiritual civilization. I see myself doing this kind of work for the nation."

I left Chen Zhi impressed, not only by his sincerity, warmth, and bevy of elegant, disciplined, technically superb, and musically sophisticated disciples, but by his dedication to the guitar and to China. He is proud of himself, and with good reason. By returning to the mainland in the 1980s and investing in a guitar school, despite the persecution he suffered for his family background, Chen demonstrated a unique patriotism and, indeed, vision. I was about to meet someone I thought would be very different: a lead guitarist in the heavy metal bands Spring and Autumn (Chunqiu) and Suffocated (Zhixi), a young man who, I had been told, "totally shreds."

. . .

Truth be told, I was a little apprehensive about meeting Kou Zhengyu. Kaiser Kuo suggested I talk to him and showed me pictures from the liner notes of Suffocated's new CD, *Dead Wind Rising*. Photographed eerily from below against a bleak, blasted landscape, the four band members were an even split between skinhead bruisers with pointy goatees, and head-whirling guitar warriors with sleek black manes. I had heard a track or two: a nasty growl with all the tunefulness of throat-singing Tibetan monks, set against a crunching tattoo of distortion. Suffocated's sound reminded me of an MRI I once underwent to rule out a possible brain tumor. Kou and I were to meet up at 3 P.M.

in central Beijing, and I wondered what back-alley bar or smoky basement crash pad we would conduct our business in.

My worries were misplaced. Xiao (little) Kou, as he asked me to call him, gave my hand a soft shake and escorted me into a KFC on the northern end of Wangfujing, Beijing's main and increasingly ritzy shopping district, dense with international hotels and department stores. He insisted on buying me, the foreign guest, coffee and French fries. We sat by a tiled wall at a plastic table under fluorescent lights, where toddlers from a neighboring booth scurried happily all around us. Xiao Kou wore a black T-shirt, requisite uniform of Chinese rockers, but that was the darkest thing about him. This Chinese thrash metal rocker is a sweet guy.

Kou, then thirty, came of age a decade after the post–Cultural Revolution *liumang* hooligans first took up the guitar. He saw the *liumang* through the eyes of his elder siblings, who were entrenched in that countercultural milieu.

"In those days, people who wanted to play guitar would hang out and *chaqin.*"

"*Chaqin?*" I asked.

"It was like a contest for playing guitar." I thought of Chen Zhi's students in their pretty recital dresses winning international competitions.

"Except," Xiao Kou added, "if you lost, you got beaten up and your instrument was smashed."

"Ah."

Despite the incentives of competition, Xiao Kou told me, nobody could play very well in those days. In a few years, the guitar became more acceptable. The pop song (*liuxing gequ*) emerged in China, and by the mid-1980s, hits of a more or less global style came in from Hong Kong and Taiwan. There were "pictures in the magazines of a stupid girl hugging a guitar." Kids asked their parents to pay for guitar lessons at their schools, and though parents were willing to do so, none of the teachers were very good. "They were just those same *chaqin* guys who'd been smashing each other's guitars a few years earlier," Xiao Kou laughed.

Xiao Kou told me how he got his first electric guitar, started playing metal music, and put a band together. It was, in many ways, a typical story, the teenage male rock fantasy satirized in the movie *Wayne's World*—but with Chinese characteristics I was now beginning to recognize. At first, Xiao Kou fooled around on old acoustic guitars with his friends and barely knew what an electric guitar sounded like. He had heard foreign rock music, especially Metallica, on copied and recopied cassettes, but he didn't put the distorted sounds together with his image of guitars. He thought it required many people playing together to make such a loud noise. Eventually, he saw pictures of the first Chinese metal bands, Black Panther and Tang Dynasty, in a music store, and suddenly realized, not only that electric guitars were making the sounds, but that "Chinese can do this too!"

By the time he graduated from middle school, he had to go electric. A co-worker in the bar where he worked part-time offered him an old electric guitar, but Xiao Kou still needed money to buy an amplifier. He raised the 110 yuan by selling all his old electronic games with an advertisement that read, "Please help support Chinese Rock Music!" Funds in hand, he and a friend picked up the guitar and amp and wheeled the gear home strapped to the back of bicycles, because they couldn't afford to hire a cab. At home, they discovered that only the three highest strings on Xiao Kou's new guitar actually sounded because of a wiring problem. All six strings worked on his friend's guitar, so he played rhythm, and Xiao Kou became, by default, the lead guitarist.

Xiao Kou and his friends progressed through the usual stages of rock band development, learning about effects boxes, studiously ignoring the giggly high school girls smoking and acting cool around the gym where they practiced, gradually getting more organized, growing long hair, writing their own material, all the while upgrading their gear. (Korean guitars were thought to be better than Chinese, and Japanese better than Korean, though Japanese guitars were largely made in Taiwan.) They'd all left school by now. Xiao Kou had a good position in the Beijing office of a Japanese firm—his father had helped him get the job—but he often called in sick to play the guitar, and one day in 1997, he just quit. If he'd stayed at the job, he mused to me, by now he'd have been able to buy a nice apartment. But he wanted to try working full-time at music.

It was a decision with serious consequences at home. When his father found out that his son had walked away from a job that had taken so many favors from acquaintances to get, he was furious. "My parents said to me, 'What are you doing? You haven't got a job, you're growing long hair, you think you're an artist, but you're nothing.'" They asked him to move out, and he did.

But Suffocated gradually began getting gigs at more prominent venues. They made a little money, and together with income from the guitar students he taught (and a loan here and there from girlfriends), Xiao Kou got by.

"If there was a poster saying Suffocated was playing somewhere, I'd go home when my parents were out and leave it on the table," Xiao Kou said. "They'd see it and think, 'Hmmm, what's this?' At first they thought if I wasn't making any money, what was the point? Later as we developed, if there was an item in the paper or a magazine, I'd leave it for them to see. Slowly they've come around to accept that I'm really doing something—not like ten years ago when I first quit the job."

I asked Kou whether he was socially accepted, or if people saw him as a *liumang* playing foreign music.

"I don't think about it too much. In my mind, the electric guitar is itself a foreign thing. But sounds of the electric guitar, with distortion, were coming into China already with Taiwan and Hong Kong pop, in the 1990s. And the electric guitar is so versatile, it can get so many different tones, it can play accompaniment or solo, and the sound with bends and all that can't be mimicked by synthesizers. So there has to be a guitar in a band."

He paused to eat a couple of the now-cold fries.

"Chinese rock music has become more and more developed. I just heard news that next year there will be a big festival of Chinese rock put on by the Beijing Organizing Committee for the Olympic Games"— he was referring to the 2008 Games, then up-coming and on everyone's mind. "For the Organizing Committee to take notice is really something—I think Chinese rock music will begin internationalizing. And now the people can accept it too, not like before. They see it as a genre of music." No Olympic Committee–sponsored concert ever took place, but Kou's excitement at gaining Chinese and even international recognition for his music was palpable.

We bussed our trash and left the KFC. Evening had fallen, and Beijing's homeward rush hour was in full spate. I was struck by the parallels emerging from my conversations with Chen Zhi and Kou Zhengyu, between the elderly father of classical guitar in China and the young heavy metal practitioner. The China historian in me noted the Confucian colorings of their stories: both men, albeit in very different ways, had pursued their guitar careers in complex relationships with their fathers and other authorities. But more than that, their goals were tied up with China's position vis-à-vis the rest of the world. Where else but in China could the electric guitar still be called a "foreign thing" in the twenty-first century? For Chen and Kou, and others developing the guitar from the 1970s to the 1990s, you couldn't just be a guitar player in China. You were, especially if you excelled, a *Chinese* guitar player. You might be a latecomer to the global band, but now you were challenging the world to *chaqin*.

Xiao Kou wanted to show me where he was playing his current gig. We walked a short distance to the Beijing People's Arts Theatre, one of the main venues for Western-style drama in the city. Suffocated was playing there in a modern production of Shakespeare's *Coriolanus,* translated into Chinese and accompanied by dueling musicians performing heavy metal and hardcore, he told me. I later read a glowing review of the performance beside a picture of Xiao Kou in *Beijing Wanbao* (Beijing Evening News), one of the capital's main dailies. His star turn came in act 5 during the climatic dialogue between Coriolanus and his mother, Volumnia. Kou Zhengyu "swept the strings to maintain a clock-like rhythm, which not only paced the actors' lines, but influenced the audience's mood, maintaining a tense atmosphere." The paper dubbed him "Suffocated's Kou Zhengyu, China's Number One Metal Guitarist." I knew Xiao Kou's father would see this review.

Xiao Kou posed us in front of the theater billboard. In the gathering dusk, a passer-by took a blurry photo with my camera. Xiao Kou threw the horns, holding up his index and pinky fingers in the universal hand gesture of heavy metal fans. But it seemed more like a victory V.

Afterword

ANGILEE SHAH

I met with Megan Shank on the Upper East Side of Manhattan when we were making final revisions to this book. Over Darjeeling in delicate teacups, she explained compound annual growth rates and the ins and outs of an initial public offering. This quick lesson in finance was prompted by Ray Zhang, the founder of the car rental company eHi. Zhang had just told her that he planned to take his company public in the United States, and Shank realized that she needed to make some changes to her chapter.

It should not have come as a surprise: China's fast-changing lives don't slow down for book editors and contributors. We always knew that trying to pin down the stories of the protagonists of *Chinese Characters* would be an impossible task. The best we could do, we decided, was to narrate these lives as they were being lived in a fascinating moment in history. By the time this book reaches readers, we know, many things about the people in it will have changed.

When he initiated economic reforms in the 1970s, Deng Xiaoping envisioned prosperity as a bicycle for every household. Now Chinese citizens can ride a maglev train that breaks 250 miles per hour. The pace of change in China is so rapid, and the inequities and breadth of experiences so vast, that the human stories are unforgettable. Adam Hersh, an economist at the Center for American Progress, told me that what we are seeing in China is not new—the United States and Europe went through industrialization periods that parallel China's experience now—but China's economic rise is, he said, "the most rapid socioeconomic transformation in the history of human civilization."

Stephen Mihm, a historian of American economy and culture, explained further that China today is a lot like New York City in the mid-1800s, which began as a modest seaport and bloomed into a densely populated metropolis. In China, migrants are moving into cities, liberated from back-breaking farm labor. Some five hundred million people have been raised out of poverty since the 1980s, the greatest achievement in poverty reduction in the shortest amount of time ever. But like New York City's growth spurt, China's boom is not good news for everyone. In emerging economies, people's perspectives are skewed by where they stand. For some, like Ray Zhang and the artist-for-hire Chen Meizi, China's growth is an economic opportunity. For others, like Old Lady Gao and her son in their Beijing *hutong,* the boom has come with displacement and disenchantment. And for many, China's roaring economy has been a mixed blessing.

It is not just people's socioeconomic lives that are evolving. Identities in and around China are also being formed and reformed. As China takes greater strides into the rest of the world, trying to decide what constitutes "Chinese" for the purposes of this book was a challenge in and of itself. Is it a nationality, an ethnicity, a language? A film scholar once told me that in his field, they have begun to use the term "Chinese-language cinema," instead of "Chinese cinema," for precision's sake. How else could they distinguish between films from Taiwan or Singapore, or Chinese American films, often in Mandarin but not from the mainland? When Jeffrey Wasserstrom and I first began talking about this collection, we wrangled over what its boundaries would be. Could an expat or an immigrant teach us something about how people live in China today?

While I was waiting to board the plane that took me from my home in Los Angeles to New York, where I met with Shank, I got an e-mail from James Carter. His chapter's main character, the globalized monk Lok To, had passed away. There would be a wake on Saturday night and a funeral on Sunday in Queens. It just so happened that I was on my way to Queens, where I was to be a bridesmaid at the wedding of two Chinese American friends. After finishing tea with Shank on Friday afternoon, I took three trains to get out of trendy Manhattan and into Flushing. When I exited the subway an hour later, it was bright and humid. The sidewalks were spilling over with men and women carrying large grocery bags and students with giant backpacks. Pedestrians walked at varying speeds, sometimes slowly, maddeningly, arm-in-arm in the middle of the sidewalk. Vendors on the street side sold roasted nuts covered in caramelized sugar. The smoke mingled with the scent of seafood on ice and the sounds of fishmongers yelling their wares in Mandarin and Cantonese. Nothing could cover the smell of the pungent durian displayed by grocers under green and orange awnings. I had a half-mile to go—and it would be slow going—down Main Street to the wedding rehearsal in the Queens Botanical Garden. I felt as though I were walking down a boulevard in an Asian megacity. As I navigated the crowd, I was glad that, thanks to Carter, we could include the story of a monk from the Bronx in our "China" anthology.

Around that time, I e-mailed Ian Johnson to see if there was any news of the Daoist Xianfo Shengren. Johnson responded that when he had returned to the North Peak to find Xianfo: "One Daoist said he had gone back to the Zhongshan mountains. Another added, 'Forever.'"

Harriet Evans visited Old Lady Gao that September as well. Gao, now in her ninth decade, had just moved from her *hutong* in Dashan-lanr to a temporary, rented apartment on the first floor of a 15-story building near the Temple of Heaven and the local hospital. The new apartment is spacious and concrete with a shower and toilet. Gao's daughter-in-law is pleased with the arrangement, though she realizes they will have to move again within three years. Evans says that when she arrived, "Old Lady Gao was installed on a large bed in front of a large television, in a spacious bedroom adjacent to the main room where her family was gathering. She looked much the same, but seemed quieter and more drawn into herself, and there was no smile on her face when she greeted me."

Anna Greenspan's son Max, now aged six, started at Aiju Primary School in Shanghai in the fall of 2011. Things are going well, Greenspan wrote in an e-mail: "He is memorizing Tang poetry, learning calligraphy and has homework every day but, so far at least, has plenty of time to play."

Not long after Lok To passed away, Christina Larson e-mailed me from China to say that the environmentalist in her essay was still working to ease the burdens of China's economic boom. Yong Yang, she wrote, was "focusing on documenting the impact of climate change in western China, still venturing out on long missions with his SUV packed full of canned foods and cigarettes." A June 1, 2011, report in the *New York Times* chronicled some of the early effects of the South-to-North Water Transfer Project that Yong researched. Three hundred and fifty thousand people are being relocated to build a canal that will drain water from already parched parts of the country. The canal's eastern and middle routes are scheduled to begin operations in 2013 and 2014.

While Yong meets his challenges with science, not everyone who wants change in China has the opportunity to influence policy makers through scholarship. Larson had just completed a story for the *Atlantic* about protests in the northeastern Chinese city of Dalian, where 12,000 residents had gathered in the main plaza to call for the relocation of a chemical plant that they believed was an environmental and health threat. Meanwhile, the dangers for Tibetans and Uyghurs in China have increased since Alec Ash and Ananth Krishnan wrote their chapters. Both Tibet and Xinjiang have experienced many violent incidents, though reports are sparse and reporters have been largely blocked from the regions. Twelve people died in a spate of violence in Xinjiang at the end of February 2012, but the government has not released many details about who they were and what happened. The situation in the western part of Sichuan Province, which Tibetan independence advocates call Eastern Tibet, has also deteriorated. From the spring through the fall of 2011, seven Tibetan monks immolated themselves to protest years of increasing government surveillance and interference. At least four monks died, among them a 19-year-old named Choepel. Advocacy groups say that from that spring through early 2012, more than 20 Tibetans have set themselves on fire; local Chinese officials have called them criminals and blamed the Dalai Lama for orchestrating the self-immolations.

In this book, we have taken great care to obfuscate the identities of Tibetans and Uyghurs who agreed to tell their stories, but have also done our best to illuminate their lives. While writing his chapter, Ash had had the good fortune to meet the Dalai Lama in Oxford. He sent a photograph of the two of them together to his Tibetan friend Tashi, who had written a poem about the Dalai Lama's former residence, the Potala Palace. Tashi was excited, Ash said, but "perhaps a bit unwise in showing the photo off to his friends." Tashi still lives in Xining but now works for a publishing company. He returned to Shuangpengxi for the last Tibetan new year, in February 2012, to see his grandmother. It was the first time he had been back to his home village in almost two years.

Bo Xilai, the Chongqing party boss introduced at the end of Xujun Eberlein's chapter, became an even greater figure in China's political scene. His "red songs" campaign garnered a great deal of attention, both inside and outside of China, and the pros and cons of his "Chongqing model" of development and local control generated great debate. Analysts believed that the charismatic politician was angling for a seat on the Politburo Standing Committee in 2012. But the historian He Shu was critical of Bo's campaigns, so when the Chongqing leader was swiftly ousted from his position in the spring of 2012, Eberlein was relieved. That He Shu chose to tell his story, for now, carries much less risk.

This is all to say that China and its people are in political flux. The Communist Party is not immutable. Ever since Mao took power, its messages and priorities have been evolving. Scholars, such as Harvard University's Elizabeth Perry, argue that we should see experimentation and reinvention as one of the defining features of the Party. China has never been as centralized or as hegemonic as images of Party leaders in black suits and orderly rows gathered in the Beijing Great Hall of the People to vote in unison might lead observers to believe. There is much more to the story of politics in contemporary China, including political infighting, mass protest, and the netizens who push ideologies and make influential critiques. Since meeting Evan Osnos in 2008, the nationalist Tang Jie has become a web editor and writer for M4 Media, formerly called Anti-CNN.com, adding yet another vision of what China should become to the dialogue.

Oversimplified views, which too often pit Communist Party loyalists against a few famous dissidents, have done much to fuel cartoonish understandings of China. They keep Yellow Peril and Red Menace fantasies alive and encourage the political posturing that leads to poor foreign policy decisions. In truth, China today is a place of great diversity and incredible people who are living through an unprecedented time. We hope that this collection helps bring their stories, and the writers who take the time to tell them, to greater prominence.

Notes and Readings

FOREWORD

John K. Fairbank is quoted from Stephen R. MacKinnon and Oris Friesen's *China Reporting: An Oral History of American Journalism in the 1930s and 1940s* (University of California Press, 1987), 182–84, a book that views China's Republican era (1912–1949) through the eyes of reporters who were on the scene at the time. See also, for the broader sweep of international press coverage of China, Paul French's *Through the Looking Glass: China's Foreign Journalists from Opium Wars to Mao* (Hong Kong University Press, 2009). For additional background on contemporary journalism dealing with China, see the latest volume in Lionel Jensen and Timothy Weston's "China beyond the Headlines" series, *China in and beyond the Headlines* (Rowman & Littlefield, 2012), especially the chapters by David Bandurski (on the Chinese press) and Gady Epstein (on foreign correspondents). For a valuable comparative perspective that looks at foreign correspondents in China and India, see Pankaj Mishra's "Pre-Fab Reporting," *Outlook India,* November 1, 2010.

INTRODUCTION

The best detailed yet accessible overview of the broad sweep of modern Chinese history remains Jonathan Spence's *The Search for Modern China* (1990; 2nd ed., Norton, 1999), which begins with the rise to power of the Qing Dynasty (1644–1912) and ends near the close of the twentieth century. Rana Mitter's *Modern China: A Very Short Introduction* (Oxford, 2007), Timothy Cheek's *Living with Reform: China since 1989* (Zed Books, 2007), and anthologies such as Kate Merkel-Hess et al.'s *China in 2008: A Year of Great Significance* (Rowman & Littlefield, 2009) carry the story forward past the turn of the millennium. Several contributors to *Chinese Characters* have written books that focus on specific issues and people. Notable other works of this kind include Robert Gifford's *China Road: A Journey into the Future of a Rising Power* (Random House, 2007), Duncan Hewitt's *Getting Rich First: A Modern Social History* (Pegasus, 2008), John Pomfret's *Chinese Lessons* (Holt, 2006), James Fallows's *Postcards from Tomorrow Square: Reports from China* (Vintage Books, 2008), and John Gittings's *The Changing Face of China: From Mao to Market* (Oxford University Press, 2006).

Two works that share the biographical style of *Chinese Characters* are Sang Ye's *China Candid: The People of the People's Republic of China* (University of California Press, 2006), translated by Geremie R. Barmé, and Zha Jianying's *Tide Players: The Movers and Shakers of a Rising Power* (New Press, 2011). The transformation of Chinese cities, a backdrop to many chapters in this book, is covered well in Thomas J. Campanella's *The Concrete Dragon: China's Urban Revolution and What it Means for the World* (Princeton Architectural Press, 2008). Information about many specific topics addressed in *Chinese Characters* (and a much more extensive set of suggestions for further reading than is offered here) can be found in Jeffrey Wasserstrom's *China in the 21st Century: What Everyone Needs to Know* (Oxford University Press, 2010).

PART 1. DOUBTERS AND BELIEVERS

One of the best general introductions to China's competing philosophic traditions is Benjamin Schwartz's *The World of Thought in Ancient China* (Harvard University Press, 1985). On Taoism, see Ian Johnson's "The Rise of the Tao," *New York Times Sunday Magazine,* November 5, 2010, and Sam Crane's blog "The Useless Tree" (http://uselesstree.typepad.com [accessed January 26, 2012]). James Carter's *Heart of Buddha, Heart of China: The Life of Tanxu, a Twentieth-Century Monk* (Oxford University Press, 2010) also deals with the issue of religious belief.

A good place to start for an understanding of contemporary Tibet and the beliefs and experiences of ethnic Tibetans living in the PRC is Robert Barnett's *Lhasa: Streets with Memories* (Columbia University Press, 2006). Donald S. Lopez Jr.'s *Prisoners of Shangrila: Tibetan Buddhism and the West* (University of Chicago Press, 1998) and Orville Schell's *Virtual Tibet: Searching for Shangri-La from the Himalayas to Hollywood* (Metropolitan Books, 2000) discuss how Tibetan realities overlap with and diverge from the Tibet conjured up in the Western imagination.

For background on Chinese nationalism, see Henrietta Harrison's *China: Inventing the Nation* (Oxford University Press, 2001), and for its changing meaning in the PRC today, see various contributions to Merkel-Hess et al.'s *China in 2008*. And for an overview of issues associated with spiritual beliefs in the PRC, past and present, see Vincent Goossart and David A. Palmer's *The Religious Question in Modern China* (University of Chicago Press, 2010), which shows how often religion has been at the center of China's crises during the past century and illuminates the current spiritual vacuum.

PART 2. PAST AND PRESENT

A window on the meaning of the past in contemporary China is provided by the Australian National University's wide-ranging online journal *China Heritage Quarterly* (www.chinaheritagequarterly.org [accessed February 2, 2012]). Roderick MacFarquhar and Michael Schoenhals's *Mao's Last Revolution* (Belknap Press of Harvard University Press, 2006) treats the Cultural Revolution in depth. *Picturing Power in the People's Republic of China: Posters of the Cultural Revolution* (Rowman & Littlefield, 1999), an illustrated volume edited by Harriet Evans and Stephanie Donald, discusses the period's cultural, artistic, and gendered aspects, while Philip P. Pan's *Out of Mao's Shadow: The Struggle for the Soul of a New China* (Simon & Schuster, 2008) covers the way it is remembered and forgotten. Michael Dutton et al.'s *Beijing Time* (Harvard University Press, 2008) looks at the transformations in that city. He Shu's book *Wei Mao zhuxi er zhan* (Combating for Chairman Mao: A Factual History of Chongqing's Large-Scale Armed Fights), referenced at the end of Xujun Eberlein's chapter, "Another Swimmer," is available in Chinese from Joint Publishing (HK). And for general background on the political events of the era following the Cultural Revolution, see Ezra Vogel's *Deng Xiaoping and the Transformation of China* (Belknap Press of Harvard University Press, 2011).

PART 3. HUSTLERS AND ENTREPRENEURS

On Chinese car culture, see Peter Hessler's *Country Driving: A Journey through China from Farm to Factory* (Harper, 2010) and Karl Gerth's *As China Goes, So Goes the World* (Hill & Wang, 2010). On migrant workers, see Leslie T. Chang's *Factory Girls: From Village to City in a Changing China* (Spiegel & Grau, 2007) and Michelle Dammon Loyalka's *Eating Bitterness: Stories from the Frontlines of China's Great Urban Migration* (University of California Press, 2012). For more on Lishui, see Peter Hessler's 2009 audio slide show "Art Factory" (www.newyorker.com/online/multimedia/2009/10/26/091026_audioslideshow_artfactory [accessed February 2, 2012]).

PART 4. REBELS AND REFORMERS

On intellectual life in contemporary China and the need to think in terms of more than just a simple divide between "dissidents" and apologists for the regime, see the compendium of views showcased in *One China, Many Paths,* edited by Wang Chaohua (Verso, 2005), and for the adaptability of the Chinese Communist Party, see *Mao's Invisible Hand: The Political Formation of Adaptive Governance in China,* edited by Sebastian Heilmann and Elizabeth J. Perry (Harvard University Asia Center, 2011). On Xinjiang, see James Millward's *Eurasian Crossroads: A History of Xinjiang* (Columbia University Press, 2007) and Gardner Bovingdon's *The Uyghurs: Strangers in Their Own Land* (Columbia University Press, 2010). For moving accounts of crusading lawyers, see Ian Johnson's *Wild Grass: Three Stories of Change in Modern China* (Pantheon Books, 2004) and Susan Jakes's "China Behind the Headlines: Xu Zhiyong," The China Beat, August 6, 2009 (www.thechinabeat.org/?p=563

[accessed February 2, 2012]). For background on Chinese environmentalism, see Elizabeth Economy's *The River Runs Black: The Environmental Challenge to China's Future* (Cornell University Press, 2004), Jonathan Watts's *When a Billion Chinese Jump: How China Will Save Mankind—or Destroy it* (Scribner, 2010), and China Dialogue (www.chinadialogue.net [accessed February 2, 2012]). And for updates on China's water crisis, see the "Choke Point China" section of the Circle of Blue web project (www.circleofblue.org/waternews/featured-water-stories/choke-point-china [accessed February 2, 2012]).

PART 5. TEACHERS AND PUPILS

On educational pressures in general and the toll that these take on children, listen to Marketplace's special multi-part report, "China: Obsession with the Test" (http://marketplace.publicradio.org/projects/project_display.php?proj_identifier=2011/06/07/china-standardized-test [accessed February 2, 2012]) and read Rob Schmitz's June 7, 2011, post "How Now Gaokao?" (www.publicradio.org/columns/marketplace/china-blog/2011/06/how_now_gaokao.html [accessed February 2, 2012]) that accompanies the series. On classical music's history in China, see Sheila Melvin and Jindong Cai's *Rhapsody in Red: How Western Classical Music became Chinese* (Algora, 2004), and for rock music, see Jon Campbell's *Red Rock: The Long Strange March of Chinese Rock and Roll* (Earnshaw Books, 2011). A fascinating window on life in a Chinese elementary school—as well as on life in a changing alleyway neighborhood—can be found in Michael Meyer's *The Last Days of Old Beijing* (Walker, 2008).

Contributors

ALEC ASH is a freelance writer in Beijing, where he studied Mandarin and wrote a blog about China's youth. His articles have been published in the *Economist* and *Prospect* magazine.

JAMES CARTER teaches Chinese and Asian history at Saint Joseph's University in Philadelphia and has written on the history of nationalism, religion, and colonialism in modern China. He is the author of *Heart of Buddha, Heart of China: The Life of Tanxu, a Twentieth-Century Monk* (Oxford University Press, 2010) and *Creating a Chinese Harbin: Nationalism in an International City, 1916–1932* (Cornell University Press, 2002). He holds a Ph.D. in modern Chinese history from Yale University.

LESLIE T. CHANG lived in China for a decade as a correspondent for the *Wall Street Journal*. She has also written for *National Geographic* and *Condé Nast Traveler*. Her book *Factory Girls: From Village to City in a Changing China* (Spiegel & Grau, 2008) has won numerous awards and been translated into ten languages.

XUJUN EBERLEIN is a writer who grew up in China, then moved to the United States. She is the author of the award-winning short-story collection *Apologies Forthcoming* (Livingston Press, 2008). Her stories, essays, journalism articles, and book reviews have been widely published. Her blog, insideoutchina. blogspot.com, discusses literary topics and current events related to China.

HARRIET EVANS is professor of Chinese Cultural Studies and director of the Contemporary China Centre at the University of Westminster. Her publications include *Women and Sexuality in the China: Female Sexuality and Gender since 1949* (Continuum, 1997) and *The Subject of Gender: Daughters and Mothers in Urban China* (Rowman & Littlefield, 2008). Her current research interests are on gender, urban change, locality, and cultural heritage in China.

ANNA GREENSPAN is adjunct professor at New York University Shanghai where she teaches about globalization and the city and co-founded the Institute of Shanghai Studies. She is writing a book on Shanghai's "neomodernity" and researching cross-cultural education.

PETER HESSLER is a staff writer at the *New Yorker* and the author of *River Town: Two Years on the Yangtse* (HarperCollins, 2001), *Oracle Bones: A Journey Between China's Past and Present* (HarperCollins, 2006), and *Country Driving: A Journey through China from Farm to Factory* (Harper, 2010).

IAN JOHNSON first went to China in 1984 as a student and has lived there off and on for a dozen years. He won a Pulitzer Prize for international reporting in 2001 for his coverage of the Falun Gong movement and has written two books, one on grassroots China and another on Cold War Islam. His essays and reviews have appeared in the *New York Review of Books,* the *New York Times Sunday Magazine,* the *Journal of Chinese Religion,* and the *Journal of Daoist Studies.*

ANANTH KRISHNAN has been the China correspondent for *The Hindu,* one of India's leading national dailies, since 2009. During his time reporting from Beijing, he has covered issues ranging from protest to Communist Party congresses and tensions between China and its neighbors. He previously worked for *The Hindu* in Mumbai and Chennai.

CHRISTINA LARSON is a contributing editor to *Foreign Policy* magazine and a Schwartz Fellow at the New America Foundation. She has reported widely from across China and Southeast Asia; her essays and reportage on China, the environment, climate change, and civil society have appeared in the *New York Times,* the *Boston Globe, The Atlantic, The New Republic, Foreign Policy, Smithsonian, Time,* the *Washington Monthly,* and the *Christian Science Monitor,* among other publications.

MICHELLE DAMMON LOYALKA is a freelance journalist and editor with an MA from the Missouri School of Journalism. During the thirteen years she has lived in China, she has launched a business consulting company, co-hosted a radio talk show, and headed the educational products division of a Chinese software company. Her book *Eating Bitterness: Stories from the Front Lines of China's Great Urban Migration* (University of California Press, 2012) focuses on the challenges and contributions of China's growing population of rural migrants.

JAMES MILLWARD is professor of Intersocietal History at the Edmund Walsh School of Foreign Service, Georgetown University. He has lived and traveled extensively in China and elsewhere in Asia and has written and edited four books on China and Central Asia, including *Eurasian Crossroads: A History of Xinjiang* (Columbia University Press, 2007). He writes a blog called "The World on a String" (www.worldonastringblog.blogspot.com) and is currently working on a history of stringed instruments on the Silk Road and the globalization of the guitar.

PANKAJ MISHRA is a novelist and writer of literary and political essays who has visited China often in recent years. His books include *Temptations of the*

West: How to be Modern in India, Pakistan, Tibet and Beyond (Farrar, Straus, and Giroux, 2006), *The Romantics: A Novel* (Random House, 2000), and, most recently, *The Revenge of the East.* When not traveling, he divides his time between London and Mashobra, a village in the Himalayan foothills in India.

EVAN OSNOS is China correspondent for the *New Yorker.* Previously, he worked as the Beijing bureau chief of the *Chicago Tribune,* where he contributed to a series that won a 2008 Pulitzer Prize. Before his appointment in China, he worked in the Middle East, reporting mostly from Iraq. He was born in London and educated at Harvard. He has lived in Beijing since 2005.

JEFFREY PRESCOTT is a specialist in U.S.–China relations, law, and human rights. He has been visiting professor at Fudan University in Shanghai and at Peking University in Beijing and deputy director of Yale's China Law Center. Most recently, he served as special advisor on Asia to the U.S. vice president. The views expressed in his essay are his own, and do not necessarily reflect the views of the U.S. government or any organization with which he is or has been affiliated.

ANGILEE SHAH is a freelance journalist and editor in Los Angeles. She has reported from across Asia, including China, Thailand, Indonesia, and Sri Lanka, and was a South Asian Journalists Association Reporting Fellow in 2007–8. She is a former editor of the online magazine *AsiaMedia* and a consulting editor to the *Journal of Asian Studies.* Her writing has appeared in the *Far Eastern Economic Review, Mother Jones Online, Miller-McCune Magazine, TimeOut Singapore,* and *Global Voices.*

MEGAN SHANK is a writer whose work has appeared in *Newsweek,* Bloomberg News, *Dissent,* and *Ms.,* among other publications. She helped launch the pilot issue of the *Current Digest of the Chinese Press* and formerly served as an editor at the Chinese-language edition of *Newsweek.*

JEFFREY WASSERSTROM is the author of *China in the 21st Century: What Everyone Needs to Know* (Oxford University Press, 2010) and three other books. He is professor of history and chair of the Department of History at the University of California, Irvine, editor of the *Journal of Asian Studies,* a co-founder of The China Beat (www.thechinabeat.org), Asia editor of the *Los Angeles Review of Books,* and an associate fellow of the Asia Society. His commentaries and reviews have appeared in many publications, including the *New Left Review,* the *Wall Street Journal, Foreign Policy, Time,* and the *TLS.*

Credits

Evan Osnos's "The New Generation's Neocon Nationalists" (chapter 2) has been adapted from his essay "Angry Youth: The New Generation's Neocon Nationalists," *New Yorker,* July 28, 2008.

Michelle Damon Loyalka's "The Ever-Floating Floater" (chapter 7) has been adapted from her book *Eating Bitterness: Stories from the Front Lines of China's Great Urban Migration* (University of California Press, 2012).

Peter Hessler's "Painting the Outside World" (chapter 9) has been adapted from his essay "Chinese Barbizon: Painting the Outside World," *New Yorker,* October 26, 2009.

Christina Larson's "Yong Yang's Odyssey" (chapter 11) has been adapted from her essay "Geologist Yong Yang and the Middle Kingdom's Dilemma," *Washington Monthly,* January 2008.

Leslie T. Chang's "Gilded Age, Gilded Cage" (chapter 14) has been adapted from an essay that appeared in *National Geographic* in May 2008.

TEXT
10/13 Sabon

DISPLAY
Sabon Open Type

COMPOSITOR
Toppan Best-set Premedia Limited

PRINTER AND BINDER
Maple-Vail Book Manufacturing Group